Parapsychology

Parapsychology
A Concise History

JOHN BELOFF

ST. MARTIN'S PRESS   NEW YORK

First published in the United States of America in 1993

Printed in Great Britain

ISBN 0–312–09611–9

Library of Congress Cataloging-in-Publication Data

Beloff, John.
    Parapsychology: a concise history / by John Beloff.
        p.   cm.
    Includes bibliographical references.
    ISBN 0–312–09611–9
    1. Parapsychology – History. I. Title.
BF 1028. B45 1993
133 09–dc20

                                          92–47274
                                             CIP

*This book is dedicated to Brian Southam
whose idea it was and without whose encouragement
it would never have got written.*

Contents

Acknowledgements

I wish to thank the following for reading and commenting on portions of the work in progress: Alan Gauld, the late Brian Inglis, Ian Stevenson and the late Charles Honorton. They are not to blame, of course, for the finished product. I would also like to take this opportunity to thank all of my friends and colleagues who encouraged me to persevere.

Foreword

When I had occasion to mention that I was working on a history of parapsychology, the usual response I got was 'at what point does your history commence?' There was, presumably, never a time when people were not concerned with phenomena that we would now call 'paranormal'. On that basis our history could have begun with the earliest recorded activity of this kind. On the other hand, before the advent of the Scientific Revolution of the seventeenth century, the distinction between what was normal and paranormal was too fluid to justify distinguishing a separate discipline devoted to the latter. Magic and the occult arts were, after all, still part of received knowledge.

Parapsychology as such, therefore, that is as a challenge to the existing world view, could not have arisen before the Age of Enlightenment. On that basis there is a case for regarding Mesmer as the first parapsychologist. Although he prided himself on being a man of the Enlightenment, and believed that his concept of 'animal magnetism' would prove a valuable addition to existing science, his learned contemporaries repudiated his new science and dismissed him as a charlatan. Hence, the whole subsequent history of mesmerism takes place outside the pale of the official sciences until finally, shorn of its more intractable claims, it becomes absorbed into medical psychology under the rubric of 'hypnotism'. Yet, during the half – century or so of mesmeric activity, not only were there a large number of reported cures, where official medicine was powerless, but all the phenomena that we, today, would classify under the heading of ESP (extrasensory perception), plus some that we no longer find, became the focus of systematic experiment and demonstration.

If, on the other hand, we take as our starting point the period when people first started to *specialize* in studying the paranormal, then the founding of the Society for Psychical Research in London in 1882 would represent as good a marker as any. By then, of course, the rift with orthodox science had become even more pronounced, although this initiative aroused the curiosity of a number of eminent scientists, including Fellows of the Royal Society. On this reckoning, we would have to say that Myers, Gurney and their fellows, who did so much of the initial spadework, qualify as the first accredited parapsychologists.

Yet others, again, might argue that parapsychology as such did not exist before J.B. Rhine came along. He, after all, introduced the term to the English-speaking world, together with much of its technical vocabulary, and it was he who developed what became standard experimental procedures. Furthermore, he established the first long-term centre for parapsychological research at a university. Nevertheless, to take Rhine as one's point of departure would, indeed, open one to the charge of being parochial. In the event, we have tried to solve the problem of where to begin by letting our first chapter deal with the mesmerists but preceding it with a prologue in which we try to depict the climate of opinion before and after the Scientific Revolution. In this way we try to show how it was that parapsychology came to fall outside the enclave of conventional science where, indeed, it has ever since struggled to survive.

The next question I had to consider was one of length. This

is *not*, emphatically, a comprehensive or definitive history of the field. The problem of what to *ex*clude was no less crucial than the problem of what to include. There are, roughly, three categories of phenomena that go to make up the study of parapsychology: first, the familiar spontaneous incidents that crop up unbidden and unexpected in everyday life, e.g. premonitions, telepathic messages, crisis apparitions, hauntings, poltergeists, etc; secondly, effects that are elicited intentionally in the laboratory, be they extrasensory or extramotor; thirdly, a mixed category of phenomena, associated with specially gifted individuals, which can, hopefully, be observed under more-or-less controlled conditions, albeit in a form, or at a time, that can never be precisely specified in advance. Our policy here has been to concentrate on the second and third of these three categories, not because the spontaneous phenomena are unimportant – on the contrary it is the persistence of such spontaneous phenomena that has kept alive interest in the field among the broad public who know nothing of the published evidence – but because it is the experimental findings and the controlled observations that have, in the event, proved to be the cutting edge of the discipline.

As will also become evident, we have tended to devote more space the closer we come to the present. This is due partly to the fact that the evidence tends to become both more plentiful and more reliable as we progress, and as parapsychology strives to meet the challenge of its critics, but partly to the fact that, for the ordinary reader, the present state of the field is likely to be of more concern than forgotten episodes that may have little bearing on anything that has happened since. On the other hand, I do not belong to the school of thought that holds that what no longer obtains ceases to be of interest. If we want to gain a view of the whole landscape of the putatively paranormal, it is vital that we include cases from the past that have no contemporary counterparts.

My choice of what to include must also, inevitably, reflect the fact that I am an English speaker. Fortunately, this is a field where, by common consent, the English and American researchers have been in the forefront.

On the question of nomenclature, the word 'parapsychology' is not to everyone's liking, indeed, many parapsychologists dislike it. They complain that it links the field too closely to psychology when, in fact, it has implications that go far beyond. Language, however, is full of misnomers. Psychology itself no longer represents the 'science of the soul' (if, indeed, it ever did!). There is every reason to think, however, that, for good or ill, the term 'parapsychology' has come to stay, if only because there is no plausible contender in the offing. 'Psychical research' is almost obsolete (except in connection with 'societies of psychical research') although the word 'psychic', for someone claiming paranormal powers, still enjoys wide currency. As for the numerous suggested neologisms: psychotronics, psychoenergetics, paraphysics, psychophysics, parascience, psiology, psi research, etc., none of these has come anywhere near to ousting 'parapsychology'. It would be wiser, surely, to settle for what we have got.

In general, I have tried not to assume any specialized knowledge on the part of the reader and technical information has, as a rule, been relegated to the Notes section. Accordingly I use as few technical terms as the text will permit and, when they cannot be avoided, I try to explain them as they arise. There are, however, three technical expressions with which the reader, however new to the field, would be well advised to take on board from the outset: namely 'ESP', 'PK' and 'Psi'. The words 'telepathy' and 'clairvoyance' entered the English language during the nineteenth century (although 'clairvoyance' is still too often confused with 'precognition'). The expressions in question, however, belong to the post-Rhinean era. 'ESP' or 'extrasensory perception' is an umbrella term that covers all the mental phenomena of parapsychology, be it telepathic or clairvoyant, precognitive, contemporaneous or retrocognitive. 'ESP' is contrasted with 'PK' which, in turn, covers all phenomena involving paraphysical or extramotor activity. Finally the term 'psi' embraces both ESP and PK so that one could say, quite simply, that parapsychology is *the study of 'psiphenomena'* or, harking back to the words of the founders of the Society for Psychical Research: 'those faculties of man, real or supposed, that appear to be inexplicable on any generally recognized hypothesis'. Readers should also note that the initials 'SPR' stand for Society for Psychical Research.

It is, no doubt, unfortunate that the basic phenomena of parapsychology should have to be defined in this negative way, but it is important to remember that, besides being 'inexplicable on any generally recognized hypothesis', they are also said to be 'faculties of man'. Now the question of whether there exist mental abilities that transcend a physicalist explanation is surely one of supreme theoretical and philosophical importance, quite apart from whatever practical applications such abilities may be found to have.

In the case of something as controversial as parapsychology, it is, of course, futile to pretend that one can adopt an attitude of complete neutrality or objectivity. A foreword provides a useful device for allowing the author to step aside and acknowledge his or her personal bias. Having devoted so much of my academic career to the study of what, elsewhere, I have called 'the relentless question', I can say that I, for one, am satisfied that the basic phenomena we shall be discussing are indeed real, not imaginary, although of course there is always room for argument as to which of the particular historical cases that we here consider can be accepted at face value and which are spurious. My history will, accordingly, differ from one written by a sceptic (or rather, as my colleague Robert Morris would call such a person, a 'counter-advocate') who regards the entire venture as a blind alley and all paranormal phenomena as illusory. Thus Ray Hyman, endorsing a position taken by Antony Flew, maintains that 'a single, unreplicated event that allegedly attests to a miracle [read: paranormal phenomenon] is simply a historical oddity that cannot be part of a scientific argument'. In what follows, I adopt the contrary view that even such singular occurrences should not be ignored unless we can offer a reasonable normal counter-explanation. Critics may consider that I have not given enough prominence to such counter-explanations as abound in the sceptical literature. I can only plead that, in the limited space I have available, I have done my duty by the sceptics in providing references and annotations to alternative interpretations of the evidence.

The fact that opinions differ should never be an excuse for not expressing an opinion. One needs also to remember that scepticism is not necessarily a badge of tough-mindedness: it may equally be a sign of intellectual cowardice.

John Beloff
Department of Psychology
University of Edinburgh
George Square, Edinburgh EH8 9JZ

Prologue

Is it possible to influence the outside world to make it conform more closely to one's desires, otherwise than by the appropriate physical intervention? That is, after all, the key issue for parapsychology but it is also the underlying assumption of magic as this has been practised down the centuries. Primitive man understood well enough what was needed to be done to obtain food, to grow crops, to build shelters or to fashion tools and utensils. But what was he or she to do if what was needed was to increase the rainfall or to cure a sickness? It was at such points, when practical activity was powerless, that recourse was had to those rituals, ceremonies and practices that fall under the heading of magic. Keith Thomas even goes so far as to suggest that we may define magic as the employment of ineffective techniques to allay anxiety when effective ones are not available.[1]

Magic is much older than religion. If the archaeologists are right, then the cave paintings – the earliest art-form known to us – fulfilled a magical function with respect to the hunt. Religion is a product of civilization. It fulfilled three needs of a settled community: a common mythology and cosmogony, a morality, and a cohesive set of rituals and ceremonies. At the same time, it was always, as it still is, intertwined with magical ideas and practices at all levels.

Ironically, just before the advent of the Scientific Revolution that was effectively to put a stop to it, we find an unprecedented flowering of magic and of the occult sciences. Renaissance magic, moreover, attracted some of the most remarkable personalities of the time. For the magic we are here discussing was not the perennial folk magic of the populace or of the countryside but the sophisticated magic of a learned and dedicated élite. All the key texts of this magic were in Latin. It is hard for us, at this remove, to enter into the minds of its protoganists but we can respond readily enough to the art and literature of that period which reflects this outlook, whether in the paintings of Botticelli or in the plays of Shakespeare. Shakespeare was a true child of the English Renaissance and, in the character of Prospero, in *The Tempest*, he gives us an alluring portrait of the benign Renaissance magus.

Let us begin by distinguishing between two main branches of Renaissance magic: 'natural magic' and 'supernatural (also known as "supercelestial") magic'. The former invoked only such properties or virtues deemed to be inherent in the objects themselves, whether pertaining to the terrestrial or to the celestial realm. The latter invoked superior beings whose aid could be solicited if one knew the correct spells or incantations. And here we must remember that, in the medieval cosmos that still prevailed, there was a veritable hierarchy of such beings – angels, spirits, demons, invisible to the human eye but more potent than man – and an accomplished sorcerer could, like Faustus, compel them to do his bidding.

Let us consider first, natural magic, which was closer to science and less embroiled with religion. The philosophical basis of natural magic was a world view usually designated by the term 'neoplatonism', a legacy of late Hellenistic thought. For a neoplatonist, virtually everything in creation possesses a soul of some description. Even the world itself could be credited with an *anima mundi*. A key doctrine in this connection was the supposed relationship between the 'macrocosm' and the 'microcosm'. Thus man, the microcosm, mirrored the universe or 'macrocosm'. Indeed, to a convinced neoplatonist, nothing was totally separate from anything else. It was up to the student of natural magic to learn about the sympathies or antipathies that might exist between objects of diverse kinds. This became of special relevance to the practice of medicine. And, given this outlook, one can see why both astrology and alchemy, the two most important branches of natural magic, made very good sense. Indeed, these two venerable occult sciences complemented one another. Every substance, every plant and every animal could, in principle, be assigned a special sympathetic relationship with one or other of the heavenly bodies.

The Renaissance, as its name implies, was a *rebirth* of learning rather than a revolution that would imply a break with the past. One of the cardinal texts of Renaissance magic was the so-called *Corpus Hermeticum*. This was a translation into Latin, by the fifteenth-century scholar, Ficino, of certain Greek treatises which purported to represent the wisdom of the ancient Egyptians. Its name derived from its supposed author, Hermes Trismegistus (Hermes being the nearest Greek equivalent of the Egyptian god Thoth, and 'trismegistus' meaning thrice great). Actually, these writings originated in the late Hellenistic period but this was not known until much later when, in 1614, the scholar Isaac Casaubon assigned them correctly to the Christian era. At the time, the student of the hermetic texts imagined that he was imbibing knowledge far older than that of the Greek philosophers, perhaps older even than Moses. It may seem curious to us that what was in fact a literary hoax should have proved so influential. However, it was typical of Renaissance culture in general to want to dignify one's own aims and activities by attributing them to some ancient authority and this mythical Hermes seemed as good as any other. It was

only later, after the Scientific Revolution, that such importance was attached to the question of priority.

And yet the Renaissance magi were never slavish copiers
of the authorities. Just as the great artists and architects of
the Renaissance soon surpassed in their daring and imagination their classical models, so the Renaissance magi were able
to impress their contemporaries with the novelty and audac-
ity of their approach. They were, moreover, thoroughly
cosmopolitan, moving from one European centre of learning
to another, producing all the while their hefty tomes. One
such was the German known as Henry Cornelius Agrippa
who, in 1553, published his *De Occulta Philosophia* which
Frances Yates has called the handbook of Renaissance occult sciences.[2] Another German, even more celebrated in his
day, was Phillipus Theophrastus Bombastus von
Hohenheim who adopted the name 'Paracelsus' (Celsus,
whom he claimed to surpass, was a physician famous in
Ancient Rome). Our word 'bombast' is his unflattering legacy to the English language. And yet he was a man of deeds
not just of words who scoffed at those who were content to
base their medicine on books rather than on observation and
experiment and insisted, ahead of his time, that nature, not
evil spirits, was the source of all diseases.[3]

Another intriguing figure of that era is the Italian-Neapol-
itan, Giordano Bruno. His immortality, as a pioneer
freethinker, was assured when he fell into the hands of the
Venetian Inquisition. They were obliged to hand him over
for punishment to the Inquisition in Rome who sentenced
him to be burnt alive as an impenitent heretic, and he was
duly executed on the Campo di Fiori in February 1600.
Among the many heresies for which he paid with his life was
a belief in the plurality of worlds (i.e. the problem of whether
there are rational beings on other planets, a problem that has
resurfaced in our own day with the advent of space-travel
and radio-telescopes) and, more fraught at the time, a belief
in the heliocentric theory. It is not surprising that, when

Galileo likewise fell into the hands of the Inquisition, some 16 years later, he decided to play it safe and recant, the more so as he was examined by the same Cardinal Bellarmine who had condemned Bruno.[4] Hence he suffered only imprisonment. It is noteworthy, however, that, although both these bold thinkers were condemned for what was then regarded as the Pythagorean heresy of putting the Sun rather than the Earth at the centre of the known universe, they arrived at their beliefs from very different directions. As Frances Yates points out, Galileo took his stand on mathematical and mechanical grounds that are intelligible to us today, whereas Bruno was influenced much more by the Sun magic of the ancients.

It is of interest to learn that Bruno was a welcome guest at the court of Queen Elizabeth when he visited England in 1583. Indeed, one of the charges that the Inquisition levelled against him was for lavishing praises on a heretic Queen![5] The most celebrated English magus of the period was John Dee, court astrologer in the Queen's retinue. He was also a mathematician of some note, who published the first English translation of Euclid, as well as being a practical scientist and inventor. Although much in Renaissance magic was derivative, it absorbed contemporary scientific discoveries. In 1600, William Gilbert, the Queen's personal physician, published (in Latin) his treatise on the magnet, which one authority has called 'the first major original contribution to science published in England'.[6] Yet Gilbert was very much in tune with the animistic world of the neoplatonist. Thomas comments, in connection with Gilbert: 'the magnet seemed to open the possibility of telepathy, magical healing and action at a distance'.[7] Indeed, nearly 200 years later, when Mesmer (another physician) was setting out on his fateful career, magnetism still seemed mysterious enough to provide him with the analogue he needed to launch his 'animal magnetism' as the principle of a new healing technique (see Chapter 1).

Now let us turn to that other branch of magic which I mentioned previously: supernatural or supercelestial magic. It derived from Judaic rather than Hellenistic sources, notably the Cabala, the work of Spanish Jews of the period before the Expulsion of 1492. It represented a compendium of Jewish mystical beliefs but its main relevance in this context was its claim that, by manipulating the letters of the Hebrew alphabet in various ways, one could spell out the secret and sacred attributes of God, or of His angels, and thereby conjure up spirits to do one's bidding. Thus the Cabala was a species of word-magic but, since the letters of the Hebrew alphabet also correspond with numerals, it also served as a system of number-magic or numerology and this could be used for prophecy.

A Christian version of the Cabala was devised by one Giovanni Pico de la Mirandola. Pico, like Ficino, the translator of the hermetic texts, belonged to that scholarly circle at the court of the Medicis at the end of the fifteenth century. His particular gimmick (if one may be allowed the expression) was to demonstrate how, by an appropriate juggling of Hebrew letters, it was possible to prove that Jesus was, indeed, the Messiah. Hence Christians need feel no qualms about studying the Judaic Cabala. His initiative was developed by other scholars, both in Italy and Germany, until eventually most of the Renaissance magi became versed in Cabala. This was notably the case with Bruno and with Dee. Dee, in fact, kept what he called his spiritual diary in which he recorded seances he held at which, by cabalistic means, he had summoned angels. He had a rough time, however, trying to convince his enemies that his sorcery was benign and not diabolical and, with the backlash against magic that was gaining pace towards the end of the sixteenth century, he fell out of favour at court and ended his days in poverty and disgrace. He also seems to have been the victim of some mischievous chicanery – a hazard to which explorers of the paranormal have always been exposed – as his assistant and confidant, Edward Kelly, did not scruple to deceive his master about what was going on.

Obviously, in an era so obsessed with witchcraft and demonology, supernatural magic was a risky business. But we must not imagine that people like Dee or like Bruno who were prepared to take that risk were, like the legendary Dr Faustus, motivated by cupidity. On the contrary, as Yates is at pains to stress, they were inspired by lofty ideals. For, in a Europe increasingly torn asunder by Protestant and Catholic, by Reformation and Counter-Reformation, they fondly hoped that their precious magical heritage, with its roots in so many diverse traditions, Christian, Pagan or Jewish, might serve to bridge the deepening religious divide. It was a vain hope. The wars of religion persisted for another century, the persecution of witches intensified, amounting, among elderly and single women, to a veritable holocaust, and magic, especially supernatural magic or sorcery, remained under a cloud as a subversive heresy.

It may seem strange today that Renaissance conjuration appears to have stopped short of communing with named deceased individuals. After all, the biblical story of the Witch of Endor and the deceased King Saul would have been common knowledge, and belief in ghosts or apparitions, especially of murdered persons, was as familiar then as now – Shakespeare uses it to good effect both in Hamlet and Macbeth. I can only suppose that it would have been regarded as a form of necromancy too impious even for the Renaissance magus to contemplate. It is not until we reach the mid-eighteenth century, by which time religious conformity was greatly relaxed, that, in the person of Emanuel Swedenborg – scientist, seer and latter-day magus – we meet someone claiming to have detailed visions of the after-life and the other world and to be personally in communication with those who have departed thence.[8] And it took another full century before the Spiritualists devised a practical guide for the ordinary person who sought to contact deceased relatives.

SCIENCE AND SCEPTICISM

What we are calling here the Scientific Revolution represents perhaps the most momentous mutation in human affairs since the advent of agriculture or the dawn of civilization. Here, however, we shall not be concerned with the specific discoveries and inventions that originally brought it about, still less with its awesome historical significance or its implications for the future of life on this planet. Rather, we shall focus on the new world view to which it gave rise, a view which, as we shall see, introduced a sharp distinction between normal and paranormal, between science and pseudoscience, reality and magic.[9] In the aftermath of this revolution an 'enchanted boundary'[10] has ever since divided parapsychology from conventional science.

The revolution itself, as an episode in the history of science and ideas, spans the period between Galileo (who was born in 1564, the same year as Shakespeare, and died in 1642) and Newton (who, as it happens, was born in 1642, the year of Galileo's death, and died in 1727). It could be said to have culminated in 1687 with the publication of Newton's *Principia*. It was a revolution brought about not just by scientists and inventors but also by metaphysicians. Indeed, before the establishment of the scientific academies, like the British Royal Society (which received its first charter in 1662), there was as yet no firm distinction between the philosopher and the 'natural philosopher' (the word 'scientist' was a mid-nineteenth century coinage). Descartes, for example, a key figure of the Scientific Revolution, though nowadays usually thought of as a philosopher, made important contributions both to mathematics and to physiology. Equally, Robert Boyle, though now best remembered as a scientist (e.g. Boyle's Law) had much to say on the distinction between mind and matter. Most of its other progenitors, e.g. Bacon, Hobbes, Gassendi, Spinoza, Leibniz and Locke, belong primarily to the history of philosophy but were strongly influenced by developments in the sciences. However, each sought to promote his own distinctive version of the new outlook and it took another century before anything resembling a scientific orthodoxy took shape.[11]

What became known as the Enlightenment, which came to fruition in the eighteenth century, can be considered the ideological aftermath of the Scientific Revolution.[12] Its salient feature was the idea that life should be conducted on the basis of reason as opposed to dogma, revelation or tradition. It was the precursor of modern secular humanism. It took its stand on the success of the natural sciences and it found an influential mouthpiece in the French Encyclopaedia edited by d'Alembert and Diderot (the first volume of which appeared in 1751) and in that formidable spokesman and international propagandist, Voltaire.[13] From our point of view, its significance lay in its uncompromising mechanism or determinism which left no room for free-will or, ultimately, for any intervention of mind in nature be it human or divine.

The key feature of Enlightenment thinking was the belief, encouraged by the success of the scientific enterprise, especially after the publication of Newton's *Principia* in 1687, that the universe was a coherent and intelligible system whose workings could be known accurately, and eventually in full, through observation, calculation and the due exercise of reason and reflection. This, at a stroke, disposed of the awe and mystery with which an unfathomable nature had been shrouded in the past and, more particularly, of the possibility of any extraneous intervention whether by the Deity or by the caprice of any other supernatural agent. It also discredited the residues of magical thinking or practices derived from esoteric, occult or obscurantist sources. Religion as such was not renounced, but the dominant deist position reduced the role of the Deity to that of a creator who, having initially set everything in motion, then allowed his creation to proceed autonomously in accordance with his laws. Atheism did not become common until late in the nineteenth century, and outspoken atheists, such as d'Holbach or Diderot, were regarded as extremists. Spinoza, though often taken for an atheist by his contemporaries, was in fact a pantheist.

It followed that miracles, conceived as an interference with the natural order, whether divinely, diabolically or just humanly inspired, could not be tolerated. Accordingly, since miracles were still reported, they could only, in the robust words of that great luminary of the Scottish Enlightenment, David Hume, be attributed to the 'knavery and folly of mankind'. Hume, however, was less concerned with the inviolability of the laws of science as such (his scepticism was, indeed, all-embracing), rather he could conceive of no instance where it would not be more rational to suspect one's informant of bad faith than to discount, at a stroke, everything that past experience had taught one about the way things actually work (he does not, unfortunately, discuss the ideal case where one is oneself the key witness, though doubtless he would then have invoked the possibility of trickery as sufficient reason to doubt one's own senses). Hume was, of course, primarily concerned in his essay with religious miracles but he recognized 'the strong propensity of mankind to the extraordinary and the marvellous' and he certainly intended his analysis to apply to those secular miracles that today we would call paranormal events.[14] As this history will show, the quest for the paranormal has, indeed, at all times been dogged by 'knavery and folly' – all the more credit, then, to those intrepid explorers who have sought to penetrate the smoke-screen and the camouflage with an open mind.

It was not, however, merely the progressive secularization of Western culture that was inimical to a belief in the supernatural. More subtle, for what Max Weber called 'the disenchantment of the world (*die Entzauberung der Welt*)', was the relegation of mind to a marginal position within the scheme of things. Before the advent of the Scientific Revolution, no firm line had yet been drawn between the mental and the physical, between man and nature; the microcosm and the microcosm were all of a piece. The decisive step was taken by Galileo himself when he insisted that only that which could be counted or measured pertained to the physical realm – the book of nature, he proclaimed, was written in mathematics – hence the sensuous qualities we attribute to external objects actually belong to the mind of the perceiver and have no independent objective existence. The distinction was elaborated in Descartes' epistemology where he points out that, whereas it is always logically possible to doubt the existence of the external physical world, it is *not* logically possible to doubt one's own existence or the immediate deliverances of one's own consciousness. In Locke's empiricist epistemology[15] the distinction is further codified in terms of the primary and secondary properties of the perceived object where only the former correspond to aspects of the external world and so are of concern to physicists.

The big question that then confronts one, however, is: what then are minds for? What role, if any, do they play in the workings of nature? A brave attempt to answer this question was given by Descartes when he relegated mind to the pineal gland of the brain. There its function could be confined to regulating the outgoing nerve impulses ('animal spirits') which, by activating the muscles, controlled the movement of the limbs. The pineal gland was chosen because it appeared to be the one organ of the brain that was not bilaterally duplicated. This ingenious solution to the question of what the mind could do served at one stroke to salve his conscience as a good Catholic, in that it allowed some latitude to the operation of the will, while, at the same time, limiting the mind sufficiently to avoid embarrassing his fellow physicists. Descartes, however, could contemplate the possibility that non-human animals might just be mindless automata and, in due course, his successors did not hesitate to ask whether man himself might not prove, in the final analysis, to be nothing more than a self-regulating machine.[16]

It was not until the late nineteenth century, however, that the progressive demotion of mind reached its consummation in Huxley's doctrine of epiphenomenalism which, in effect, deprived mind of any functional significance whatsoever. And it was not until the twentieth century that attempts were made to eliminate mind altogether, as in the various formulations of behaviourism, materialism, functionalism and kindred doctrines which, however nonsensical or misguided they might sound to the layman, were not only taken seriously by the learned but achieved the status of an orthodoxy for some of the most influential psychologists, physiologists and philosophers of our time.

Thus it was not only miracles which, by definition, are rare and extraordinary events, that had to be discarded under the new dispensation, but any power attributed to mind that could not be understood in mechanistic terms. The Enlightenment was, of course, the ideology of an educated élite. The general populace was as ignorant and credulous then as it has always been. The eighteenth century had its quota of hauntings, poltergeists, miraculous cures, spells, prophecies and superstitions. Renaissance magic did not so much disappear as go underground. We find echoes of it in the rituals of the Masonic lodges or in the activities of secret societies such as the Rosicrucians. The difference lay only in the attitudes they now invoked. To the sophisticated, anything that smacked of the miraculous had either to be dismissed as imposture or else explained away as, at best, a misunderstanding, or in some instances a failure to grasp the implications of coincidence.[17]

Parapsychology, as we shall follow its progress in the ensuing chapters, can best be understood as challenging the mechanistic and reductionistic implications of official science by reaffirming the autonomy of mind.[18] Its main opponents at the present time are those who, claiming to be the heirs of the Enlightenment, see themselves as the guardians of rationality or, at least, of robust common sense who must, at all costs, discredit any dangerous backsliding into superstition and obscurantism. To this end they freely resort to mockery – that formidable weapon which the great Voltaire had wielded to such good effect. Unfortunately, in their zeal, they too often blur the distinction between scientific parapsychology and popular occultism and 'New Age' cults which perpetuate the magical tradition.[19]

Parapsychologists are often accused of magical thinking. The accusation has this much substance, that parapsychology shares with traditional magic the idea that events in the external world can, in special circumstances, be influenced by purely inner mental events. Where the parapsychologist parts company with the magus lies in the treatment of the evidence. Failures in alchemy, astrology or the other occult arts could always be explained away as due to special countervailing circumstances so that the doctrines remained intact. A parapsychological hypothesis must be open to rejection if it is to be taken seriously. The problem of falsification is, of course, much more contentious in the social and psychological science than it is in physics or chemistry. But the idea of experimentation and readiness to question received opinion or unsubstantiated claims aligns parapsychology with science as opposed to magic and pseudoscience. It is necessary to stress this point if only because there are at the present time many voices urging us to adopt a neo-hermeticist view of the world, often invoking the latest trends in fundamental physics in support of their contention.[20]

ROMANTICISM AND THE RESURGENCE OF THE OCCULT

By the close of the eighteenth century the impetus that had given rise to the Enlightenment had begun to flag. It now began to look as if Newtonian science, though it might well be unchallengeable in the domain of inanimate nature, had little to offer that was of human or social relevance.[21] What we have learnt to call, broadly, the Romantic revolution was a tidal wave that had profound and lasting effects on European culture and sensibility. Even if, in one of its aspects, it might represent no more than a nostalgic yearning for an imaginary pre-industrial age, in another it could involve a liberation from artificial conventions and a readiness to explore new realms of thought and self-expression (this is specially evident in the music of that period). Of special relevance in this context was the rise of German philosophy.[22] From Kant onwards, the Idealists had striven to turn materialism on its head and demonstrate that mind, not matter, was the paramount reality, or even that mind alone could be said to exist – the material universe being, in the final analysis, no more than a construction of mind.[23] Schopenhauer, for example, found no difficulty accommodating the paranormal into his scheme of things.

In the end, however, it was not the metaphysicians who were responsible for the advent of parapsychology. Rather it was the success of empirical science which convinced certain dissident thinkers of the late nineteenth century that, only by taking on the scientists at their own game, that is by accepting strict scientific criteria for distinguishing between genuine phenomena and bogus claims, that any serious challenge to the mechanistic universe could be mounted. In the mean time, however, what the Romantic revolution did accomplish was to make the cultural climate more propitious for paranormal phenomena to arise. This applies especially to the rise of the mesmeric movement which we look at in our next chapter. For this went far beyond its significance as a 'fringe medicine'. The so-called 'Societies of Harmony' which sponsored it offered a new vision of what was possible in interpersonal communication and, over and above whatever medical services they could provide, the mesmerists were concerned to explore and demonstrate new-found human potentials of the kind we now call parapsychological.

Science, on the other hand, was not to be deflected by this new permissive climate of opinion. The nineteenth century was, after all, a period of unprecedented progress both in the physical and in the biological sciences, culminating as it did in the work of Faraday, Maxwell and Helmholtz on the one hand and Darwin and Pasteur on the other. These giants of nineteenth-century science saw no need to disown the mechanistic world view that had served them so well out of any deference to romantic or religious susceptibilities. Inevitably, science underwent its own changes and paradigm-shifts so that the physics that we profess today, especially at its more fundamental levels, is remote, indeed, from that of the Newtonian synthesis. Nevertheless, the basic materialist assumption, that the physical world is a closed system, impervious to anything falling outside the domain of space – time events, has never been renounced. None of the attempts we describe in the remainder of this book, which purport to cast doubt on this tenet, has so far succeeded in upsetting it, not, at any rate, in the eyes of the arbiters of official science.

Thus the history we are about to survey ends in an uneasy stalemate unsatisfactory to all concerned. What, I submit, *does* emerge from these pages, at least for those sufficiently open-minded, is that the question remains wide open and, so long as this remains the case, it would be an unforgivable failure of nerve to call a halt to further efforts to come to grips with it.

CHAPTER 1
The mesmeric era

Mesmerism was, in the first instance, a branch of what nowadays we would call fringe medicine. Its founder, Franz Anton Mesmer, a Viennese physician, believed that he had discovered a fundamental type of energy in the universe, one so subtle and elusive that it had hitherto escaped detection. Although all pervasive, its distribution in the body, where it was identified as 'animal magnetism', as opposed to the familiar mineral magnetism, governed the health and well-being of each individual. Accordingly, treatment for diseases and disorders of all kinds involved a transfer of this magnetic fluid from the body of a healthy magnetizer to that of his sick patient. Originally, Mesmer had used actual magnets but soon discovered that he could obtain the same results using a system of stroking or making passes with the hands across the patient's body. The effect of such a procedure, he found, was that a crisis or convulsion was produced in the patient after which relief and improvement could be expected to follow.

It may seem strange that such a bizarre form of therapy could ever have attracted a following, yet Mesmer and his disciples were never at a loss for eager patients – often those who had despaired of what orthodox medicine could do for them. Indeed, given the dubious nature of so much of what was then approved medical treatment, some benefit may well have accrued if only as a result of its cessation. Be that as it may, the mesmerists were able to claim a remarkable number of successful cures, however we may choose to interpret the fact.

A new era in mesmeric practice came about when it was discovered that, instead of eliciting a crisis or convulsion, the treatment could induce a trance-like state in the patient which, on the analogy of sleep-walking, came to be known as 'somnambulism' or, sometimes, as 'lucid sleep'. One important advantage of this was that such a trance-like state was often accompanied by an insensibility to pain so pronounced as to allow for painless surgical operations. In the days before the discovery of chemical anaesthetics its appeal needs no explanation.

The historical importance of mesmerism, however, goes far beyond its utility as fringe medicine. Its legacy was such that it can, as Ellenberger has shown, be regarded as the forerunner of modern dynamic psychiatry.[1] It can also, as I shall try to show, be regarded as the forerunner of modern parapsychology. The link with dynamic psychiatry is based on the fact that mesmerism was the precursor of hypnotism which, in turn, gave rise to the concept and theory of the unconscious culminating in the work of Freud. Also, the somnambulistic state served to reveal the multiplicity of personality and its unsuspected hidden depths. As regards parapsychology, the focus of interest lies in the activities associated with certain gifted individuals who, in the somnambulistic state, displayed a capacity for extrasensory perception. Indeed, one could say that, perhaps for the first time in history, a procedure was available for eliciting paranormal powers under controlled conditions of observation. The so-called 'higher phenomena of mesmerism' are what we would now call parapsychological or psi phenomena. We may still argue about the authenticity of their claims but the importance of the precedent which the mesmerists thus created should not be underestimated.

The advent of mesmerism

The whole history of mesmerism is full of bitter ironies. Mesmer, himself, wanted to be regarded as a man of the new Enlightenment. He went out of his way to challenge the exorcist, Father Gassner, who then enjoyed a thriving practice in Germany, and tried to show that he, Mesmer, could do all that Gassner could without invoking the supernatural.[2] At the same time, the magnetic fluid, which Mesmer invoked as an explanation, had an uncomfortable resemblance to those occult agencies to which the discredited alchemists and astrologers of an earlier period appealed in the days when when magic was still taken seriously. At all events, Mesmer's medical colleagues in Vienna derided his efforts and treated him as a mystagogue and a charlatan. 'Mystagogue', he may have been, for Mesmer, throughout his life, was notoriously secretive about his discoveries in a way that is more in keeping with the magus than with the modern scientist. But if by the word 'charlatan' we impute deliberate deceit, that charge would be harder to sustain. Married to a wealthy woman, Mesmer had no need to resort to fraud in order to lead a comfortable life and to enjoy the amenities of Vienna where he was known as a patron of music and a friend of Leopold Mozart and his prodigy of a son. Yet his fanatical faith in the importance of the discovery that bears his name turned him into a refugee. In 1778, he left Vienna for good and settled in Paris, a city which, at that time, was less conservative and more receptive to exciting novelties.

In Paris, he was fortunate to gain as a disciple Charles d'Eslon, a much respected physician who also happened to be personal physician to the King's brother, the Comte d'Artois. Very soon, both Mesmer and d'Eslon built up fashionable and lucrative practices although, to do them justice, it should be said that they both, at times, treated poor patients without any fee. Soon their services were so much in demand that they devised a system of group therapy. This involved the celebrated *baquet*, a tub filled with 'magnetized' water around which the patients sat grasping iron rods that protruded from the water while joined to one another by a cord. The analogy with ordinary magnetism could hardly have been more blatant. Yet, all the while, the magnetizers would move from one patient to another, sometimes touching an affected limb, and all to a background of harmonious music. In such an atmosphere, so conducive to suggestibility, it would not be hard to excite emotional crises leading to cathartic relief.

The medical profession in France reacted strongly against the new movement which they resented as a rival and an intruder. D'Eslon was stripped of his position in the Paris Faculty of Medicine but he was still confident that, given a fair hearing, he could vindicate the mesmeric doctrine and his own integrity. In due course, the King (Louis XVI) agreed to set up an independent commission of inquiry. Actually, two such commissions were appointed, one with nominees of the Royal Society of Medicine, the other composed of assorted savants associated with the Academy of Sciences plus members of the Paris Faculty of Medicine.[3] Both issued their findings in 1784; both returned a negative verdict. It is, however, the latter commission, headed by J.S. Bailly, the astronomer, whose deliberations are now chiefly remembered. For it was this commission that contained so many distinguished names, including Benjamin Franklin (formerly ambassador from the newly constituted United States but now living in retirement at Passy outside Paris) as well as the great A.L. Lavoisier, the chemist.

Basically, the commissioners found no evidence for the existence of this hypothetical magnetic fluid. Accordingly, the effects that they had observed on the patients must, they concluded, be attributed to the ever-pervasive, ever-forceful power of the human imagination. The only dissenting voice was that of the botanist, A.L. de Jussieu, who in a minority report claimed that the patients sometimes reacted to the pointing of a finger or a rod even when they were not in a position to see what was happening. But de Jussieu (a parapsychologist before his time?) was overruled. A short confidential report was also circulated emphasizing the moral dangers of the magnetic therapy where most of the practitioners were men, most of the patients were women, and where so much stimulation by touch was involved and so much excitement generated.

It fell to d'Eslon himself to cooperate with the commissioners and he had willingly put his clinic and his assistants at their disposal. Mesmer, who had already left Paris in 1782 for the Belgian health resort of Spa, was furious when he learnt that d'Eslon, rather than he, was in command but, in fact, d'Eslon was far better equipped for such a delicate diplomatic task than the egocentric and overbearing Mesmer. Naturally, d'Eslon was devastated at the outcome of this affair which was to prove a crushing blow to the hopes of the mesmerists. D'Eslon never abandoned the practice, but the Royal Society of Medicine forbade its members to engage henceforth in the forbidden art.

Nevertheless, mesmerism continued to gain support among the lay public and this was encouraged by the so-called 'Societies of Harmony' which Mesmer himself established and which had chapters in various parts of France and in other countries. Mesmer never returned to Paris but continued to wander and proselytize in various parts of the Continent, eventually settling in Switzerland where he took Swiss citizenship. His last few years were spent at Meersburg on the German side of Lake Constance where he died in 1815 only a few miles from the place where he was born.

The discovery of somnambulism

Credit for discovering that the magnetic treatment could bring about a trance-like state must go to the foremost of

Mesmer's French followers, the Marquis de Puységur.[4] He was by all accounts a likeable and benign individual. He had had no medical or scientific training but had learned about mesmerism from his brother. He was by profession a soldier, an officer of the artillery, but he was also a member of one of the oldest aristocratic families of France. He used his mesmerism mainly for the benefit of the peasants on his estate at Busancy near Soissons. Despite a spell in prison he survived the French Revolution and lived on to become the Mayor of Soissons.

His breakthrough came in 1784 when he was treating one of his peasants, a lad of 23 by the name of Victor Race, who was suffering severely from an inflammation of the lungs. Victor responded by going into a trance during which his personality and behaviour underwent a remarkable change. This happened repeatedly throughout the period of his convalescence but Victor had no recollection of what had transpired when awakened from the trance. What specially impressed Puységur was that, while in trance, Victor displayed powers far exceeding those he had ever evinced in the waking state. Normally a dull-witted and tongue-tied peasant, in the somnambulistic state he immediately became highly fluent and articulate. He even took over the management of his own case, diagnosing and prescribing for the disease as well as predicting its course. Even more incredible, he appeared able to do as much for other patients and was indeed used in this capacity. Eventually this became a recognized function of many notable somnambules of the early nineteenth century: Victor was just the first of this line. Puységur speaks of Victor's 'clairvoyance' in this connection but he would have repudiated any suggestion that anything paranormal was involved. Like all the mesmeric phenomena it was to be explained naturalistically as a function of the magnetic fluid.

The fame of this case soon spread and Puységur was besieged by would-be patients. Only a group therapy, he decided, would meet their needs but, instead of the *baquet*, he duly magnetized a tree on his estate to which the patients could be placed in contact. It is strange, perhaps, that Puységur took so literally the magnetic hypothesis because his writings show that he had a keen understanding of the psychology involved. He realized that success depended on the magnetizer having complete confidence in what he was doing and wanting fervently to succeed. But he stopped short of supposing, as we would now presume, that it was the patient's faith that effected the cure.

The first to break publicly with the magnetic tradition was a much-travelled Portuguese priest who, reputedly, had spent some time in India, the Abbé J.C. de Faria.[5] He settled in Paris towards the end of his long life and died there in 1819. He wrote a book in which he discusses the nature of lucid sleep, laying emphasis on the mental impressionability of the subject. More to the point, however, he gave a long series of well-attended public lectures to illustrate his theories. Dispensing with the time-consuming manual passes of the mesmerists he would demonstrate how one could impose the trance state on an impressionable subject simply by forcefully commanding him or her to go to sleep. Faria qualifies as the first of a long line of stage hypnotists in a tradition that is still with us. Inevitably, the sceptics of his day suggested that his volunteer subjects must have been in league with him. Such insinuations are still made today with regard to stage hypnotism and, in the nature of the case, are almost impossible to refute.

Another early dissident of a less flamboyant kind was a young physician, Alexandre Bertrand, who, in 1819, began a series of public lectures on animal magnetism and, in 1823, published a treatise on somnambulism which aroused considerable interest.[6] It was one of the first critical treatises that tries to examine impartially the claims made for the somnambules. Bertrand does not by any means rule out the possibility that some of the higher phenomena may be real.

What he *does* try to do is to reinterpret mesmerism along psychological lines rather than falling back on a quasi-physical interpretation. However, although Bertrand was not ignored, he failed to carry the day among the mesmeric fraternity and his pioneering efforts were not properly appreciated until reassessed in the later part of the century by the physiologist, Charles Richet, who did so much to re-awaken interest in mesmerism and hypnotism.

Thus J.P. Deleuze, who had published one of the earliest histories of animal magnetism, in 1813, was still clinging tenaciously to the fluidic hypothesis in 1819 as offering the only hope of an explanation. More important still, the principal purveyors of mesmerism in foreign parts never deviated from the fluidic assumption. Such was the Baron Du Potet from whom John Elliotson learnt about mesmerism when in 1837 the former visited London, where Elliotson held a Chair of Medicine at University College. Such too, was C. Lafontaine who visited Manchester in 1841, little knowing, however, that among his audience was James Braid, a Scotsman who practised as a surgeon in Manchester, and who then went on to make the decisive break with mesmeric doctrine when he introduced his psychological notion of 'nervous sleep'– to which the term 'hypnosis' soon came to be attached.[7] Hypnosis, though still regarded with suspicion, was less offensive than mesmerism, and Braid took good care not to antagonize the medical profession – unlike Elliotson who was forced to resign his post at University College.

Yet, like so many beliefs that have once acquired wide currency, the mesmeric doctrine died hard. James Esdaile, the greatest exponent of painless mesmeric surgery, who ran his own mesmeric hospital in Calcutta, still insisted to the end (he died in 1859) that hypnotism was one thing, mesmerism was something else again.[8] At all events, it would be rash to treat mesmerism as no more than an archaic version of hypnotism. Whatever the rationale behind it, the mesmerists seemed able to elicit phenomena that are hard to match in the annals of hypnotism. Moreover, as Dingwall puts it, 'with the disappearance of the magnetic fluid much of the more mysterious side of mesmerism vanished'.[9] And it is precisely to this 'more mysterious side' that we must now turn in our quest for the precursors of parapsychology.

Elliotson, a tough-minded materialist and atheist was, nevertheless, a firm believer in the 'higher phenomena'. In 1843 he founded his own journal, *The Zoist*, an annual which ran to 13 volumes until 1856 and served as the official organ of British mesmerism. It is a treasure-house of records of ostensibly paranormal performances. A victim of intolerance, Elliotson was not, unfortunately, himself a tolerant man and he pointedly excluded from his journal the work of Braid whom he accused of betraying the cause; Braid being sceptical alike of the magnetic hypothesis and of the paranormal.

What, precisely, then, were the manifestations that earned the name 'higher phenomena'? They comprise certain special feats connected with the performance of a gifted somnambule. Thus we have, in the first instance, the phenomenon of 'eyeless sight' or, as it was then sometimes called, 'lucidity'. This involved essentially being able to see through a blindfold or screen and could be tested by means of 'billet reading' (i.e. reading the message inside an opaque envelope) or by means of a 'book test' where the book might be open but the passage to be read was situated further on in the unopened portion of the book. Related to eyeless sight was the phenomenon known as 'the transposition of the senses'. Here the paper bearing the message might be placed on the subject's stomach and a reading given. All this would, today, be classified as varieties of clairvoyance but, at the time, the term clairvoyance was often reserved for certain special tasks such as clairvoyant diagnosis, to which we previously alluded, which implied a kind of X-ray vision of the affected organs of the patient. But the supreme achievement in this line was 'travelling clairvoyance', where the target was a distant place or person (what today we would call 'remote perception'). This could be a very useful accomplishment and was, indeed, often exploited for detective work concerned with the recovery of lost objects or the identification of the culprit. It was often elicited by getting the clairvoyant to handle a relevant object or to grasp the person who was seeking the information. Finally, we may mention in this context 'community of sensation'. This was supposed to come about when the subject had been put in rapport with another individual, usually the magnetizer, and would then respond to whatever sensations were experienced by the latter, whether they be tastes,smells or pinpricks. Most of these phenomena are illustrated in the case histories of the once-celebrated somnambules of the period, some of whom we shall now describe.

Some outstanding Somnambules

The case of Dr J.W. Haddock's subject: Emma L.[10]
Dr Haddock was a general practitioner of Bolton, Lanca- shire, who used mesmerism in his general practice. He was familiar with the work of Dr Braid of Manchester but did not consider that there was any worthwhile distinction to be made as between hypnotism and mesmerism. He was also a firm believer in phrenology, but for that period this does not suggest that he was specially gullible. Both Elliotson and Braid took phrenology seriously and, since there is a natural affinity between unorthodox sciences, it should not surprise us to learn that a science of 'phreno-mesmerism' had by then emerged. Thus, if the mesmerized subject is touched on the part of the head above the 'organ of veneration', a display of religious behaviour could be expected!

Emma was a young woman of somewhat frail health who had entered his service as a maid in 1846 at the age of 20. In that year Dr Haddock was experimenting with ether-vapour as an anaesthetic. Emma offered herself as a subject for these experiments and he then observed that not only did she become completely insensible to pain, even when he thrust pins under her fingernails, but she would go into a sort of trance where she appeared to relive her childhood in Worcestershire. It soon dawned on Haddock that Emma was, in fact, a promising somnambule and he started carrying out all the usual tests and demonstrations including those drawn from the phreno-mesmerist repertoire.

By the beginning of 1848, Emma's powers of eyeless sight or 'lucidity', as Haddock liked to call it, were so far advanced that he was even using her for demonstrations when giving his public lectures at the Temperance Hall in Bolton, at which she would try to describe objects inside boxes for members of the audience. But, while experimenting with her at home, he also found that she was capable of 'travelling clairvoyance'. In this connection her attention was directed to a female relative of Haddock's in London.

Emma's chance to show her mettle in solving a real-life problem came in December of that year when Haddock was approached by a neighbour of his, a Mr Henry Wood, tea-dealer and grocer, whose cash-box had been stolen. The police had been unable to help and, having heard about Emma from a business acquaintance, he asked Haddock if she might be used to throw some light on the matter. Accordingly, Haddock, to oblige, put her into 'mesmeric contact' with Mr Wood and asked her to say, if she could, where the box had been taken from, what was in it and who had taken it. In what followed she duly described where the box had been placed and what was in it, mentioning certain documents that it contained, all to the satisfaction of Mr. Wood. More astonishing, however, she appeared to be conversing with an imaginary individual whom she clearly took to be the thief and her description was so vivid that Mr Wood was able to identify the man in question who, be it noted, was *not* the man whom Mr Wood had suspected. Further questions were then put to her, including a request to say whether she could see any name-plate on the door of the culprit's home. Although Emma was still illiterate at that time, she duly traced the letters with her fingers (although doing so in reverse!). As the name fitted the description, Mr Wood duly apprehended the man and brought him to Haddock's house under the threat of turning him over to the police. At first the man denied his guilt and attempted to brazen it out but, later that day, he duly confessed and confirmed the truth of all Emma's statements concerning the theft.

Emma's most spectacular coup, however, came in 1849 and was reported in the *Bolton Chronicle* for 8 September, from where it found its way into a Liverpool paper and thence even into *The Times*. In July, the firm of Arrowsmith & Co. of Bolton received a letter from a firm in Bradford, Yorkshire, containing the sum of £650 made up from a banknote for £500, another banknote for £50 plus a bill-of-exchange for £100. The Arrowsmith cashier, a Mr William Lomax, duly deposited the amount with the Bank of Bolton but, about five weeks later, after comparing his own ledger with the bank-book, he was disturbed to note that no entry had been made for this deposit. When he tackled the bank manager about this omission, the latter staunchly denied ever having received the sum in question. Naturally poor Mr Lomax was most upset, the more so as he could no longer recall whether he had made the deposit in person or via the customary messenger.

From a friend he had heard how Emma had helped Mr Wood to recover his missing cash-box so, in desperation, he entreated Haddock to secure Emma's services in this case. At her very first session Emma showed that she was on the ball by correctly describing the missing contents of the letter from Bradford even though, while she was doing so, Haddock himself thought she must be wrong, assuming that a cheque rather than banknotes would have been sent. Emma also said that the missing sum was truly with the Bank of Bolton and persisted with this assertion during a subsequent mesmeric session, when she went on to say that the missing notes were in a red pocket-book, wrapped in a paper along with many other papers, in a private part of the bank.

At this point, Haddock advised Mr Arrowsmith, the head of the firm whose money it was, to go to the bank and insist on a further search. Although the bank protested that this was useless, a search was carried out and the missing notes were found exactly as the clairvoyant had described. They were in an inner room of the bank where they had been carelessly mislaid and, doubtless, would have remained there undetected for years.

This incident, says Haddock, 'caused considerable sensation in the neighbourhood, where all the parties were so well known and the main facts so well authenticated'. Apparently, a Manchester paper sought to discredit the idea that Emma's clairvoyance had played any part in the recovery of the money but this was duly answered by the Bolton correspondent of the *Manchester Guardian* who insisted that, whatever interpretation one might choose to put on the case, the facts were undeniable.

The case of the Didier brothers[11]

There were many other private clairvoyants, like Emma, at that time. Another example one could cite was that of Ellen Dawson, a patient of a London physician, Dr J. Hands. She, too, seems to have had a remarkable flair for travelling clairvoyance and the recovery of lost objects.[12] But we must now turn to a very different case where we are dealing with two international celebrities who were also public entertainers. Both their way of life and the magnitude of the claims made on their behalf inevitably demand cautious assessment.

Both Alexis and Adolphe Didier came to public attention as young men in the early 1840s (it was alleged that their father had had clairvoyant powers). They operated quite independently, however. Alexis had a regular magnetizer in the person of J. Marcillet (who had originally been his business employer when Alexis was a clerk) while Adolphe used a number of different magnetizers including J. Richard and C. Lafontaine. Both travelled extensively, both eventually published books about animal magnetism and somnambulism, both books were published in the year 1856 (Adolphe's in London, Alexis' in Paris) and both died in the same year, 1886. For simplicity's sake I shall concentrate on the case of Alexis as he was, in fact, the better known of the two. I shall consider his case from two angles: that of his public performances and that involving his private consultations.

The regular public performances, which were rather frequent – sometimes there would be more than one a day – followed a somewhat stereotyped pattern. After he had been duly magnetized and blindfolded, his first demonstration would be to take part in a game of cards! This was usually followed by a 'book test' in which Alexis would try to discern a phrase printed on some specified later page than the one at which the book had been opened. After that would come tests provided by members of the audience involving 'billet reading', 'token object reading' leading up, finally, to a test of travelling clairvoyance where the person's private home would constitute the target area.

Aside from the sheer incredibility of all this, there was much in Alexis' behaviour to arouse suspicion. He was often observed to fiddle with his blindfold, quite apart from the fact that, as we now know, there *is* no such thing as a foolproof blindfold, or not, at any rate, of the traditional kind. Then when he did start making his guesses he was often very wide of the mark and only gradually would he home in on the actual target. Such a procedure would, obviously, allow for all manner of unwitting hints that the audience might supply and, indeed, a common objection raised by the sceptics at that time was that the supposed clairvoyant only ever gives the sitters information that they had, unwittingly, conveyed to the clairvoyant.

Certainly, not everyone was impressed by Alexis. Sir John

Forbes, a Fellow of the Royal Society and physician to the Queen's Household, had two sittings with Alexis in 1844 and four with his brother, Adolphe, the following year. Like most of the medical establishment, he was sceptical about mesmerism, although he did accept as irrefutable the evidence for anaesthesia in the trance state. But he drew the line at the higher phenomena and his experience with the Didier brothers did not suffice to change his mind. Although unable to put his finger on how they did the trick, he felt sure that trickery must be involved.

On the other hand, someone whom, of all people, one would have expected to be sceptical, confessed that he was completely baffled. I allude to J.E. Robert-Houdin, the most famous conjuror of that time (in deference to whom Houdini adopted his own stage name). His pronouncement was all the more extraordinary since his own repertoire was so similar. Asked by the Marquis de Mirville whether he had ever attended any of the performances given by touring somnambules he replied that he had done so but considered them all purely entertainers like himself. De Mirville decided that it was time he met Alexis and duly effected an introduction. Robert-Houdin eventually held two private sittings with Alexis in 1847 at which he brought his own pack of cards and contrived the blindfolding to his own satisfaction. He even brought along a trusted friend just in case he might overlook anything himself. At the end of these sessions, he handsomely acknowledged that Alexis' phenomena went beyond the art of conjuring as he knew it, which could produce nothing to compare with what Alexis constantly demonstrated.[13]

But I would agree with Dingwall that it was his demonstrations of travelling clairvoyance that are the most impressive, at any rate for us who can only read about his exploits. I shall, in what follows, discuss, as an illustration of this, a surprise visit he received from the Rev. C.H. Townshend in 1851.[14]

Townshend was a wealthy man who owned a sumptuous house in London, near Park Lane, as well as a country house near Lausanne in Switzerland where he spent part of each year. He had some reputation as a poet and he took an interest in mesmerism. That year, while *en route* for Switzerland, he decided, on a whim, to make a detour via Paris and try there to meet Alexis about whom he had heard contradictory reports, some alleging that he was a 'mere sham'. In Paris he contacted Marcillet and introduced himself as a friend of Elliotson but, from the conversation that ensued, he was satisfied that Marcillet had little idea who he was. Marcillet agreed to try and find Alexis and then bring him to Townshend's hotel that same evening.

When Alexis arrived, Townshend himself undertook to mesmerize him, and Marcillet then withdrew, much to the satisfaction of Townshend since there would then at least be no talk of collusion. Townshend plunged straight into a test of travelling clairvoyance by asking Alexis if he would proceed mentally to visit his house – whereupon Alexis demanded, in turn, which house was intended, the one in town or the one in the country? On being directed to the country house, Alexis proceeded to give a description of it from the outside which satisfied Townshend as regards its accuracy. He was then urged to enter the house and go into the drawing-room. Alexis then said that there were many paintings on the walls but that they were all modern apart from two, one a seascape, the other a religious picture. As regards the religious picture (which Townshend had in fact recently purchased from an Italian refugee) he could see three figures: an old man, a woman and a child. The woman held a book on her lap and the child was pointing to something in it. There was also a distaff in the corner. All these details were correct – it was a picture of St Anne teaching the Virgin Mary to read. Then, on being asked what it was that the picture had been painted on, Alexis replied that it was neither canvas nor metal but something else which he eventually identified as stone. The colour of this stone was neither black nor grey but it was rough behind and convex in shape. Again, all of this correct as the picture was (unusually) painted onto a piece of curved marble.

Alexis' efforts with respect to the house in London were no less impressive, but then Townshend decided to try him on some of the other kinds of test on which he was supposed to excel. After he had scored a success with a book test, Townshend then handed him a letter in an opaque envelope. Alexis stated that it contained the words 'brotherhood of nations' (which was correct) and then added that the lady who had sent it lived in Suffolk at an address which he proceeded to write down (correctly). Since the address was on the letter, Townshend wondered whether Alexis might not have contrived to take a surreptitious peek at it. However, when Alexis went on to talk about this lady, mentioning 'many minute circumstances', and when he also spoke about the character of her sister and finally came out with the correct Christian name and surname of her father, Townshend was forced to waive any lingering doubts.

The Didier brothers remain an enigma to this day and I know of no serious attempt to deflate them. It has, indeed, been suggested that Alexis and Marcillet might have operated an intelligence network concerning the homes of potential clients, when necessary bribing servants to provide details of their possessions, but, apart from the fact that there is not a shred of evidence for such a speculation, it would never have worked. Gauld, who discusses this possibility, has this to say:

> One can only say that while, for a given individual case, such an explanation might be made to work, for the *ensemble* of recorded cases, the idea is impossible..the scale of the operations would have been so large, the expense so great, the risk of being betrayed so acute, and the difficulty of retaining all the information and

producing individual items of it for the right persons at the right times so enormous, that the whole enterprise would have collapsed before it had been properly started.[15]

The case of Justus Kerner's subject, Friedericke Hauffe, the 'seeress of Prevorst'[16]

Our third example is of interest, not for its evidential value, but because it has important historical repercussions. It belongs to a tradition which Gauld calls 'mystical magnetism' which flourished especially in Germany, then in the throes of the Romantic movement. The facts of the case are as follows. Justus Kerner, who was both a poet and a physician, was the medical officer for the district of Weinsberg in the State of Wurttemberg. He is credited with being the discoverer of a type of food-poisoning that we now know as 'botulism'. Friedericke, the daughter of a game-keeper of Prevorst, was, from an early age, given to prophetic dreams, nocturnal visions and such like odd experiences. Following an unhappy arranged marriage she became de-pressed and contracted a severe fever. Significantly, she occasionally entered spontaneously into the somnambulistic state when, as somnambulists were wont, she would then prescribe for her own malady. As she wasted away, however, her life was feared for and eventually, in 1826, Kerner was called in. He had her moved to Weinsberg so as to keep her under close observation and, thereafter, he kept a detailed diary of her condition.

As conventional remedies only seemed to make her worse Kerner (who as a child had himself been cured by a mesmer-ist) took to magnetizing her. Her somnambulism, as it then developed under Kerner, took unusual forms. For example, she was much given to propounding cosmological and theo-logical teachings which even managed to impress some of Kerner's learned friends. She was also prone to confabulate about other worlds and other types of being and to discourse at times in an unknown language. There is sporadic evidence of some genuine psychic ability. For example, she sometimes exhibited something akin to Scottish second sight when she would have a prevision of an impending death. She was also credited with being a ghost-seer and seems to have solved a mystery connected with one local case of haunting. There are, too, accounts of physical phenomena occurring in her presence such as the displacement of objects.

Unfortunately Kerner failed to save her life and she died in 1829 at the early age of 28. Kerner then published his case-history of her with the title *Die Seherin von Prevorst* which appeared in 1832. It was a runaway success. Ellenberger calls it 'the first monograph devoted to an individual patient in the field of dynamic psychiatry'.[17] Furthermore, on the basis of the correspondence it generated and the fresh cases it brought to light, Kerner founded a journal, *Blatter von Prevorst*, which ran from 1831 to 1839, followed by another journal, *Magikon*, which ran from 1840 to 1853. Ellenberger describes them as: 'probably the first journals devoted mainly to parapsychology'.[18]

Mesmerism: A retrospective reassessment

Mesmerism remains an enigma. What was it, one wonders, that lay behind this movement which Mesmer ushered into the world at the end of the eighteenth century and then virtually disappeared again by the end of the 1850s? Its one abiding legacy, hypnotism, does not provide the answer. There is an obvious affinity between the deeply hypnotized subject and the mesmeric somnambule, but both the medical potentialities of hypnotism, which lie largely in the field of psychiatry, and its parapsychological applications, largely a matter of boosting ESP scoring, are so low key by comparison with those associated with mesmerism that the latter seems to point to a quite different order of phenomenon. And this difference become all the more pronounced as we come closer to the present time when hypnotism, itself, has been so far demystified that it is now commonly treated as a socio-psychological phenomenon involving a compliant subject who indulges an authority figure.[19] Basically, then, we are left with two mysteries on our hands. First, how to account for the therapeutic successes claimed by the mesmerists with respect to a wide range of organic illnesses. Secondly, what to make of the astonishing displays of clairvoyance such as we have noted in connection with some of the more remark-able somnambules of that period which have no parallel in recent times.[20]

As I explained, mesmerism always purported to be, in the first place, a branch of medicine, although it has always been tempting to suppose that mesmeric cures are just another example of the power of suggestion, such as we find with the 'placebo effect'. Such, indeed, was the interpretation of the original Royal Commissions of 1784 when they attributed the effects to the 'power of the imagination'. Nevertheless, I would agree with Gauld, who has made an extensive exami-nation of the records kept by the nineteenth-century mesmerists, that this cannot be the whole story. As he points out, most of their patients were rejects from a medical pro-fession that could do nothing for them. If the treatment they got from physicians of imposing status and credentials was unavailing, how was it that the despised mesmerists so often got impressive results?

Gauld offers one ingenious suggestion. Perhaps the exten-sive stroking that accompanies a mesmeric cure releases those natural opiates which, as we now know, the brain can secrete and are now widely thought to explain the efficacy of acupuncture.[21] Like the mesmerists, the acupuncturists also claim to be able to anaesthetize a patient for surgical opera-tions. But, whatever the merits of this suggestion, it is unlikely to solve more than one aspect of our problem. It seems more likely to me that we are, in fact, dealing with cases that would now come under the heading of 'psychic healing.'

And, although the latter may be controversial, as, indeed, is everything that falls into the category of the paranormal, evidence for such healing continues to accumulate. To say this, is not, of course, to solve the mystery of mesmerism, but it does at any rate set it in a wider context and one that remains a live issue at the present time.

What does seem to me to be incontestable is that the mesmerists were sadly mistaken in adhering to Mesmer's conviction that the mesmeric influence could be explained in terms of a mysterious energy or fluid or, indeed, of any physical force, however subtle. In Mesmer's own day, when magnetism itself, along with electricity and galvanism, were still exciting novelties, the idea had an understandable appeal. Yet even today, many parapsychologists believe (mistakenly in my view) that paranormal phenomena are all potentially explicable in terms of some principle of physics that has yet to be clarified – usually some of the more paradoxical implications of modern quantum theory are invoked to provide an answer.

The closest parallel with mesmerism at the present time, I would suggest, is to be found in the Chinese system of *qi-gong*, a branch of traditional Chinese medicine now again widely practised in China. The Chinese concept of *qi*, as a vague but universal form of energy, invites comparison with the mesmeric concept of a magnetic fluid. In both cases, health is held to be dependent on its proper distribution. What makes the comparison even more inviting is that both mesmerism and *qi-gong* are closely associated with paranormal phenomena. Indeed, at the present time, China is perhaps the one country in the world where one hears persistent claims for the occurrence of strong paranormal effects under controlled conditions.

But perhaps the biggest mystery of all is the virtual disappearance of strong paranormal phenomena in the rest of the world. Where could one now even begin to look for another Alexis Didier? Not that the likes of Didier were ever common even at the best of times. Yet the somnambules flourished for a while until they, in turn, were succeeded by a string of no less amazing mediums. Eventually, mediumship, too, slowly degenerated until it barely presented a challenge to the student of the paranormal. One can only suggest that we are, here as elsewhere, dealing with phenomena that are peculiarly culture-bound and which, with the decline or disappearance of the culture that produced them, eventually cease to be attainable. This may sound a lame and defeatist note on which to conclude but, if so, it is one which a study of the mesmeric era makes it hard to resist.

CHAPTER 2

Spiritualism

The importance of spiritualism in the history of parapsychology is twofold. First, it revived the age-old question of a life after death in an empirically testable form. Secondly, from the seance-room there issued a steady stream of puzzling phenomena, much of it of a physical nature, which, irrespective of its implications for the survival problem, cried out for impartial investigation.[1]

If the burial customs found by archaeologists are anything to go by, there was probably never a time when belief in an after life did not exist and, to my knowledge, there is no society known to anthropology where it is absent. This suggests that, for whatever reason, such a belief has deep-seated roots in human nature. Most religions incorporate this belief into their doctrines, often linking it to the idea of posthumous rewards or punishments. Christianity is the most salient example. Communication with the deceased, however, was another matter. Although something of the kind is part of the shamanistic tradition, a shaman being an intermediary with the spirits of the dead and the living, all three of the great monotheistic religions frowned on such practices, and none more so than the Christian Church. What distinguishes the movement we call 'spiritualism' from previous attempts to come to grips with the problem was not only its encouragement of such communication, as affording comfort and hope to the bereaved, but its matter-of-fact attitude towards that other world. So far, indeed, was the spiritualist after-life from any sort of Dantesque scenario, it strikes one as hardly more than a cosier version of the world we know![2]

The fact is that by the 1850s, when spiritualism got going, the Romantic movement was a thing of the past and the prevailing ethos was one befitting the extraordinary rate of progress taking place in industry and in science. Although spiritualism was, of course, scorned by most of the established figures and leading thinkers of that era as too preposterous, nevertheless spiritualism could justly claim to be considered the first religion to base itself on concrete evidence (however questionable) rather than on revelation or faith.

As with any movement in the history of ideas, one can trace its antecedents. During the previous century the celebrated Swedish savant and seer, Emanuel Swedenborg (1688–1772), propounded his own teachings based on visions of Heaven and Hell and on his experiences of holding intercourse with departed souls that included some of the famous names from history. These gave rise to a Swedenborgian Church that still exists.[3] Somewhat later, some of the mesmeric somnambules attracted attention by retailing their visions of the life to come. But the idea of holding routine commerce with one's deceased relatives and friends, as a facility open to all, was something undreamt of before the Fox sisters got their act together around 1850.

The spiritualist movement is often taken as commencing with the mysterious rappings heard at the house of John Fox in Hydesville, Upper New York State, in 1848. But similar poltergeist outbreaks had been known since antiquity. At most it provided the impetus that set the whole thing in motion. Nothing illustrates this more clearly than the rapidity with which it spread. The first notable converts, around

1850, were Judge J.W. Edmonds, of the New York Court of Appeals, and Horace Greely, editor of the *New York Tribune*. The former had lost a wife, the latter a son.[4] By the mid-1850s, spiritualism had taken Europe by storm so that mediums and 'home-circles' were to be found in almost every European country and in every stratum of society. Whatever the ultimate verdict of posterity may be as to the nature of spiritualistic phenomena, it is doubtful whether any other movement in history, be it magical or occultist, religious or mystical, or, like mesmerism, quasi-scientific, ever produced such a profusion of puzzling phenomena or made such outrageous claims as did spiritualism at the height of its success in mid-Victorian England.

One must keep in mind, however, the distinction between the message and its manifestations. The message – that death is not the end of personal existence – whether true or false is one thing. It must not be confused, however, with the question as to whether the manifestations that purported to convey this message are indeed paranormal or can be explained in terms of the ingenuity of the mediums and the gullibility of their clients. That question, too, remains controversial but it is, at least, much more amenable to a solution. Parapsychology has, for better or worse, inherited the survival problem, which it cannot disown, but, for the most part, it has concentrated on the paranormality of phenomena among which spiritualistic phenomena constitute no more than one special category. It took a rare determination, it must be said, to examine such phenomena objectively instead of dismissing them out of hand. Conditions were never ideal. Most mediums insisted on performing in darkness or semi-darkness and observers were constrained in what they were permitted to do. It required all one's ingenuity to overcome such obstacles, and positive findings would invariably be challenged. Yet, whatever mistakes the early pioneers may have made, they cannot be accused of lacking intellectual courage.

In its dealings with spiritualism, two distinct phases can be discerned in the development of psychical research. In the first phase it was the physical phenomena as such that preoccupy the investigators, rather than their putative significance as coded messages or manifestations of the spirits. In the second phase it is the information imparted by the medium herself, whether in spoken or written form, that becomes the focus of attention as providing evidence for survival.

Spiritualistic phenomena

The key figure of the first phase was Daniel Home (or D.D. Home as he is generally referred to in the literature) (1833–1886). Born in Edinburgh but brought up in America, he became incomparably the most celebrated medium of all time, judging by the number and impressiveness of the seances of which we have records and by the calibre of the observers whom he attracted in the many countries he visited. Virtually all Home's phenomena fall into the physical category.[5]

The key figure of the second phase was Leonora Piper of Boston (1859–1950). She was discovered in 1884 by no less a person than the great William James, psychologist and Harvard professor, but she spent her entire career as a retainer of the Society for Psychical Research, of London, who early on steered her away from physical phenomena and encouraged her development as a trance medium who could act as a mouthpiece for deceased communicators.[6]

It may seem odd that, in the early exuberant days of spiritualism, so much prominence should have been given to the physical phenomena. If communication with the departed was to be the object of the exercise, the production of raps, even when coded to spell out messages, seems clumsy as compared with verbal messages conveyed by a medium. There were, it is true, the odd cases of supposedly direct

spirit-writing on slates or of direct voice, but such manifestations were exceptional. Even when materializations were
introduced, they were more likely to be legendary figures or
unknown spirit-controls rather than known deceased individuals. However, the aim presumably was to impress. Most
religions, after all, recognize the propaganda value of miracles – none more so than Christianity – and one could regard
the seance-room in this light as pre-eminently a power-house
of miracles. The implication was that, since such wonders
exceeded mortal powers, they could only be the work of
spirits. It is true that some of the more sophisticated sitters
who attended Home's seances acknowledged the phenomena
as genuine without ascribing them to the work of spirits, but,
to the ordinary sitter, they were a striking and reassuring
confirmation of his or her own immortality.

The variety of spiritualistic phenomena of this physical
kind was very wide. Among the more spectacular we may
note the following: the playing of musical instruments by
unseen hands; the movement of objects and items of furniture by an invisible agency; the levitation of furniture and,
occasionally, of persons; the sudden inexplicable intrusion of
objects into the seance-room (apports) or sudden displacement of an object from one locale to another (teleportation)
and, most provocative of all, materializations. At first these
were mostly partial materializations, usually hands that
ended at the wrist or elbow; full form materializations, such
as were ultimately to become indistinguishable from a living
human being, were a feature of the 1870s. And, since materialized objects did not outlast the seance, one must add here
the phenomenon of *de*materialization. A dematerialization,
moreover, could be harder to fake than a materialization. A
materialized hand might, after all, prove to be an inflated
rubber glove, but what is one to say of a hand that simply
melts away in one's grasp?

That all such phenomena (what parapsychologists nowadays call 'macro-PK') lack credibility goes without saying.

For one thing we know of nothing comparable at the present time (unless we include the occasional poltergeist case). Nevertheless, objectivity and open-mindedness oblige us to take such claims seriously. Home was the great virtuoso in this connection. A typical seance with Home, where there might be perhaps a dozen sitters, would include the following sequence of demonstrations. First, the room itself together with the chairs on which the sitters were seated would shake and vibrate (this was known as the 'earthquake effect').[7] Next, various tiltings of the table might occur when it would be observed that objects placed on the table would stay put instead of sliding off. This might be succeeded by the invisible playing of musical instruments. The accordion was a regular feature of Home's seances. Sometimes he would hold the instrument by the end away from the keyboard but sometimes it was said to play of its own accord without anyone visibly touching it. The climax of a Home seance, however, was the levitation of a large table. Such, briefly, was the act which won Home his entree to society and which made him a fêted guest at the courts of Europe.[8] This does not, by any means, cover the full range of his phenomena. There was also his handling of live coals, for example, his self-levitations and the elongations of his body, but these peculiar marvels would be kept for special occasions and for selected sitters.

Was he for real? There was much in the personality of Home and in the circumstances surrounding him that invites suspicion, quite apart from the sheer incredibility of what he was supposed to have done. It is hardly surprising therefore that today it is taken for granted by writers of a sceptical bent that Home was nothing more than a skilled illusionist. Yet, if that is so, the question arises: how was it done? For it is important to realize that, when we talk, for example, of Home's table-levitations (his most consistent phenomenon) we are not talking about a flimsy card-table or the like that can be hoisted with one foot, but rather of a massive Victorian mahogany dining-room table such as would require more than one person to lift it off the ground. Moreover, the table often rose to a level that obliged the sitters (whose hands would be resting on the table in full view) to rise from their chair – and even then they could not always reach. Moreover, unlike most of the other mediums of that time, Home normally operated in good light, usually gaslight, and it was only with special phenomena such as materializations or self-levitations, which were usually reserved for sympathetic sitters, that the lights were turned down (it being a tenet of spiritualist lore that light was inimical to the process of materialization). His seances, it should be noted, were held in private houses or, occasionally, in hotels, often at short notice that did not allow for any preparation, and it goes without saying there could be no question of accomplices.

Now, while mediumship of this order is a thing of the past, conjuring techniques have made consistent progress since the mid-nineteenth century. If Home were doing all this by sleight of hand, one wonders why some enterprising magician of today does not offer to perform similar stunts in similar circumstances.[9] An alternative scenario, and one that would avoid invoking massive concealed machinery, is to suggest that everyone who came into his presence invariably became hallucinated. But when we consider the hundreds of named individuals who, in the course of his career, witnessed his phenomena, this is hardly easier to credit than levitating tables. For we do not even have one instance of someone who failed to see what everyone claimed to see. Even his bitterest critics, like Robert Browning, whose animosity towards Home was notorious, freely admits, in an account of a seance he attended, that: 'I don't know at all how the thing was done.'[10] And, so far, Browning's puzzlement has gone unanswered.

In view of the prominence accorded to physical phenomena during the early period, it is not surprising that, among scientists, it was the physicists, or physical scientists, who were most keen to investigate what, at first blush, must have looked like a new force in nature. Later on, when the focus shifted to mental mediumship,it was, again not surprisingly, the specialists in abnormal psychology who led the way.

Perhaps the first scientist of repute to show an interest in spiritualism, as well as the first to test Home, was Robert Hare (1781–1858) who was Professor of Chemistry at the Medical College of the University of Pennsylvania.[11] Hare could hardly be described as a pushover for spiritualist propaganda. On the contrary, he was also the first to denounce it in the name of science in the American press. There he declared that it was his duty 'to stem the tide of popular madness which, in defiance of reason and science, was fast setting in favour of the gross delusion called spiritualism'[12] Where he differed from the great majority of his colleagues and contemporaries was in thinking that one ought, nevertheless, to investigate the claims that one was denouncing.

Using his ingenuity as a designer of apparatus he devised a number of contrivances for eliminating deception during a seance. In particular, he built what he dubbed a 'spiritscope' which consisted of a disc about a foot in diameter on which were placed the letters of the alphabet in random order. This disc would revolve when the table tilted by dint of a system of springs and pulleys that brought the various letters of the alphabet successively under a pointer, thus spelling out a message. The disc was so positioned that he alone, not the medium or the sitters, would be able to see the letters. Using this device Hare obtained many such messages which were not only coherent but which yielded factual information which could later be verified. But what finally clinched the matter, so far as Hare was concerned, was the discovery that he, too, possessed mediumistic ability and so could himself activate the spiritscope on his own and obtain evidential information.[13] The upshot was his book, which appeared in 1855, whose full title was *Experimental Investigation of the Spirit Manifestations Demonstrating the Existence of Spirits and their Communion with Mortals.* Although, as the title indicates, Hare had, after much deliberation, accepted the spiritualist interpretation of such phenomena he pleads that those who are not prepared to go that far should try these experiments for themselves. These, he assures them, will 'not only affirm the existence of the sounds and movements but also their inscrutability.'

Hare was made to pay dearly for his empiricism. The professors of Harvard, far from wanting to try his experiments, passed a resolution denouncing him and 'his insane adherence to a gigantic humbug'. Similarly, when he attempted to address the American Association for the Advancement of Science, when it met in Washington in 1854, he was howled down. Soon afterwards, he resigned his Chair.

At much the same time as Hare was engaged in this work in the United States, systematic investigations of table tilting or 'table turning' were going on in Europe. One of the pioneers in this connection was a French politician and scholar, Count Agenor de Gasparin, who had left France after the revolution of 1848 and settled in Switzerland. In 1854 he published a book *Des Tables Tournantes* in which he describes a series of experiments which he had carried out with his own family and friends as sitters, where the upward or downward pressure on the table was registered on a balance. He claimed that his results precluded any obvious normal explanations but he refused to ascribe them to the intervention of spirits. His work came to the attention of Marc Thury, then Professor of Physics and Natural History at the University of Geneva, who, in turn, conducted his own investigations under still more stringent conditions before endorsing de Gasparin's findings. Thury was the first to posit a hypothetical substance – he called it a 'psychode'– whereby the mind might act on material objects.[14]

The first British scientist of note to evince an interest in spiritualism was Augustus de Morgan (1806–1871). He was Professor of Mathematics at University College, London, and for many years Secretary to the Royal Astronomical Society. He seems an unlikely convert considering that his atheistic views had debarred him from a position at Oxford or Cambridge but his involvement with spiritualism was partly due to his wife, Sophia. She worked with Mrs Hayden, the first American medium to visit Britain, and, later, with her own servant, Jane, whom she discovered to possess mediumistic powers. On the basis of her findings, she published anonymously a book, *From Matter to Spirit*, in 1863, to which her husband contributed an anonymous preface (although the second edition duly disclosed both their authorships). In it, De Morgan was more cautious than Hare about ascribing the phenomena to spirits although he insisted there that 'I have both seen and heard, in a manner which should make unbelief impossible, things called spiritual which cannot be taken by a rational being to be capable of explanation by imposture, coincidence or mistake'. His positive appraisal was a factor in William Crookes' decision to enter the arena, as Crookes himself acknowledges.[15]

Crookes (1832–1919) began his investigation of Home in May 1871. It was to prove the most important step in bringing spiritualism into the laboratory. Crookes had been introduced to Home by Dr James Gully at whose well-known hydropathic clinic at Malvern, Home, a consumptive, had been a patient. Crookes, now 39, had been made a Fellow of the Royal Society in 1863 for his discovery of the element thallium in 1861 and was now regarded as one of the outstanding physical scientists of Victorian England.[16] Home was then 38 and at the zenith of his fame. In 1869 Lord Adare had published his *Experiences in Spiritualism*, an account of an extraordinary series of seances which he, together with two of his close friends, had held with Home at Adare's London residence at Ashley House, Victoria Street. It had provoked much speculation and controversy.[17]

With the help of a few intimate friends, together with his wife, Ellen, his brother, his daughter and his laboratory assistant, Crookes held a series of sittings at his home, in the course of which almost the full range of Home's phenomena were observed. William Huggins FRS, an astronomer, was one of the sitters, another was the lawyer Edward Cox (generally known to the literature as Serjeant Cox) who, once he had overcome his initial suspicions, had become a keen student of spiritualistic phenomena. Crookes lays special emphasis on a test which he devised involving a wooden beam that rested at one end on a table while the other end was suspended from a spring balance. Home had to place his fingers at the table end past the fulcrum while exerting a 'psychic force' that would be registered as a downward thrust on the spring balance. Other variations on this set-up were tried in which Home's hands were immersed in a bowl of water connected to the beam, and clear indications were recorded of a substantial downward thrust on the spring balance.

Sceptics may today speculate about the possibility of Home tugging at invisible threads, but those present, at any rate, had no such suspicions. Significantly, however, the Honorary Secretaries of the Royal Society refused Crookes' invitation to act as witnesses and when, in due course, Crookes submitted his report of his findings to the Royal Society in June of that year, even the title of his report was refused acknowledgement in the Society's publications. Fortunately, as Editor of the *Quarterly Journal of Science*, he was free to publish his report there and, eventually, in 1874, he brought it out in book form.[18] It is amusing to note that, when it was first announced in the press that Crookes was to undertake an investigation of spiritualism, there was public jubilation – it being taken for granted that he would expose it for the humbug it was assumed to be. Once it became known, however, that his findings were positive, he had to fend for himself.

It is a sad commentary on the reluctance of scientists to risk upsetting their preconceptions that so few responded to

Crookes' entreaties to witness Home's phenomena for themselves. The great Michael Faraday was peculiarly obstinate in this regard. Faraday had indeed made a promising start, in 1853, as an investigator of spiritualistic phenomena by showing convincingly, by means of some ingenious demonstrations which he devised, that, when a number of people have their hands on a table, unconscious muscular activity is quite sufficient to account for the observed movements or tiltings of that table. Effects of this kind, however, were of course a long way from the sort of things which Home was able to produce in good illumination. Following the publication, in the *Cornhill Magazine*, by the well-known contemporary writer Robert Bell, describing a seance he had witnessed with Home, Faraday was again approached to see whether he might now be willing to attend such a seance. Unfortunately, Faraday was a Christian fundamentalist to whom the very notion of spirits was abhorrent. Accordingly, he made it a condition of his cooperation that Home first acknowledge that all such phenomena were, at most, 'glimpses of natural action not yet reduced to law' and then admit 'the utterly contemptible character of them and their results, up to the present time' (as if it mattered what Home thought provided the phenomena were real!). After that one need hardly add that nothing came of this overture.

One of the few well-known scientists who *did* respond to Crookes' invitation was the wide-ranging and ever-curious Francis Galton. He attended three seances at which both Home and Kate Fox (or Fox-Jencken – as she now was, following her marriage to H.D. Jencken, an English barrister) were the mediums. Galton was so impressed that he wrote to his cousin, Charles Darwin, urging him to see for himself what was going on. His letter, dated 19 April 1872, is worth quoting at length if only because it dispels the common stereotype of a seance as a situation where observation is necessarily clouded by emotion or excitement. After mentioning that it was conducted in 'full gas-light', and describing the playing of the accordion when 'held by *its base*', he goes on to say:

> What surprises me is the perfect openness of Miss F. and Home. They let you do whatever you like within certain limits, their limits not interfering with adequate investigation. I really believe the truth of what they allege, that people who come as men of science are usually so disagreeable, opinionated and obstructive and have so little patience, that the seance rarely succeeds with them. It is curious to observe the entire absence of excitement or tension about people at a seance. Familiarity has bred contempt of the strange things witnessed ... Crookes, I am sure, so far as is just for me to give an opinion, is thoroughly scientific in his procedure. I am convinced that the affair is no matter of vulgar legerdemain and believe it is well worth going into, on the understanding that a *first rate medium* (and I hear there are only three such) puts himself at your disposal (author's italics).[19]

Darwin was duly impressed, and Galton then wrote to Home enclosing a letter from Darwin. When no reply was forthcoming Crookes explained that Home had gone to Russia and they should wait until the following spring, as no other medium could be relied on to produce comparable results. In the event, Home, whose health had deteriorated, never returned to England and so we shall never know what might have happened had there been such an historic encounter between Darwin and Home. What *did* happen was that Galton eventually lost interest in psychical research and settled back into a position of conventional scepticism.

Yet, even before Crookes got going, the London Dialectical Society, a rationalist debating club, had undertaken its own investigation of spiritualism in 1869. Depositions were taken from witnesses and, in addition, six sub-committees were set up to investigate for themselves diverse phenomena. One such committee, on which no professional medium was admitted, obtained some striking effects, involving raps and movements of the table in good light, even when all hands had been withdrawn some distance from the table. Curiously, the one committee which *did* use a professional medium – none other than Home himself – got only rather feeble results. Even Home could not always be counted on to deliver the goods! Not that he was easily put out by sceptics. He had put up a brilliant display before a group of Dutch rationalists and sceptics who tested him in Amsterdam in 1858.[20]

Despite dissenting opinion from the chairman of the general committee and from three other members, the London Dialectical Society duly issued its report in July 1870 declaring that 'in the absence of any proof of imposture or delusion as regards a large proportion of the phenomena' and despite the fact that 'no philosophical explanation of them has yet been arrived at..the subject is worthy of more serious attention than it has hitherto received'. The fact, however, that neither Thomas Huxley nor George Lewes deigned to accept the Society's invitation to participate, did not augur well for the prospect of such phenomena receiving 'more serious attention'. The Society's efforts were predictably lambasted in the press by journalists who were disappointed that the report had not done more to discredit what the *Saturday Review* called: 'one of the most unequivocally degrading superstitions that has ever found currency among reasonable beings'. It was not until 1882, with the founding of The Society of Psychical Research in London, as a meeting-point of spiritualists, scholars and scientists, that the topic did at last gain the attention it deserved and a measure of respect.

In the preface of his 1874 volume on his experiments with Home, Crookes had declared that 'I cannot, at present, hazard even the most vague hypothesis as to the cause of the phenomena', adding 'Hitherto I have seen nothing to

convince me of the truth of the "spiritual" theory.' In this
regard he was in line with earlier investigators of a scientific
outlook such as de Gasparin or Thury whom we have already
mentioned. In the ensuing chapters he does, indeed, talk of
a 'psychic force' but that is about as far as he was then willing
to indulge in speculation. His subsequent career, however, is
an example of what his critics would see as a rake's progress.
His initial attempt to distance himself from the spiritualist
camp gives way to a greater readiness to adopt the spiritualist
outlook as the phenomena he investigates become ever more
bizarre. Although he never went as far as Alfred Russel
Wallace or Cromwell Varley (to name two of his contemporary Fellows of the Royal Society) he began to realize that
something even more subversive was involved than a new
force in nature. Moreover, as Brandon (1983) has pointed
out, the loss through illness of a much-loved younger
brother, in 1867, may well have made him receptive to the
spiritualist message.

The turning-point of Crookes' career as a psychical researcher came in December 1873, when he took up with the
young medium, Florence Cook, then under a cloud following
accusations of blatant fraud. She was only 17 at the time but
already her fame had spread abroad. Now it is one thing to
talk about a 'psychic force' when one is dealing primarily
with alterations in the weight of objects, as Crookes had been
in his experiments with Home. But when one is dealing with
materialization, that is, with the sudden emergence and subsequent dissolution of a complex organism, something more
way-out is indicated. Yet with young Florrie, nothing less
was at issue than a full-form materialization.

'Katie King' (putative daughter of John King, who
claimed to have been Henry Morgan, the seventeenth-cen-
tury buccaneer, and who was, for some reason the favourite
spirit-control among mediums)[21] was, to all appearances, a
duplicate of her medium, albeit a finer specimen of woman-
hood. Crookes held numerous seances with Florence in his

own home in Newington Road (off Regents Park), London, until 'Katie's' final manifestation in May 1874. Then, already in June of that year, Crookes published an account of his findings in the *Spiritualist* in which he declared unequivocally that: 'I have the most absolute certainty that Miss Cook and Katie are two separate individuals so far as their bodies are concerned' and proceeded to list a number of physical differences which he had duly noted.[22] Was he lying? Was he deceived? Or, was this, *per impossibile*, a genuine phenomenon?

What makes this case so truly baffling is that, however disconcerting it may be for those who cannot tolerate ambiguity, there *just is no* plausible explanation! In 1962 the late Trevor Hall published his book *The Spiritualists*[23] in which he put forward his much discussed thesis that Florence Cook and William Crookes were lovers and that his endorsement of her mediumship was the price he had to pay for her sexual favours. This bold conjecture impressed even that eminent historian of psychical research, Eric Dingwall, and more recently it has been favourably canvassed by Ruth Brandon.[24] Perhaps the most telling piece of positive evidence in its favour is that Florence herself is alleged to have said as much, twenty years later, in 1893. She confided this to a young man, Francis Anderson, her then lover, who in 1922 related her disclosure to the SPR. Anderson, however, had no interest in psychical research and so never bothered to interrogate Florence on the details of the case.

While, no doubt, this thesis could explain much, there are as I see it a number of fatal objections. In the first place, not only would Crookes have had to deceive his wife, under her very nose, so to speak, but, more to the point, he would have had to deceive some of his most loyal friends, like Cromwell Varley or Dr Gully. Varley had devised for him an electrical test whereby, if Florence were to quit the chair where she was supposed to remain throughout the seance, this would show up as a break in the electrical resistance. Hall suggests that

Crookes coached her as to how to elude this test.[25] Gully was present at many of these seances and is presumed to have actively assisted Crookes with the photography. Curiously these seances were the occasion for one of the earliest exercises in flashlight photography, and the sheer amount of effort involved in obtaining the numerous photographs is difficult to reconcile with the idea that the whole venture was nothing more than a charade to cover up an illicit assignation. Certainly nothing that we know about William Crookes – and we know a fair amount – would lead us to suppose that he was capable of such audacious cynicism and mendacity as Hall's thesis implies. It would, after all, have meant making a mockery of the two causes which meant most to him in his life: science and psychical research.

But, however cynical we may be about Crookes, where the thesis becomes completely unstuck (although its supporters have curiously failed to notice this), is with the involvement of Mary Rosina Showers. Miss Showers, in contrast to Florence with her working-class background, was the daughter of a high-ranking Indian Army officer, but the two young women were good friends for all that. Now Miss Showers also claimed to be able to produce a full-form materialization who went by the name of 'Florence Maple' and she and Miss Cook held certain joint seances under Crookes' supervision at which 'Katie King' and 'Florence Maple' paraded arm-in-arm! At first Crookes was much impressed. He then discovered that Miss Showers was shamming and that her 'Florence Maple' was none other than Miss Showers in disguise! Through an intermediary, Crookes was able to extract a full confession from her to this effect. Crookes' detractors have commented on the absurdity of the idea that a genuine 'Katie King' would consort with a phoney 'Florence Maple' although, granted the premise that Katie was, to all intents and purposes a normal woman (at least for the duration of the seance) there would be nothing to stop her from consorting with anybody. What these critics *failed* to notice is that, if the Katie King seances were a mere cover-up for his surreptitious amours, why on earth should Crookes have risked everything by involving someone like Miss Showers – with all the opportunities for blackmail that that would open up? Even more to the point, why, having got her involved, would he then go out of his way to accuse her of cheating? How indeed would he dare to do so, assuming as he must have done that she was privy to what was going on? And, anyway, why would he bother,if he knew all along that such phenomena were fraudulent? Thus, on the collusion hypothesis, it is impossible to make any sense at all of the Showers episode.

There remains the possibility that Crookes was the innocent dupe of Miss Cook's machinations. There is, certainly, much that we know about Florence Cook that should make us highly suspicious. She consorted with mediums who were exposed in fraud, and her later career, after she had parted with Crookes, degenerated into a tomfoolery that was both fraudulent and farcical. Nevertheless, the fact is that, during the seances at his home, Crookes had a total freedom of manoeuvre. If she were indeed masquerading as Katie King, how are we to explain, for example, the dye-test in which Katie had to dip her hands in dye but Florence was found to be unaffected (a test which Miss Showers notably failed to pass)? If, on the other hand, 'Katie' was a confederate who had been surreptitiously insinuated into the Crookes' household, where on earth could Florence have found a confederate who was virtually her double (she had no twin sister)?

Whatever the truth of this strange episode (which must now remain for ever a matter of surmise),[26] the upshot was that Crookes was subjected to a barrage of criticism and ridicule, not just from his fellow scientists but from some of his fellow psychical researchers, like Edward Cox. If his report on Home had been met with disdainful silence, his account of Cook was treated with open derision and contempt.

At all events, he must have felt by then that he had done his bit for the paranormal, for he soon returned to more orthodox pursuits. Whatever psychical research may have lost thereby, physics and chemistry certainly gained. He did pioneering work on the properties of highly rarefied gases and on spectroscopy, while his work on cathode rays paved the way for J.J. Thomson's discovery of the electron.[27] The nation duly recognized his worth,he was knighted in 1897, was awarded the Order of Merit in 1910, and served as President of the Royal Society from 1913 to 1915.

Even so, Crookes never turned his back on psychical research nor on Florence Cook. To the end he never retracted any of the claims he had made for her, always insisting that there was more he might have said had he chosen to do so. Moreover he and his wife continued to befriend her until her lonely death from pneumonia in April 1904. Nor did he ever lose his wider interest in psychical research. He remained friendly with Home until the latter's death in June 1888, and served as President of the SPR from 1886 to 1889. The *Dictionary of National Biography* nicely sums it up when it remarks: 'His excursions into psychical research have been strongly criticized and they certainly led him into some curious situations, but they show that he thought all phenomena worthy of investigation and refused to be bound by traditions tradition or convention.'

The vogue for full-form materializations during the 1870s, as exemplified by such exponents as Florence Cook, Rosina Showers, Eva Fay, Elizabeth d'Esperance, Francis Monck and William Eglinton, represents a high-water mark of the more florid type of spiritualistic phenomena. These mediums were, on any reckoning, a rum crew and they were all, at one time or another, detected in, or suspected of, fraud. Yet it was not only Crookes but others of impeccable integrity and reputation, such as Alfred Wallace or Hensleigh Wedgwood (the philologist and cousin of Charles Darwin) who were prepared to vouch for one or other of them.

Undoubtedly, however, such claims made it even harder for psychical research to gain an unprejudiced hearing in scientific circles. This was partly on account of the nature of the phenomena – and spirit photographs did nothing to lessen their ludicrous aspect – and partly on account of the fact that, by then, spiritualism was known to be riddled with malpractices. Indeed, Home himself complains bitterly (Home, 1877) that fraudulent practitioners had brought the entire movement into disrepute and made a mockery of its mission.

Proving survival

It was this scandalous aspect of physical mediumship which persuaded the founders of the Society for Psychical Research (SPR), about which we shall have much more to say in our next chapter, to concentrate henceforth on the more salubrious phenomena of mental mediumship. It is not that the Sidgwick group were indifferent to physical phenomena. Thus both Myers and Gurney held sittings with a pair of female materializing mediums from Newcastle, Annie Fairlamb and C.E. Wood (they operated as a duo) between April 1875 and January 1877 but, although some striking effects were observed, conditions were never as tight as they would have wished, there were strong suspicions of fraud, and, in the end, they gave up in sheer desperation![28]

Physical mediumship never disappeared and we shall have occasion, later,to discuss the careers of some of the more remarkable physical mediums of the late nineteenth and early twentieth centuries. But when a truly first-rate mental medium came along, in the person of Leonora Piper, she was expressly discouraged from exercising any physical powers by the leaders of the SPR in London who had engaged her on a permanent basis by paying her a retaining fee to devote herself exclusively to research. Their object now was to discover whether there was some substance to the spiritualist claim that survival was more than a mirage. But, to attain such proof, more was needed than just paranormal phenomena suggestive of spirit intervention, namely information paranormally acquired that was not yet known to any of the sitters. And this was something that only a first-rate mental medium could provide.

In 1887 Richard Hodgson was sent to Boston by the SPR in London to take charge of their newly formed American branch. He arrived with the reputation of a ruthless sceptic, following his visit to India on behalf of the Society to investigate the activities of Mme Blavatsky. His devastating report on her was such that her reputation as a physical medium never recovered.[29] He was certainly ruthless in his treatment of Mrs Piper. He had her tailed by detectives who opened her mail and he made sure that she could pick up no visual or auditory cues from her sitters. Indeed it became customary for the anonymous sitters to enter the room only *after* she had gone into trance and, even then, to sit behind her rather than facing her. Indeed, James Hyslop, of Columbia University, the first American to devote himself full time to psychical research after he took over the running of the American SPR, always insisted on wearing a mask when he visited Mrs Piper.[30] But despite all such precautions Mrs Piper was so often on target that Hodgson came round to the view that she must, after all, be in touch with the deceased persons who, ostensibly, were seeking to communicate through her.

What proved the turning-point for Hodgson were the so-called 'GP' communications. George Pellew (or 'George Pelham' as he is known in the literature) was, in life, a young Bostonian lawyer and a personal friend of Hodgson's. It is said that, like many modern intellectuals, he considered survival as not just improbable but inconceivable![31] All the same, he made a pact with Hodgson that, if he were to die first and were to find that he had, after all, survived, he would do what he could to let his friend Hodgson know about this. In the event, he *did* die soon after, in February 1892, at the early age of 32, from an accidental fall.

Already in March of that year, a communicator calling himself George Pellew began to manifest through Mrs Piper who was now increasingly operating through automatic writing. Thereafter, GP's career as a 'drop-in' communicator persisted until 1897. During this period he invariably greeted anyone whom he had happened to know during his lifetime (there were 30 such persons) but never once greeted anyone he had *not* known (of such there were 120). Hodgson was impressed also with the sheer amount of information coming from GP, which exceeded that of any other communicator. By 1898, when he published his report for the SPR,[32] Hodgson had become a firm adherent of the survival hypothesis.

Then, in December 1905, Hodgson himself died, also unexpectedly, at the age of 50, of heart failure following a game of hand-ball at his sports club. A week later, messages purporting to come from the deceased Hodgson began to be relayed by Mrs Piper and, for a long time thereafter, she had few sittings at which this 'RH' control did not manifest to some extent. In 1908 it fell to his friend, William James, to evaluate this material and his report was published the following year in the *Proceedings* of both the English and American Societies.[33] By then there had been some 75 sittings to consider. James found much of this material impressive evidence of supernormal knowledge, but whether it betokened the continued existence of his friend Hodgson, he declined to speculate. Unlike Hodgson, James never committed himself to a belief in survival. He had gone on record as saying that 'taking everything that I know of Mrs P. into account, the result is to make me feel absolutely certain as I am of any personal fact in the world that she knows things in her trances which she cannot possibly have heard in her waking life'[34] but he stopped short of committing himself to the view that what she knew derived from discarnate entities. After all, Mrs P. had known so well the living Hodgson. At all events James' reservations were shared by Mrs Sidgwick, Sir Oliver Lodge and J.G. Piddington, all of whom were to go further than James in their commitment to the survival hypothesis (Lodge, indeed, was a passionate believer).

Curiously, if it *had* truly been the post-mortem Hodgson who was trying to get through, he would have achieved the unique distinction of having tackled the mystery of survival in three different capacities. For, like Robert Hare, he too claimed to have acquired mediumistic powers before he died. Thus the erstwhile investigator turned medium would then have figured as communicator!

The discovery of Mrs Piper inaugurated an era in which a good many outstanding mediums, many of them amateurs, put their services at the disposal of researchers instead of cultivating a clientele. At the same time, most of the leading figures, both in America and England, gave high priority to survival as a research problem. The supreme achievement of this era, and the high point in the history of survival research, was an episode known to all students of psychical research as the 'cross-correspondences'.

It all began in 1901 with the death of Frederic Myers. Posthumous author of *Human Personality and its Survival of Bodily Death*,[35] first Honorary Secretary of the newly founded SPR, Myers is arguably the most important pioneer of psychical research, besides being an ardent believer in personal survival. The idea for this method of demonstrating survival purported to come from the deceased Myers through communications received by Margaret Verrall. She was a lecturer in classics at Newnham College (her husband, Dr Arthur Verrall, was also a lecturer in classics at Cambridge) but she also happened to be, since childhood, a gifted automatist. She had, of course, known Myers during his lifetime, which might seem to lessen the evidentiality of whatever communications she might receive from him, but there were others who had *not* known Myers in his lifetime who were soon co-opted into this scheme. The idea was to exploit Myers' knowledge of classical literature in such a way that items belonging to some theme in classical mythology or classical history appearing in the scripts of a number of different automatists could be collated by an expert team appointed by the Society, whereupon the significance of the individual communications would, hopefully, become apparent. Hence the term 'cross-correspondences'. In this way, evidence of a concerted *purpose* on the part of the ostensible communicator would become apparent.

The mediums involved were, as far as possible, to be kept in ignorance of each others' participation and of the use to be made of their scripts. They were, certainly, widely scattered. There was, to start with, the indispensable Mrs Piper in Boston. She was, however, the only professional medium regularly involved. Most of the others, like Margaret Verrall or her daughter Helen (later Mrs W.H. Salter), were highly educated women who had an interest in psychical research and who practised automatic writing in their spare time. Such, for example, was 'Mrs Willett', the pseudonym adopted by Mrs Coombe Tennant, a Welsh woman well known in public life (she was the first woman delegate from Britain to the League of Nations),[36] and such was 'Mrs Holland', the pseudonym adopted by Mrs Alice Fleming who, as it happens, was the sister of Rudyard Kipling and was then living in India.

This weird experiment proved to have extraordinary staying power. Commencing in 1901, it reached its apogee around the time of the First World War and eventually petered out during the 1930s. During this time others, besides Myers, who had during their lifetime been associated with the Society, also appear as communicators. These include Henry Sidgwick, its first President, Edmund Gurney (who had worked so closely with Myers until his accidental death in 1888), Richard Hodgson, Dr Arthur Verrall, Henry Butcher (Professor of Greek at Edinburgh) and others. But, throughout, Myers remained the dominant communicator. Since all these individuals had had a classical education, they were equipped to participate in this erudite game. The investigative team, whose duty it was to evaluate the scripts, included several of the Society's most prominent figures, notably J.G. Piddington, Gerald (later Earl) Balfour, Sir Oliver Lodge, Frank Podmore, Eleanor Sidgwick and Alice Johnson.[37]

It is not, here, my remit to assess the cross-correspondences as evidence for survival. Inevitably they have have come in for their share of criticism from posterity. Some have deplored the extent to which the time and energy of so many of the ablest members of the SPR was absorbed by such a quixotic and convoluted enterprise. Others have pointed out the futility of even trying to discriminate between a communication that is the work of an actual post-mortem entity and one that is the product of a medium's ESP (or, to use the preferred expression in this context, 'super-ESP'). All one can say, for sure, is that, whatever the cross-correspondences may or may not prove, they cannot be dismissed lightly as a product of coincidence or over-interpretation and that they undoubtedly made an impression on those who studied them in detail. Perhaps what Piddington said in 1908 still stands as the best verdict we can hope for, in the circumstances, when he remarked: 'The only opinion which I hold with confidence is this: that if it was not the mind of Frederic Myers it was one which deliberately and artistically imitated his mental characteristics'.[38]

Up to the Second World War, most of the leading psychical researchers in England, apart from a few notable dissidents, could broadly be described as 'survivalists', even if few of them held to their opinion with as much conviction as Lodge. Does this make them spiritualists? Obviously not. There is a crucial difference between a survivalist and a spiritualist. The former could be defined as one who adopts survival as the most plausible hypothesis. The latter, on the other hand, regards survival as an established truth and adopts a missionary attitude towards its propagation. The career of Sir Arthur Conan Doyle (1858–1930) nicely illustrates the distinction. He had already become interested in psychical research in the closing years of the century and duly joined the SPR. But, after 1922, when he resigned from the Society, he threw in his lot wholeheartedly with the spiritualists and thereafter devoted himself unsparingly to purveying their message.

The point to remember is that spiritualism was essentially practical, not academic. It sought to put its adherents in touch with their loved ones who, in the lingo, had 'passed over'. It had its own organizations, even its own churches. It impinged on psychical research only to the extent that mediumship is, in the nature of the case, of concern to students of the paranormal and that it raised, in a more acute form than ever before, the question of survival which, after all, and whatever our personal position may be, is still an open one.

Today spiritualism is at a low ebb and provides little scope for the serious psychical researcher. The one country where it took root and continued to flourish as an indigenous movement is Brazil. And it is significant that Brazil is one of the few places today where strong paranormal phenomena are still regularly reported.[39] Unfortunately, it remains difficult to evaluate them, as the tradition of scrupulous investigation that arose in Victorian England never gained a firm foothold in that country.

CHAPTER 3

Psychical research: First fruits

We have now to consider the emergence and growth of a new discipline and those dedicated pioneers who made it their avocation. Its purpose, as set out by the Society for Psychical Research founded in 1882, was, to use the words now enshrined in every issue of its journal, 'to examine without prejudice or prepossession and in a scientific spirit those faculties of man, real or supposed, which appear to be inexplicable on any generally recognized hypothesis.' At the present time it is often said of parapsychology that its weakness is that it has to be defined in negative terms. Hence, to the extent that it succeeds in explaining the mysteries which it addresses, they cease to fall within its remit, becoming part of regular science. It is thus the fate of parapsychology, say these critics, either to disappear, having disposed of its subject-matter, or else to remain in a state of permanent puzzlement and frustration. Accordingly, parapsychologists – or psychical researchers, to use the earlier designation – are often accused of being obscurantists who cling to anomalies for their own sake and resist their incorporation into genuine science.

To make this accusation, however, betrays a lack of understanding as to the true aims of this new discipline and to confuse 'explaining' with 'explaining away'. It might have been the case that, when such 'faculties of man' came to be studied objectively, they turned out to be no different in principle from such noncontroversial faculties as come under the rubric of conventional psychology or neurophysiology. For example 'telepathy' (the word was coined in 1882 by Frederic Myers and came to supersede expressions such as 'mind-reading' or 'thought-transference') *might* have been explained away in terms of coincidence, sensory cueing or some other convenient formula, as the pioneers were well aware, but, surveying the evidence, they concluded, rightly or wrongly, that such was *not* the case. Similarly, the even more controversial paraphysical phenomena, associated with spiritualistic seances or with poltergeist disturbances, *might* all have been explicable in terms of sleight-of-hand on the part of the perpetrators or of malobservation and slips of memory on the part of the investigators – as much of it clearly was – yet enough stubborn evidence remained to give substance to the profound and time-honoured belief that the mind may, after all, have powers that surpass those of the brain and body.

So long as religion was paramount, there was little incentive to try proving what most people took for granted, that we are more than just complex automata. But late Victorian England was plunged into the fateful aftermath of the Darwinian doctrine, and faith could no longer be counted on to sustain belief in a transcendent soul. It is surely no accident that many of the founding fathers of psychical research were themselves the sons of clergy who, as a result of a secular education and some knowledge of science, had lost the religious faith on which they had been brought up. Their fascination with the paranormal, even when it took on disconcerting or unsavoury forms, was not, for most of them at least, the outcome of some kind of intellectual perversity: it was due, rather, to the hope it offered of a universe that might not, after all, be the soulless machine which the new scientific materialism was propagating.

Of course, psychical research was not the only recourse open to an intellectual of that time who was eager to combat scientific materialism. Idealist philosophy, emanating from Germany, had supplanted traditional British empiricism at the old universities and had succeeded in turning materialism on its head, arguing that mind alone was real and that even the so-called material world was itself no more than a product of some ubiquitous mind or Absolute. However, those imbued with that down-to-earth empirical disposition, for which the British are renowned, wanted to defeat materialistic science at its own game. If there *were* any phenomena *at all* that defied a mechanistic explanation, the duality of body and mind might still be vindicated and the universe would no longer appear so inexorable or so indifferent to human aspirations.

For the past hundred years, some such dualism has remained the dominant philosophy among psychical researchers, but it has never been the only one. As physics moved on, the view of reality that it disclosed became everstranger and further removed from commonsense notions. The possibility, therefore, that paranormal phenomena, even if they could not be explained by 'any generally recognized hypothesis' might yet turn out to be reconcilable with the new physics was one that many physicists themselves found attractive. The invention of wireless communication provided an almost irresistible (albeit misleading) analogy with telepathy.[1] Oliver Lodge, whose own work anticipated Marconi, regarded the existence of the luminiferous ether itself as some kind of justification, not only for a belief in the paranormal, or in 'mental radio', but even for the belief in the survival of death.

In due course, however, with the advent of relativity theory, the ether itself was swept away as otiose. At the same time, the implications of relativity and then of quantum theory represented a far greater departure from the commonsense view of the world than anything that had arisen previously within classical physics. This aspect of the new physics was inevitably seized upon by certain apologists for the paranormal. As we shall see in a later chapter, many parapsychologists at the present time believe (rightly or wrongly) that only a relatively minor modification to existing quantum theory is all that we now need to explain all psi phenomena – even if they have yet to convince orthodox physicists that such a modification is either necessary or legitimate. But, whatever view might be taken as regards the ultimate nature of psi, a belief in the importance of ascertaining the facts and of distinguishing fact from fantasy or chicanery was the common ground on which psychical researchers, from many different walks of life and from many different countries, took their stand. And, in general, one can say they were an earnest and dedicated lot, willing to withstand ridicule and discouragement in pursuit of what they saw as a vital and compelling challenge. And, apart from the odd maverick who might succumb to the lure of publicity, they were, unlike the promulgators of so many new creeds, admirably cautious in coming to any firm conclusions.

The scope of psychical research

The phenomena that required attention may, in the first instance, be divided into two main categories. First, there were those spontaneous incidents that crop up uninvited in people's lives as typified by premonitions or precognitive dreams or sudden unaccountable urges to go to some place or to contact some person. At a more dramatic level, this category would include the seeing of apparitions, especially where these seemed to convey veridical information such as the unexpected demise of the person who had manifested in this way. On the physical side, it would cover the inexplicable movements of household objects which, if it persisted, would constitute a 'poltergeist outbreak'.

As against such spontaneous cases, our second category

involves the deliberate induction of psi phenomena in those
individuals who appeared able to produce them more or less
on demand. Such individuals were often products of the
spiritualist movement and could be either physical mediums
– the supreme example being D.D. Home – or mental mediums such as Leonora Piper or even both at once. But not all
those who were deemed to be specially gifted were mediums.
Some were clairvoyants who continued the tradition of the
somnambules of the mesmeric era but with the added advantage of not needing a mesmerist to put themselves into the
requisite state of mind. Some were children or young persons
with a seeming flair for telepathy. Whatever the case, one
could say that the history of psychical research, as discussed
in this and in the following chapter, is largely composed of
encounters between seasoned investigators and these rare,
outstanding subjects whatever their particular gift or origin.

Experimentation with ordinary volunteer subjects is an
approach that was occasionally used but which did not come
into its own until the next phase of our history, the one we
shall call 'experimental parapsychology'. But we already find
examples of card-guessing experiments using estimates of
probability from the 1880s onwards. More important, however, are the experiments concerned with the so-called
'higher phenomena' of hypnotism. By the time the SPR was
founded, the idea of the magnetic fluid had lost its credibility
and mesmerism had been superseded by hypnotism conceived as a purely psychological technique. But hypnotism,
like mesmerism, still gave rise to various claims of a paranormal nature, e.g. hypnotism-at-a-distance, obedience to
unspoken commands or community of sensation between
the hypnotist and the hypnotized. It was these 'higher' or
anomalous phenomena associated with hypnotism that specially attracted the psychical researcher.

Although Britain took the lead in psychical research, the
example it set was quickly followed by other countries both
in Europe and America, especially those countries where

spiritualism had taken root. For spiritualism continued to produce phenomena that could not readily be ignored. The problem was that few mediums are content to be passive, docile subjects. Usually they insist on conditions that are by no means those which an investigator would choose. However, as interesting mediums have always been hard to come by, psychical researchers have usually had to compromise as the price of obtaining any phenomena at all. Whether they are wise to do so is another matter. Sceptics could always allege that they were the victims of the deceits and trickeries that made up the medium's repertoire and enabled the medium to gain the upper hand. On the other hand, those who, in the absence of any convincing specific counter-explanation, are satisfied that some, at least, of the phenomena *are* genuine, have put forward possible psychological explanations for the medium's special demands. Paranormal phenomena, they suggest, can never be elicited routinely or automatically under arbitrary conditions, they arise only within the constraints of a particular belief-system. Be that as it may, so much that we find in the annals of psychical research reads like a battle of wits between hunter and hunted!

Unfortunately, with the virtual disappearance of strong paranormal phenomena at the present time, the controversy remains an open one. For example, modern technology, that now enables us to see and to record photographically what goes on in the dark, could no doubt settle the argument as to the reality of materialization – if only there were still mediums around at the present time on whom it could be deployed! In the event, the historical record is all that we can fall back on. In the remainder of the next two chapters we shall take a look at certain seminal episodes in the history of psychical research and at selected protagonists on both sides of the divide: investigators and investigated.

The first learned society

The year 1882 is rightly regarded as the key date in parapsychological history because it was in February of that year that the Society for Psychical Research was established in London, the first learned society of its kind in the world. The idea for such a society seems to have come initially from a leading spiritualist, E. Dawson Rogers, who was hopeful that, by attracting the support of reputable scholars, scientists and savants, spiritualism might gain a new respectability. He discussed the idea first with William Barrett, then Professor of Physics at the Royal College of Science in Dublin, who was known to be sympathetic toward spiritualism and who had already carried out his own experiments on 'thought-transference'. It was Barrett who then took the initiative in bringing together those who were to constitute the new Society. He and Rogers agreed that the person who should be invited to become the Society's first President was Henry Sidgwick, that eminent Cambridge moral philosopher whose reputation for caution and scepticism would amount to a guarantee that the Society would not become just a front organization for spiritualism, even though, in the event, a large proportion of its initial membership and funding was drawn from the ranks of the spiritualists.

The personnel
The choice of Sidgwick to lead the new society proved an auspicious one. For there were a number of able people with whom he was connected who, like him, were disillusioned with the religious teachings on which they had been nurtured but were temperamentally out of sympathy with the prevailing scientific naturalism to which so many of their intellectual contemporaries subscribed. In psychical research they saw the hope of vindicating, if not the persistence of the soul after death, at any rate the ontological independence of mind in relation to the body and to the physical universe. The

Sidgwick circle comprised not only his disciples, who had studied under him at Cambridge, such as Frederic Myers, Edmund Gurney and Richard Hodgson, but also the Balfour family into which he had married. His wife Eleanor Balfour was a woman of outstanding intellectual ability and distinction, a pioneer of women's education and the first Principal of Newnham College, Cambridge. Her brother Arthur Balfour, philosopher, politician and, from 1902–5, Prime Minister, and their younger brother Gerald Balfour, classicist and politician, also took an active part in the work of the Society and all three took their turn in serving as Presidents.

Besides the Sidgwick circle, the other main group who figure in the early history of the Society were the scientists. By 1887 no less than eight Fellows of the Royal Society were serving on the Council. Besides Crookes, Barrett, Lodge and Wallace, all of whom have already been mentioned, other Council members include Lord Rayleigh (John William Strutt, 3rd Baron), head of the Cavendish Laboratory at Cambridge and discoverer of the gas argon, who became a Nobel Prize winner and holder of the Order of Merit, and that other Nobel laureate, J.J. Thomson, discoverer of the electron, who was knighted for his services to science. Of Rayleigh, one could say that he married into psychical research. His wife Evelyn was a younger sister of Eleanor Balfour; Eleanor herself, at one period, worked under Rayleigh at the Cavendish. Among the miscellaneous celebrities who early on joined the Society we find Charles Dodgson (Lewis Carroll) and honorary members included Gladstone, Alfred Lord Tennyson, John Ruskin and the painter G.F. Watts.

The main work of the Society, however, was delegated to the 20 individuals who made up its Council and, more especially, to the officers appointed by Council. The research output of the early years, as published in the Society's *Proceedings* and in books written by members of the Society, was largely the work of a small select group who possessed both the will and the means to devote themselves wholeheartedly to this new branch of learning. Outstanding among these were Frederic Myers and Edmund Gurney (who jointly acted as Honorary Secretaries), Eleanor Sidgwick, Richard Hodgson – an Australian whom we have already encountered in our previous chapter – and Frank Podmore, a civil servant who, unlike the others, was an Oxford graduate and later became the Society's foremost historian. Of these, however, Myers and Gurney were the stars of this constellation. Both were men of wide-ranging talents who, after a chequered career, found fulfilment in their work in psychical research.

The programme

A circular to members and associates of the Society was issued in February 1883, setting out the six committees that had been set up to investigate the various phenomena that the Society regarded as falling within their remit, together with the names of those appointed to each committee.[2] It is worth pausing to consider each of these committees since they cover the full range of what initially became the subject-matter of psychical research. In order of listing they are as follows:

1. Committee on Thought-Transference
2. Committee on Mesmerism
3. Committee on Reichenbach's Phenomenon and suchlike
4. Committee on Physical Phenomena
5. Committee on Haunted Houses
6. Literary Committee.

The first of these was the one to which the Society attached the greatest importance as being the most likely to yield promising results. 'Thought transference' was here defined as 'any influence which may be exerted by one mind upon another, apart from any generally recognized mode of perception'. The evidence sought was to be based on guessing experiments using cards, numbers, words, names, colours or other such familiar symbols as lend themselves to such treatment. From the beginning, evidence was sought both from those who appeared to reveal exceptional ability in such guessing tasks as well as from those who might perform only marginally beyond chance expectation. It was the former, however, the gifted individuals, who, in the event, provided the most impressive evidence, as they have done ever since, but as always in such cases the suspicion that trickery might have been involved was never easy to dispel. The concept of thought transference, however, as the intentional influence of one mind upon another, was found to be too restrictive and the term itself was eventually superseded. Thus the first report of the Literary Committee, whose remit included an examination of various spontaneous phenomena, has this to say:

> Our phenomena break through any attempt to group them under heads of transferred impression; and we venture to introduce the words *Telaesthesia* and *Telepathy* to cover all cases of impression received at a distance without the normal operation of the recognised sense organs.[3]

Eventually, even the word 'telepathy', which still enjoys wide currency, would appear too restrictive to the researcher and was largely displaced by the term 'extrasensory perception' or 'ESP'.

It may strike one as anachronistic to set up a committee on mesmerism at a time when mesmerism as such had been rejected by science in favour of the concept of hypnotism which, during the 1880s, was gaining ground in scientific circles through the work of Charcot in Paris and Bernheim in Nancy. However, as the account makes clear, no firm distinction is here being drawn between 'mesmerism' and 'hypnotism'. What specially interested the Society was the phenomenon of 'clairvoyance' or 'lucidity' which, as we have seen in a previous chapter, was such a familiar feature of the mesmeric era. Moreover, the experiments which Gurney conducted on the telepathic induction of local anaesthesia or on 'community of sensation', with G.A. Smith as the mesmeriser, show that it was the work of the old mesmerists rather than that of the new hypnotists that most concerned the Committee on Mesmerism.

The Reichenbach Committee was the most transient of the Society's committees. Baron Carl von Reichenbach, a Moravian industrialist, took an interest in mesmerism and claimed that certain sensitives in the somnambulistic state were able to perceive luminous emanations from the poles of a magnet and sometimes from crystals or even from the human body. He regarded such emanations as physical and related to magnetism and coined the term 'odyle' or 'odic force'. Although the first report of this committee was fairly positive, it was, in the event, a false trail. The related idea of seeing auras surrounding a person is one that has been a persistent feature of spiritualism, although the occasional attempt to test it objectively has never vindicated this phenomenon. Von Reichenbach's 'odyle' is also reminiscent of Blondlot's 'N-rays' which attracted some attention among scientists during the first decade of this century before they were shown to be the product of suggestion. A recent fringe science that recalls the Reichenbach effect is Kirlian photography, although in the case of Kirlian photographs the effects are not in doubt: it is their interpretation that is at issue.

The Committee on Physical Phenomena was the one that brought the Society in closest contact with the spiritualist movement. For the term 'physical phenomena' is here defined as 'of the kind commonly called spiritualistic'. It presented the Society, however, with a delicate problem of policy. For, as explained, 'This is a subject which has been largely brought before the public through paid mediums', a fact which, as they point out, is conducive to fraud. Hence, where the medium is paid and the investigator untrained, results are, they declare 'generally worthless for scientific purposes'. In the event, the Society tended to fight shy of physical mediums and to decry the claims that were made for them. Curiously, the subject of the 'divining rod' came to be included as relevant to this committee, although nowadays we are more likely to think of it as an extension of clairvoyance. As a phenomenon it is, of course, much older than spiritualism. William Barrett took a particular interest in dowsing, which is perhaps the most practical of all paranormal activities and still has an enthusiastic following, although the phenomenon as such has never attained strict experimental confirmation.

The two final committees, the Haunted Houses and the Literary Committee, cover, between them, the domain of the spontaneous phenomena. The former deal with place-specific phenomena, especially apparitions, the latter with person-specific phenomena, notably premonitory dreams, instances of 'second-sight', spontaneous telepathic experiences and 'crisis apparitions', i.e. apparitions seen close to the moment when, unknown to the percipient, the subject of the apparition is on the point of death. The Literary Committee, as its name implies, was also intent on collecting a library of books covering such cases from diverse angles.

It is significant that the topic of survival figures nowhere on the Society's original programme of research. Even such topics as hauntings and apparitions tended to be discussed more as evidence of telepathy or clairvoyance than as communication from the beyond. No wonder the spiritualist members of the new Society who, like Rogers, hoped that the SPR would endow spiritualism with a new respectability, became restive and did not conceal their disappointment. Matters finally came to a head over the case of William Eglinton, a medium held in high esteem by the spiritualists but dismissed in a report by Eleanor Sidgwick as an obvious charlatan. Thus, in 1886, a number of prominent spiritualists, including Rogers himself, resigned from the Society in protest. Among them was the extraordinary Stainton Moses. A former clergyman, now a schoolmaster, he was also an amateur medium whose physical phenomena were said, by those fortunate enough to be allowed to sit with him, to be as powerful as those of D.D. Home himself!

It is not, curiously, that the psychical researchers were indifferent to the question of survival. Most of them, and especially Myers, thought it the supreme question. But the new Society considered that the first step, if psychical research was ever to gain any credibility, was to rebut the prevailing materialism purveyed by the influential thinkers of the time. And this, they thought, could best be done by establishing, above all else, the reality of telepathy conceived as a function of a nonmaterial mind.

Publications

The main outlet for the work of the Society and its six committees was the *Proceedings*, the first issue of which appeared in October 1882, the year in which the Society had been founded. For many years issues continued to appear at the rate of two or more a year. A journal followed in 1884 but, throughout most of its history, the *Proceedings* remained the chief outlet for the Society's research publications. However, Myers, Gurney and other prominent members did not confine their output to the Society's own publications, but contributed articles on various aspects of psychical research to the leading intellectual periodicals of the day, e.g. the *Nineteenth Century* and the *Contemporary Review*.

What, however, may be regarded as the crowning achievement of the early Society was the massive two-volume opus *Phantasms of the Living* which appeared in 1886. It represents primarily the efforts of Myers and Gurney but, at Sidgwick's instigation, Gurney was allocated sole responsibility for the text so that, if the work were to come under attack (as, of course it did) one rather than two reputations would be on the line. Myers wrote the Introduction and Frank Podmore figures as third author in recognition of his extensive labours in collecting and checking the many spontaneous cases described in the book. But in many respects it could be regarded as a collective endeavour on the part of all the leading researchers of the Society.

The title of the book calls for comment. As Myers explains in his introduction,

> under the heading 'Phantasms of the Living', we propose, in fact, to deal with all classes of cases where there is reason to suppose that the mind of one human being has affected the mind of another, without speech uttered, or word written or sign made; – has affected it, that is to say, by other means than through the recognised channels of sense.

In other words, as Myers proceeds to avow, the book is really about telepathy and, in fact, the lengthy second chapter presents some of the experimental findings on what was then still best known as 'thought-transference' while the still lengthier third chapter discusses some of the evidence on spontaneous telepathy. On the other hand, much of the work, and indeed its most original contribution, deals with apparitions, that is to say, apparitions of the *living* as opposed to apparitions of the *dead* ('ghosts' in popular parlance), although this notably covers apparitions of the *dying*. Indeed, the book might have been called 'Apparitions of the Living' but, as Myers points out, an apparition or phantom is a visual phenomenon whereas the cases discussed may comprise 'auditory, tactile or even purely ideational or emotional impressions'. Hence the term 'phantasm' that does not have this specifically visual connotation. The point, however, is that, whether we call it an apparition or a phantasm, what makes it of interest to the researcher is whether it conveys veridical information. For this determines whether or not it constitutes a manifestation of telepathy.

This encyclopedic two-volume survey concludes with a Table which lists some 702 cases cited in the text with the initials of the percipient and agent involved, the nature or sense-modality of the impressions received, and the relationship obtaining between the two parties. The four-page conclusion appears less than half-way through volume 2, the remainder being supplementary material. The tone is characteristically modest and unpretentious. The author recognizes that far more needs to be done before psychical research will be able to 'surmount ridicule and prejudice, and to clear for itself a firm path between easy credulity on the one side and easy incredulity on the other'. The author recognizes 'the evidential shortcomings of many of the spontaneous cases' and that, in the nature of the case, spontaneous cases can never be conclusive. He is, however, buoyed by his conviction of a 'radical connection between *experimental* and *spontaneous* telepathy' and admits that he is more willing to accept the evidence from the spontaneous cases because he was *wholly* convinced by the evidence from the experiments.

Perhaps the most notable feature of *Phantasms* was the concept of the 'crisis apparition'. This was defined as having a hallucination of someone who, it later transpires, died no more than twelve hours before or after such an intimation. In the course of their enquiries, the Society had accumulated some '13 first-hand and well-attested cases of this kind'. The problem for Gurney and the others was whether this statistic might represent no more than chance expectation. Obviously a good many factors had to be taken into account, none of which could be accurately evaluated: the total number of potential respondents, the frequency with which people experience such hallucinations, the probability that any individual, taken at random, may die within 24 hours and so on. Gurney offers some provisional calculations on the liberal assumption that the possible catchment population for the Society's questionnaire might comprise some 30,000 individuals and arrives at the tentative conclusion that the odds against finding even 13 such cases was '*more than a trillion to 1*' (author's italics, i.e. 10^{18} to 1).[4]

Inevitably, Gurney was challenged when the book appeared. A critic, A.T. Innes, writing for the *Nineteenth Century*, raised the question of documentation. Where, he asked, were the letters in which the respondents had described their experiences? Without them, how can we be sure that our informant was not confabulating? An even more aggressive review appeared in, surprisingly, the *Proceedings of the American S.P.R.* by the eminent American philosopher, C.S. Peirce, who challenged many of Gurney's assumptions and calculations. Gurney, however, stuck to his guns and defended his claims. But, alas, his time was running out for, in June 1888, he died accidentally of an overdose of chloroform while staying at a hotel in Brighton. At first suicide was suspected, for Gurney was no stranger to melancholy, but his brother Alfred, a vicar, testified that Gurney had been in the habit of using narcotics to relieve his persistent neuralgia and insomnia, while Myers' brother Arthur, a physician, added that he had often discussed with Gurney the use of chloroform as an analgesic. So a verdict of death by misadventure was duly recorded. But, in the nature of the case, the suspicion of suicide can never be ruled out completely, and one modern historian of psychical research, Trevor Hall, has, as we shall see below, contrived to put a sinister construction on the case. Be that as it may, when Alan Gauld writes of Gurney:

'His death at the early age of forty-one was perhaps the greatest single blow that psychical research has ever suffered',[5] his words may be taken as a fitting epitaph.

Some years later, the Society undertook a more extensive

survey of 'crisis apparitions' under the aegis of Henry Sidgwick himself which was published in the *Proceedings* in 1894.[6] Answers were obtained from some 17,000 persons among whom some 300 had experienced visual hallucinations of persons known to them and, of this number, some 80 (or 0.47 percent) coincided, within twelve hours, with that person's death. These 80 cases were then whittled down to some 32 crisis apparitions that satisfied the criteria of being 'well attested'. But, again, the upshot was to confirm the original conclusion that this was far beyond what chance alone would allow. Yet, as with so many paranormal phenomena, the crisis apparition may well be, in part, culture bound. When Donald West undertook a recent survey of this kind for the SPR, albeit on a much more modest scale,[7] he obtained some 840 replies. But, although these show that waking hallucinations are not unknown today, not *one* case qualified as a 'crisis apparition' within the terms of the original study. However, on a percentage basis, he would have been lucky to get even one.

Some experiments in telepathy[8]

Since, of all the SPR committees, the Committee on Thought-Transference was the most active and the most successful, let us conclude this chapter with an account of three of its investigations which, at face value, at any rate, appeared to provide overwhelming evidence for the reality of mind-to-mind communication.

The Creery girls

A popular pastime in Victorian England was the game in which one person leaves the room, the others decide on some object in the room, and that person then has to find the chosen object when readmitted to the room. Some public performers, like Stuart Cumberland, made a name for themselves so that the phenomenon is still sometimes referred to as 'Cumberlandism'. Yet, although the game was often regarded as a case of 'thought-reading', the more perspicacious recognized that it was more a case of muscle-reading for, normally, the searcher needed to hold the hand of someone privy to the secret. At all events, it could not seriously qualify as a paranormal phenomenon.

The Reverend A.M. Creery, of Buxton, Derbyshire, knew all about Cumberlandism. What he wanted to find out was whether there was such a thing as genuine thought-transference where *no* physical explanation would be forthcoming. Accordingly, in October 1880, he tells us[9] 'I resolved to thoroughly investigate the whole question of the action of mind on mind.' Being the father of five daughters, he decided to use his family for this purpose.

> I employed four of my children between the ages of ten and sixteen, all being in perfectly robust health, and a maid-servant, about twenty years of age. Each went out of the room in turn, while I and the others fixed on some object which the absent one was to name on returning to the room.

To his astonishment the test succeeded beyond his wildest hopes:

> After a few trials the successes preponderated so much over the failures that we were all convinced that there was something very wonderful coming under our notice. Night after night, for several months, we spent an hour or two each evening in varying the conditions of these experiments, and choosing new subjects for thought-transference.

More astonishing still, the faculty did not seem to be confined to the Creery household because neighbours' children who were induced to join in were likewise successful.

Obviously the matter could not rest there so, in January 1881, Mr Creery wrote to Professor Barrett, whom he knew to be interested in such matters. Barrett visited the family the following Easter and carried out some tests with them of his own devising. Here is an extract from his report:

> one of the children was sent into an adjoining room, the door of which I saw was closed. On returning to the sitting room and closing its door also, I thought of some object in the house, fixed upon at random; writing the name down, I shewed it to the family present, the strictest silence being preserved throughout. We then all silently thought of the name of the thing selected. In a few seconds the door of the adjoining room was heard to open, and, after a very short interval the child would enter the sitting-room, generally speaking with the object selected.[10]

Among such objects successfully brought was a hairbrush, an orange, a wineglass and an apple. The instruction for the child was simply to bring some household object about which the company were thinking. Of course the child should have been under observation all the time but these were early days and Barrett was concerned in the first instance to satisfy himself as to the genuineness of the phenomenon. At all events, a preliminary note on the case was sent to *Nature* where it was published on 7 July 1881.

Another interested party was Professor Balfour Stewart FRS, who was Professor of Physics at Owens College, Manchester. He was on the original Council of the SPR and served as President, 1885–1887. On 12 November 1881 he visited the Creerys, accompanied by a colleague, Alfred Hopkinson, Professor of Biology. Conditions were similar, the item to be guessed was written down and handed around so that no words should be spoken and the guesser, on returning to the room, was required to stand with her back to the company. The targets included playing-cards, two-digit numbers, names of towns and fictitious names of people. In the great majority of cases the girls guessed correctly at the first attempt![11]

More evidential was the visit of Myers and Gurney on 13 April 1882. Here the agents did not include members of the Creery family but were confined to Myers, Gurney and two ladies who were complete strangers to the family. This was to rule out the possibility of a conspiracy. Targets included household objects, numbers, fictitious names and playing-cards. Success was not as pronounced as previously; one would, of course, expect that the best results would be obtained when both agent and subject were members of the family. Even so, results were way beyond chance, and even some of the errors were suggestive, e.g. button-box for box of chocolates or 'Catherine Shaw' for 'Catherine Smith'. As regards the playing-cards, 'out of *fourteen* successive trials *nine* were guessed correctly the first time and only three trials can be said to have been complete failures. On none of these occasions' the authors insist

> was it even remotely possible for the child to obtain by any ordinary means a knowledge of the card selected. Our facial expression was the only index open to her; and even if we had not purposely looked as neutral as possible, it is difficult to imagine how we could have unconsciously carried say, the two of diamonds written on our foreheads.[12]

Some further experiments along these lines were carried out with somewhat similar results at Myers' house in Cambridge from 31 July over ten days with Mary, Alice and Maud, aged 17, 15 and 13 respectively. Barrett as well as Gurney was present for this series and Mrs Myers and a Miss Mason also made up the investigating team.[13]

What happened next is what always seems to happen when

things look too good to be true: the girls began to lose their ability. As Gurney tells us:

> The Creerys had their most startling successes at first, when the affair was a surprise and an amusement, or later, at short and seemingly casual trials; the decline set in with their sense that the experiments had become matters of weighty importance to us, and of prolonged strain and tediousness to them.[14]

He insists, however, that the decline 'had nothing to do with any increased stringency in the precautions adopted', pointing out that 'the decline was equally observed in the trials which they held among themselves'. Be that as it may, a few years later disaster struck when the girls were found to have resorted to signalling in tests involving playing-cards.

A few months before he died, Gurney paid a visit to Cambridge where he undertook some further tests with the Creery sisters mainly for the benefit of Henry and Eleanor Sidgwick. It was during this series that the girls were detected in the use of a somewhat primitive code of signals, visual when in sight of one another, auditory when a screen was interposed. One of the sisters confessed that a certain amount of such signalling had been used even in the earlier series which had been published, mainly on those occasions when success seemed to elude them and they were anxious not to disappoint the visitors! Gurney agreed that the discovery threw doubt on 'the results of all previous trials in which one or more of the sisters shared in the agency' but pointed out that

> How far the proved willingness to deceive can be held to affect the experiments on which we relied where collusion was excluded, must of course depend on the degree of stringency of the precautions taken against trickery of other sorts – as to which the reader will form his own opinion.[15]

Certainly it is not easy to see by what subterfuge the girls could have gained access to the targets of the series we described earlier conducted by Myers and Gurney, and no one to my knowledge has ever even attempted to suggest what manner of trick might have been used in the conditions specified. Nevertheless it was quite enough to make the Sidgwicks, ever the sticklers for strict propriety, decide to eliminate the entire investigation from the official case for thought-transference – much to the disgust of Barrett who stood by his original assessment and could never forgive the Sidgwicks their pusillanimity.

Inevitably, critics of the Society gloated over its discomfiture and, ever since, sceptics have invoked the case as evidence of how easy it is to fool even the most sophisticated believers. What actually happened, of course, we shall never know. On the one hand nothing comparable to the success of the Creery girls has ever again come to light and this alone would make one suspicious, even had they never been caught cheating. Indeed, the fact that they resorted to such a primitive trick is the least serious reason for one's incredulity. At the same time no one has yet offered a plausible account of how, right up to the final debacle, the girls could have got away with it. Moreover, if they *did* rely on a code, they ought to have become increasingly proficient in their performance, whereas in fact, as the Committee noted: 'at the end of 1882 they could not do, under the easiest conditions, what they could do under the most stringent in 1881'.[16]

The Smith – Blackburn experiments

This, too, is a case that began so hopefully and ended so disastrously. It starts with a letter published in the spiritualist journal, *Light*, from a Mr Douglas Blackburn, Editor of the *Brightonian.* He there describes the exploits of a Mr G.A. Smith of Brighton who, when the *two were in rapport* with one another, was able to 'read my thoughts with an accuracy that approaches the miraculous'.

The letter caught the attention of Barrett who reproduces it in his appendix to the very first issue of *Proceedings*.

On the strength of a full report from Blackburn of his experiments with Smith, the Committee decided to visit Brighton on 3 December 1882, where Myers and Gurney (Barrett not then being available) carried out a series of experiments in their own rooms with Blackburn as agent and the blindfolded Smith as percipient. The main targets were a series of drawings, mostly of nonsense shapes, and it is obvious from the illustrations that there is a definite correspondence. However, at this stage Blackburn and Smith were still needing to hold hands and, however hard it might be to convey in this way a description of a nonsense drawing, this clearly could not be allowed to continue.

In January 1883, and again in April of that year, a series of experiments were conducted with Blackburn and Smith at the Society's premises in Dean's Yard (next door to Westminster Abbey). The committee now comprised Myers, Gurney, Barrett and Podmore but other observers attended the sessions. In these experiments the target drawing was shown to Blackburn outside the room where Smith was seated but Blackburn was then allowed back into the room where he stood some two feet behind Smith ostensibly concentrating with eyes shut on the drawing he had just seen. After the first four trials no contact was permitted between Blackburn and Smith. Once again there is an unmistakable correspondence between the nonsense figures used as targets and Smith's attempt to reproduce them. The committee reckoned that, out of a total of 37 such trials, no more than 8 could be considered as failures. The possibility that some auditory code might be involved is discussed but dismissed. To make assurance doubly sure, however, 'we on one occasion stopped Mr Smith's ears with putty, then tied a bandage round his eyes and ears, then fastened a bolster-case over the head, and over all threw a blanket which enveloped his entire head and trunk'.[17] Even so, the illustration shows a close resemblance between the original drawing and Smith's three successive reproductions of it.

Who, then, were Smith and Blackburn, the protagonists of this remarkable act? George Albert Smith was only 18 when Myers and Gurney came to Brighton in 1883 but he had already gained a considerable reputation for himself as a mesmerist in which capacity he gave public performances. He later became active in the work of the SPR and was regularly used by Gurney as a highly skilled hypnotist in his experiments on the telepathic aspects of hypnotism. Smith also proved useful in finding suitable subjects for these experiments. Indeed, Gurney had such confidence in him that, in 1887, he made him his private secretary. Then, after Gurney's death the following year,he served for a while as Myers' private secretary. During the 1890s, however, Smith became interested in cinematography and, though he remained an associate of the SPR all his life, he ceased to be active in psychical research. He eventually won an award from the British film industry for his pioneer efforts in colour cinematography. He died in 1959 at the advanced age of 95.

Douglas Blackburn, journalist,novelist and freelance writer was a very different character who, by all accounts, was never a man to be troubled by scruples. Soon after his association with Smith and the SPR he emigrated to South Africa, but returned to Britain during the first decade of the new century. It was then that he dropped his bombshell when, in 1908, he published a 'confession' in the weekly *John Bull*, that notorious scandalmongering magazine of the Edwardian period. There he claims that he and Smith had deliberately hoodwinked the SPR with their act, the better to expose the credulity of psychical researchers. These allegations were further repeated in the *Daily News* in 1911. The question that is still being debated is: was he speaking the truth or was he creating a sensation for mercenary reasons?

One might have supposed that, before going public, he would check with his co-conspirator. His excuse, that he thought all those originally involved must by now be dead, is not very convincing, given that Smith was seven years his junior. At all events, Smith, who was still very much alive, denied all his allegations both in the columns of the *Daily News* and in an interview with Alice Johnson, then Secretary of the SPR which she duly published as a leaflet. If he *was* guilty he took his secret with him to the grave, because he was interviewed by Eric Dingwall just a few years before he died but no revelations were forthcoming.

How does Blackburn claim that they were able to pull off the trick? He describes the session we have already mentioned at which Smith was covered by a blanket and claims that he contrived to draw the target figure on a piece of cigarette-paper which he then transferred to the brass-projector of the pencil he was using and, at a convenient moment, slipped it to Smith. The point is: how workable would such a method be, considering that, in 29 of the 37 trials, Smith scored an undoubted hit? According to the Committee's report, Blackburn sat behind Smith and 'as perfectly still as it is possible for a human being to sit'.[18] But, quite apart from the committee, there would have been a dozen or so observers present whose *sole* concern was to watch the performers and would certainly have protested indignantly had they seen anything suspicious at any time, let alone on 29 occasions! Of course, by modern standards, Blackburn should never have been allowed in the same room as Smith,let alone within reach of him, but these were pioneering days and their good faith had never been in doubt. Blackburn, one can add, never demonstrated the use of his method in such a situation, although challenged to do so by Smith. But it is known that Gurney would occasionally discuss methods of cheating with his subjects and it may well be that Blackburn had recalled an allusion to the cigarette-paper ruse.

In 1964 Trevor Hall published his book *The Strange Case of Edmund Gurney* which achieved wide publicity and is, in effect, a sustained attack upon the early SPR and its founders. In his book Hall suggests that Gurney got wind of the fact of Smith's duplicity – possibly Smith's sister had met Gurney on that last trip to Brighton and had then spilt the beans – as a result of which Gurney, seeing his career in ruins, took his own life. Hall's book, however, has been mercilessly pilloried by two more knowledgeable historians of psychical research, Alan Gauld and the late Fraser Nicol.[19] As Gauld points out, it is inconceivable that, if Gurney had known that Smith had been engaging in deception, he would not have let Myers, or one of his other colleagues at the SPR know what had happened before doing away with himself, instead of letting Smith continue to fool them. Nor is there any good reason to doubt the coroner's verdict of death by misadventure. Unfortunately when mud starts to fly some of it usually sticks, and that is why the Smith–Blackburn experiments remain under a cloud.

The Guthrie experiments

Happily, our last example of these early attempts to demonstrate telepathy, which likewise involves the transmission of drawings, had no such unhappy sequel. Malcolm Guthrie was a Liverpool magistrate (a Justice of the Peace). His interest in the topic was first aroused by an article he read in 1883 in *Cassell's Magazine*. Up to that time he had, he tells us, been 'thoroughly sceptical'. He therefore decided to try some guessing tests on his son, 'a nervous and susceptible fair-haired boy of ten'. To his astonishment, the boy was soon correctly naming objects placed behind his back while he was blindfolded. However, his son quickly tired of the game and, typically, when Guthrie invited strangers to witness the phenomenon, the lad 'seemed disposed to ensure success by taking a sly peep at the object'.[20]

Guthrie's next move was to approach the Council of the Literary and Philosophical Society of Liverpool with the result that a James Birchall, their Honorary Secretary, volunteered his assistance. The question was, where would they find their gifted subject? It so happened that Guthrie was a partner in one of the large drapery establishments in Liverpool and a relative of his who worked there had been present at some playful guessing games that had been going on among the female employees of the firm. The upshot was that two of these young women, a Miss Relph and a Miss Edwards, were invited to submit to testing. Various informal tests were then tried out with some success, using a variety of targets with a number of different persons acting as transmitters. These experiments were adjourned at the end of May but Guthrie had got in touch with the SPR and, in August 1883, received a visit from Myers and Gurney. The young ladies' abilities seem to have declined after the summer break but some remarkable successes were obtained, nevertheless, in experiments involving the transmission of taste sensations with either Myers, Gurney or Guthrie acting as 'tasters'.[21]

In October 1883 the reproduction of diagrams or nonsense figures as targets was attempted and, in the course of the ensuing months, some 150 such trials were duly conducted. The target was prepared in another room from where the subject was seated, but then brought into the room and placed on a stand in a position such that it would have been impossible for the subject to have caught a glimpse of it even if there had been an attempt to do so. The agents, including Gurney, were all professional men and the subjects, again, were the Misses Relph and Edwards. The outcome could not be quantified statistically but, judging by the 16 trials illustrated in the *Proceedings*[22] and then again in *Phantasms*,[23] there is no way in which such results can be attributed to chance.

At this time Oliver Lodge was the first Professor of

Physics at the recently founded University College of Liverpool. He, too, became interested and a favourable report by him of the Guthrie set-up was published in volume 2 of *Proceedings*, 1884. In December 1885 Guthrie himself published a further report for *Proceedings*. By then Miss Edwards had left to get married and Miss Relph was bearing the full weight of the investigation, but success was still forthcoming with respect to a wide range of different targets. At the same time a note of disappointment creeps in. Thus we find Guthrie remarking:

> Personally, I find I am not equal to my former self in my power to give off impressions, and if I exert myself to do so I experience unpleasant effects in the head and nervous system. I therefore seldom join in the active experiments, but leave the thinking for the most part to others. Then we have lost one of our percipients; and as the novelty and vivacity of our seances has departed there is not the same geniality and freshness as at the outset. The thing has become monotonous, whereas it was formerly a succession of surprises. We have nothing new to try. I do not know if there is a loss of power on the part of the percipient; it is just as likely that the agents are at fault.[24]

Of course, what none of those who participated in the Guthrie experiments could have known was that the performances they were witnessing would become increasingly rare as the years went by, so that by now such claims have become all but unbelievable. It is, accordingly, enormously tempting to suppose that there was some fatal flaw which none of those who oversaw the experiments spotted, but which nullified all the findings. Yet, if so, it is hard to attach blame. Perhaps Oliver Lodge should be allowed the last word: 'As regards collusion and trickery, no one who has witnessed the absolutely genuine and artless manner in which the impressions are described, but has been perfectly convinced of the transparent honesty of purpose of all concerned.' He then adds:

> This, however, is not evidence to persons who have not been present, and to them I can only say that to the best of my scientific belief no collusion or trickery was possible under the varied circumstances of the experiments … We have many times succeeded with agents quite disconnected with the percipient in ordinary life, and sometimes complete strangers to them … All suspicion of a pre-arranged code is thus rendered impossible even to outsiders who are unable to witness the obvious fairness of all the experiments.[25]

CHAPTER 4

The expansion of psychical research

The example set by the Society for Psychical Research was soon followed by the setting up of similar societies in most other countries. Throughout the period we shall be covering in this chapter, however, from the 1890s to the 1930s, the SPR remained the most important and most respected of all such societies. But it also represented a conservative approach, that is to say it was the society least likely to accept paranormal claims at face value and was particularly suspicious of claims involving paraphysical effects.

The only two other societies to become a permanent feature of the scene were the American SPR of New York and the Institut Métapsychique International (IMI) of Paris. An American SPR was set up in 1885 after a visit from William Barrett, but it failed to attract sufficient local support and in 1889 became a subsidiary of the SPR of London. It was not until 1904 that it again became an independent body under the able leadership of James Hyslop.[1] During the 1920s, however, a rift developed, on account of the uncritical partisanship of its leaders with respect to the medium 'Margery' (see below). As a result, a rival society, the Boston SPR, was set up under Walter Franklin Prince[2] with the support of

William McDougall, then Professor of Psychology at Harvard. Eventually, in 1941, a 'palace revolution' engineered by Gardner Murphy, one of the most influential figures both in American psychology *and* parapsychology,[3] restored the reputation of the American SPR[3] and the Boston Society disappeared.

Despite the pre-eminence of the French in psychiatry, and generally in the study of abnormal psychology and hypnosis, during the late nineteenth century, it was not until 1919 that the Institut Métapsychique International was founded by Jean Meyer, a wealthy industrialist, with the illustrious Charles Richet as its first President; the *Revue Métapsychique* served as its mouthpiece. In the period covered by this chapter, it is associated with some of the foremost investigators then active, among whom we may include Gustave Geley, Eugene Osty, René Sudre, René Warcollier and Robert Tocquet. For the most part, however, psychical research at this period was the work of enterprising individual freelancers. Perhaps the two who loom largest in this category are Albert von Schrenck-Notzing,[4] a German psychiatrist and an exponent of hypnotherapy, and the Englishman, Harry Price. Both men, having wisely married wealthy women, were free to indulge their passion for the paranormal.

Price set up his own laboratory which he called, grandiosely, 'The National Laboratory for Psychical Research'. As a successful self-publicist and author of many popular books[5] he was undoubtedly the best-known psychical researcher in Britain of the inter-war period. As a person, however, he was everything that a scientist ought *not* to be: he was possessive, deceitful, spiteful and self-seeking.[6] At the same time, even his enemies had to admit that he was extraordinarily energetic and enterprising and, despite having no academic credentials himself, he was remarkably successful in persuading eminent scientists to pay attention to the demonstrations that he organized.

Such, then, was the scene at this stage of our history, dominated as it was by the exceptional subjects or psychics who flourished at this time. Thanks to the international network that then prevailed, they could usually be passed from one investigator to the next and from one country to another. In 1921 the First International Congress on Psychical Research was held in Copenhagen under the aegis of the Danish SPR with representatives from England, America, Holland and Germany. A second such congress was held in Warsaw in 1923 and a third in Paris in 1927. At this period psychical research was also represented at some of the psychology conferences, such as the International Congress of Experimental Psychology held in Paris, at the Ecole de Médecine in 1889. The Chairman on this occasion was Charles Richet himself whose distinguished career embraced alike physiology, psychology and psychical research.[7] The dividing line between the abnormal and the paranormal was still a fine one and many of the cases that attracted attention were of interest to medical psychologists no less than to psychical researchers. Multiple personality is a good example of one such phenomenon that straddled the divide.

In this chapter we shall attempt to illustrate the character of this phase of psychical research by considering a few of the many episodes that have since become highlights of the literature. Some of the features that could be said to typify these episodes are:the spectacular nature of the phenomena in question, their dependence on particular gifted individuals, the exploratory or free-wheeling nature of the tests devised to study the phenomena and, finally, the recurrent difficulty of ever reaching an agreed conclusion even within the psychical research community. In all these respects this epoch stands in marked contrast to that which we shall next be considering, involving the rise of experimental parapsychology.

A celebrated case of this period which illustrates the fine line that divides the normal from the paranormal is that of

'Patience Worth'. Pearl Curran, a housewife of St Louis of no literary pretensions, took to using a ouija board as a pastime, and then one day started receiving messages from a purported communicator calling herself 'Patience Worth'. She claimed to be the spirit of a young woman who had lived in England in the seventeenth century. It was not, however, this claim that made the case of lasting interest, for the identity of this 'Patience Worth' was never in fact established, but the fact that, under her ostensible dictation, Mrs Curran managed, between the years 1913 and 1937, to write no less than seven full-length historical novels, thousands of poems, many of high quality, not to mention quick-fire epigrams, aphorisms, repartee, etc; all, seemingly, well beyond the known powers of the conscious Pearl Curran. Her case excited the attention of linguists, literary critics, historians, psychologists and, of course, psychical researchers. The classic study is that of Walter Franklin Prince. On one occasion, without any warning, he asked 'Patience Worth' to compose a poem of 25 lines, each line to commence with the next letter of the alphabet starting with A but excluding X. A plausible poem conforming to these rules was duly forthcoming without hesitation![8] Since Pearl Curran, many mediums and automatists have written books ostensibly dictated by such a spirit entity, but there has been nothing of comparable interest whether from the literary or psychical point of view.[9]

The cases that preoccupied the psychical researchers of this era may be divided into two broad categories: the mental and the physical. The latter was closely bound up with spiritualist beliefs and practices; the former, however, include a number of outstanding clairvoyants who have much in common with the somnambules of the mesmeric era, except that they did not need to be put into a trance but appeared to achieve their success by dint of intense concentration.

The clairvoyants

From 1912 to 1921, Rudolf Tischner, a physician in Munich, carried out some 182 separate tests on about a dozen different individuals from the locality, in which the subject had to ascertain the particulars of a concealed object or inscription. Tischner was well aware that such tests are open to cheating in a variety of ways. Indeed, what is known in the trade as 'billet reading' is still a popular act with stage mentalists. None of those who witnessed his sessions, however, no matter how suspicious they may have been initially, could see any loopholes in his procedure, and Tischner himself, at any rate, was in no doubt that what he called 'psychoscopy' or clairvoyance was a genuine ability.[10] He also drew attention to the work of two earlier Russian pioneers in this field, both medical men like himself: A.N. Khovrin, who had published a treatise in 1898 describing just such a faculty in a woman patient of his, and Naum Kotik whose clairvoyant experiments with a 14-year-old girl, Lydia, came out as a book in 1908, published in Munich in German.

Another German physician who discovered an outstanding clairvoyant subject was Gustav Pagenstecher. He had settled in Mexico City where he was a surgeon at the American Hospital. His subject, Maria Reyes de Zierold, known to the literature as 'Señora de Z.' had been a patient of his, and her peculiar ability came to light only after he had hypnotized her in an attempt to cure her of her insomnia! She excelled in what, in spiritualist parlance, is known as 'psychometry': an object of unknown provenance is held in the hand and the psychic attempts to produce relevant associations. Of course, if the object in question is a sealed letter, such 'psychometrizing' may approximate to a straightforward clairvoyant reading. Prince visited Pagenstecher in 1920 and carried out a study of this case. It proved a turning-point in his outlook. For example, he gave her a letter he had taken from an old file which she held between her hands while giving her associations. Subsequent checking revealed that no less than 35 of the 38 statements she had made concerning the author of the letter (a clergyman) proved to be literally correct.[11]

Two notable European exponents of this psychometric – clairvoyant faculty, both educated men of some distinction, were (*a*) the French writer and critic, Georges Cochet, known to the literature by his pseudonym, Pascal Forthuny, and (*b*) the Polish engineer, Stefan Ossowiecki. In the case of Cochet, he discovered his gift only late in life after he had been trying to contact his deceased son who had been killed in an air-crash. He was tested exhaustively by Osty, at the Institut, who then published a book on the case in 1926.[12]

Even more impressive, however, was the career of Ossowiecki who used to enjoy demonstrating his skill at medical congresses in Warsaw. He was tested both in Paris and Warsaw between 1921 and 1923 by Geley, Richet and others.[13] He was also tested, on behalf of the SPR, both by Dingwall in 1923 when he was research officer, and again by Besterman in 1933 when he held that position. In both cases the targets they used consisted of a scribbled drawing plus an inscription. This was prepared in London where it was folded over and placed inside an elaborate nest of envelopes, such that even the most powerful X-ray machine could not have revealed the target itself, and the entire package was sealed and marked with secret markings. Again, in both cases, the sealed package was presented to Ossowiecki by a third party so that there could be no possibility of Ossowiecki picking up any hints from the facial expression or demeanour of the person who had devised the target. Yet on *both* occasions, ten years apart, Ossowiecki eventually, after homing in on the target by stages, ended by producing, in the presence of a small audience, a perfect literal reproduction of the original target drawing (a scribbled bottle of wine in the first case, a bottle of ink in the second). He did *not* get the inscription under Dingwall's target drawing beyond noting, correctly, that it was in French, but he reproduced exactly the writing on the Besterman target consisting of the words 'SWAN INK'. Afterwards, both these highly demanding and sceptical researchers, after examining their test packages, expressed themselves fully satisfied that these could not have been tampered with.[14] In true psychometric fashion, Ossowiecki was never content to stop at the ascertainment of the actual target but would go on to describe the person who had produced it and even the surroundings where it had been prepared. He was killed, tragically, during the Warsaw uprising of 1944 – one of the most highly respected as well as being one of the supremely gifted individuals of parapsychological history.

The physical mediums

In contrast to the relatively sedate nature of the cases we have been discussing, the study of paraphysical phenomena has been at all times stormy and contentious. Every physical medium has been the focus of intense suspicion, indeed none escaped outright accusations of cheating. This is not, perhaps, surprising in view of two aspects of the situation: (1) the fantastic and grotesque character of the phenomena they purveyed and (2) the obstacles which these mediums insisted on introducing which effectively prevented conclusive proof of their paranormality. In this latter connection we may note that, though some mediums were more cooperative than others, all insisted on functioning in varying degrees of darkness or, at best, of suboptimal illumination. None, to my knowledge, (leaving aside the special case of Mirabelli[15]) was willing to perform in daylight or in full illumination as Home had once done. Why, then, the preference for darkness? Whether this was, in fact, a genuine necessity (be it for psychological or paraphysical reasons) or just a convenient ploy for perpetrating a deception, we can now only surmise.[16] Today, when technology enables us to observe what goes on in the dark, there are no more physical mediums or, at any rate, none so far who have permitted an objective investigation. Rudi Schneider, whom we discuss below, was, in the event, the last of the physical mediums to submit to state-of-the-art instrumentation. Their absence today inevitably fuels suspicion.

Nevertheless, for all that we may be tempted to adopt a cynical view of these alleged physical phenomena, as so many sceptical writers have done, it is our duty to keep an open mind about them at least until it can be shown that conjurors can do what these mediums are reported to have done – *under comparable conditions*, be it well understood! Here I can do no more than offer a thumbnail sketch of the principal protagonists (other than Palladino whom we discuss at greater length below) on whom the case for the reality of the physical phenomena of mediumship now mainly rests. These include a young Icelander, Indridason, a young Belfast woman, Kathleen Goligher, two Poles, Kluski and Guzik, a Frenchwoman, Eva C., two Germans, the Schneider brothers, and, lastly, the American medium, Margery, whose tempestuous career split American psychical research into two antagonistic camps and paved the way for the next phase in the history of parapsychology which sought to dispense with mediums altogether!

Indridi Indridason
Indridason was the first medium to appear in Iceland and is the only Icelandic physical medium. Spiritualism had already gained a foothold, however, when in 1905 young Indridi moved to Reykjavik to become a printer's apprentice. He was inveigled by friends into taking part in a table-tilting sitting but the outcome almost scared him out of his wits. From then on, until 1909 when he fell ill of typhoid fever, he was given no peace. A group calling themselves the Experimental Society was set up to study his phenomena, which included levitations, materializations, etc., and a special

building was erected for this purpose. Some of the leading personalities of Iceland, such as the writer and journalist Einar Kvaran, who became President of the Society, were convinced that his phenomena were real but, even more important, was the endorsement of Gudmundur Hannesson, Professor of Medicine at the University of Iceland and, later, President of the University, who tested Indridason in his (Hanneson's) own house. Unfortunately, Indridason died of pneumonia in 1912 before he had a chance to be tested outside Iceland. His case has only recently come to the attention of the wider parapsychological community, thanks to the devoted efforts of two Icelandic scholars.[17]

Kathleen Goligher

The Golighers were a working class family of Belfast, and spiritualism was the family religion. Like so many other families of that time and of that persuasion, they were wont to sit round a table to commune with the spirits. It soon became evident, however, that without Kathleen nothing much would happen. She would not have secured her niche in parapsychological history, however, had she not attracted the attention of William J. Crawford, a lecturer in Mechanical Engineering at the Belfast Technical Institute who had been awarded a Doctorate of Science by the University of Glasgow in 1911. Between 1915 and 1920, Crawford held numerous sittings with the Goligher circle (normally it comprised some seven persons) on the basis of which he published three books.[18] The main phenomenon, apart from the raps which he recorded on a phonograph, was the levitation of the seance table. This occurred to order with such regularity, and the 'spirits' appeared to be so obliging, that inevitably his claims aroused suspicion. Yet two leading members of the SPR who visited him in the early days, William Barrett and Whateley Carington, both reported favourably on the basis of their own observations. The most remarkable aspect of this case from our standpoint, however, was the way in which it illustrates how the outlook and prepossessions of the investigator can impose themselves on the phenomena – it was, one could say, a classic case of what we would now call the 'experimenter effect'. As a mechanical engineer, Crawford arrived at the theory that the levitations of the table must be effectuated by means of ectoplasmic rods extruded from the body of the medium herself. And, sure enough, he produced photographs illustrating these 'psychic structures' as well as placing the medium on a weighing-machine that duly showed an increase in her weight corresponding to the levitation of the table. Like all photographs of ectoplasm, these curious structures may look spurious, yet it is hard to figure out how they could have been used to levitate the table in any normal way even if they had been contrived.

As a result of Crawford's efforts, Kathleen soon became known all over Europe. Unfortunately the case ended sadly and on a sour note for all concerned. In July 1920 Crawford, then 39 years of age, committed suicide by drowning. A suicide note explained that he feared the onset of insanity, but it explicitly denies that his fatal decision had any connection with his work with the Goligher circle and he expresses confidence that it would stand the test of time. Also, that same year. Fournier d'Albe, a prominent psychical researcher and the biographer of William Crookes, was sent by the SPR to follow up Crawford's lead, and he held some 20 sittings with the circle. By then the phenomena had declined, as Carington discovered when he had revisited the Golighers. At all events Fournier was unable to obtain any clear evidence of paranormal phenomena and, in the book he published on his findings, he makes no secret of the fact that he strongly suspected fraud.[19] From that time on, Kathleen vowed never to have anything further to do with psychical researchers, although her family continued to support the local spiritualist society.[20]

Jan Guzik and Franek Kluski

Both these Polish mediums were pre-eminently materialization mediums; both were tested extensively, both in Warsaw by the Polish SPR and in Paris at the Institut.[21] Both mediums, unfortunately, insisted on dark seances, although, to compensate, both medium and sitters were chained to one another to form a circle. Lastly – a bizarre touch – both were associated with the production of animal and even sub-human phantoms. The two men were, however, of very different social backgrounds. Jan Guzik was a working man: he was a tanner's apprentice when, at the age of 15, he was first taken up by Polish spiritualists. Kluski (a pseudonym – his actual name, Teofil Modrzejewski, remained confidential) was a poet, writer and professional banker who only discovered his mediumistic gifts when, in 1919 at the age of 45, he attended a seance at which Guzik (then 46) was officiating. Guzik was never above perpetrating deceptions, as even his supporters acknowledged; Kluski, though his mediumship never satisfied the hard sceptics, was never, as far as is known, implicated in fraud.

The various phantoms that proliferate at seances are transient beings. There are two ways, however, whereby their existence may be put on permanent record: one is by photography (as Crookes had done with 'Katie King') the other is by inducing them to leave an imprint in wax. This is what Geley sought to do in the case of Kluski's phantom hands. The request was made to the phantoms to plunge their hands into a bowl of liquid paraffin wax so that, when their hands were withdrawn, a waxen glove would be formed, such that when their hands were eventually dematerialized, the empty glove-moulds could be filled with plaster of paris. When set, this would provide a permanent cast which, hopefully, would display the exact texture of the skin. To make absolutely sure, however, that there was no trick, such as substituting, in the course of the seance, a ready-made glove-mould, an identifying chemical was secretly put into the paraffin wax. There is today an extant gallery of these casts showing hands of all descriptions and in various positions; some consist of two hands clasped together, some are adult hands, some children's hands. Curiously many of the adult hands are somewhat smaller than they should be. All told, one may say that the Kluski casts remain among the most challenging exhibits in the storehouse of anomalous artefacts.[22]

Marthe Béraud (Eva Carrière)

Another medium of this period who specialized in material-izations is one who might be described as having two distinct careers: the first in Algiers where she grew up and where, in 1905, her case attracted the attention of Richet[23] the second in Paris, after she came under the direction of Juliette Bisson, sculptor and psychical researcher. Thereafter she was inves-tigated more intensively than any other materializing medium has ever been, first by Schrenck in Munich between 1910 and 1914, then by Geley in Paris between 1916 and 1918.[24] It was during this latter European phase that Marthe adopted the name 'Eva Carrière' usually contracted in the literature to 'Eva C'. It was not widely known at the time that she was one and the same person as Marthe Béraud.

Curiously, her phenomena, too, underwent a peculiar change. Her phantoms became more and more two-dimen-sional until they began to approximate to psychic photographs – so much so, in fact, that they were suspected of being paper cut-outs from magazines! During her Algerian period the phantoms were, on the contrary, so life-like that the flashlight photographs inevitably suggested a human impersonator. Indeed, when her father's ex-coachman (who had been sacked) claimed that he had impersonated the phantom, by emerging through a trapdoor, a scandal erupted from which Marthe never quite recovered; in vain did Richet protest that a search had revealed no such trap-door!

Whatever our conclusions regarding Eva/Marthe, and,

with the demise of materialization, it is so difficult for us *not* to be incredulous, a point we must keep in mind is that her phantoms were never static. Richet describes how her phantoms built up from an initial blob, and Geley, studying her phantom faces, notes that 'In many instances *these representations have grown under my own eyes from the beginning to the end of the phenomena*'[author's italics]. Both, moreover, produced photographs to support their claim. We should also note that the indignities to which she meekly submitted in the name of science were exceptionally severe: she was given an emetic after some sittings to make sure that she had not swallowed any matter that might have been regurgitated to fabricate the phantom; she drank bilberry syrup before some sittings to see whether her phantoms would show discolouration; and she did not even demur at body searches *per rectum et vaginam* (to use Richet's phrase). Even so, maybe she *did* find a way to evade all these controls – she remains a controversial figure – but she should not be lightly written off.[25]

Willy and Rudi Schneider

The Schneider family belonged to the little Austrian garrison town of Braunau (later to become notorious as the birthplace of Hitler) where the father, Josef Schneider, practised as a printer. They got caught up in the local craze for spiritualism and soon found that, of their six children (all boys), Willy, who was 16 when he first went into trance in 1919, was a powerful physical medium. Even so, he might never have come to wider notice had he not been discovered by a retired naval captain, Fritz Kogelnik, who had come to live in Braunau and who persuaded *Vater* Schneider (as he came to be known in the literature) to let him test Willy in his (Kogelnik's) home. Though initially a complete sceptic, Kogelnik was sufficiently impressed by what he saw to alert Schrenck-Notzing, whose book on the Eva C. case he had read. Schrenck duly rented a room in Braunau where, in 1922, he carried out a series of tests with young Willy at which a number of scientists were present as observers. At a further series of fifteen sittings, Erich Becher, Professor of Philosophy and Director of the Psychological Institute of Munich, was present and added his endorsement that something significant was going on.

The following year Willy, having completed his apprenticeship, went to work for a dentist in Munich. This enabled Schrenck to continue testing him in his own laboratory there. At some of these sittings, which were attended both by Eric Dingwall and by Harry Price, Schrenck used a cage made of black gauze. On some occasions Willy was placed inside this cage while the objects he was required to move lay outside; on other occasions the reverse situation obtained. Yet, not only did these objects mysteriously move around but a variety of materializations would ensue whose 'flowing, changing and fantastic shapes' and whose 'mode of development until they reached their final form argue' says Schrenck 'against any possibility of a fraudulent production'.[26]

By this time, however, Willy was getting bored with the endless repetitions that were demanded of him and he left Munich for Vienna where, again, he worked for a dentist. By then, however, Rudi, six years his junior, had taken over his mediumistic mantle. 'Olga', Willy's spirit-control, had transferred the seat of her operations to Rudi's organism. Like his brother, however, Rudi was not specially interested in psychical research; he was much more interested in football and in motor-cars. Indeed, eventually, he and his wife, Mitzi, ran a driving school until his death following a stroke in 1957. Rudi's phenomena were less spectacular than those of his brother (despite an occasional self-levitation!). Moreover, they became progressively weaker as time went on, so that by the late 1920s sitters might have to wait for hours for anything at all to happen. And what made the waiting still more irksome was that the imperious 'Olga' insisted that the sitters engage in a constant flow of singing and chatter! Nevertheless, despite all such drawbacks, Rudi's mediumship is now rightly considered among the best authenticated in the literature. This may be attributed to a number of facts: (*a*) he was the last physical medium to be tested on an international scale when new instrumentation had made possible additional safeguards against deception; (*b*) his sitters included more scientists and academics of repute than was the case with any previous physical medium, with the possible exception of Palladino; (*c*) despite the many suspicions and allegations that were always being voiced, he was *never* caught in any act of fraud. I would be inclined, moreover, to add to these points (*d*) the fact that the late Anita Gregory devoted much of her career to an exhaustive examination of the records and documentation of this case. She eventually published a superlative monograph (Gregory, 1985) which, in my opinion, vindicates the reality of the phenomena as conclusively as one could reasonably demand in the circumstances.

After the sudden death of Schrenck in February 1929, there was no one in Germany who could undertake the investigation of Rudi, who thus came up for grabs as far as the international community of psychical research was concerned. Harry Price, never one to miss a trick, duly went to Munich a month later and signed Rudi up for six seances in London at his 'National Laboratory of Psychical Research' in April 1929. The results were sufficiently impressive for Price to arrange for a more prolonged series of sittings in the autumn of that year and, again, early in 1930. It was indeed largely thanks to Price, whose book on Rudi came out in 1930, that Rudi became an international celebrity.[27]

In October 1930 Rudi was investigated at the Institut where Eugene Osty in collaboration with his engineer son, Marcel, had devised an elaborate set-up they believed to be fraud-proof. At this period, the phenomena consisted largely of the moving around of light objects, such as a handkerchief;

at a good sitting the target handkerchief might even be tied into into a knot! Their device resembled a burglar alarm. An infra-red beam impinges on a photoelectric cell. When the beam is intercepted, this would cause a bell to ring or trigger a camera and a magnesium flash. In this way, any fraudulent attempt to pick up the target-object that had been placed on the seance table would at once be exposed. Of course every effort was made to restrain Rudi during the sitting, but the possibility of some accomplice taking advantage of the darkness could not, in the nature of the case, be ignored. The extraordinary outcome was that, though the beam was repeatedly occluded, at any rate to some 30 per cent of its strength, and any such intervention was usually announced beforehand by Rudi's trance-personality, Olga, the flashlight photographs revealed *nothing at all*! It was as if an invisible force had been in action, although, much to Rudi's disappointment, the target-object itself usually stayed put.

Rudi next went back to London for a further 27 sittings with Harry Price from February to May 1932. Most of these were very uneventful, but enough happened to induce a number of eminent scientists to declare publicly that what they had witnessed could not be explained by normal means. Price was now using a similar set-up to that of the French investigators and it so happened that, on one occasion involving the displacement of a handkerchief, the camera was triggered producing a photograph showing Rudi with one arm free. Since Price himself was supposed to be controlling Rudi, he, if anyone, was to blame for this lapse (Price pleaded toothache!). In any case, the free arm could not have explained the various phenomena recorded at that sitting, still less at other sittings. Price, however, appreciated the whiphand which the possession of such a photograph bestowed on him.

He had learnt that arrangements had been made for another independent investigation of Rudi under the direction of Lord Charles Hope and Lord Rayleigh on behalf of the

SPR, to be held that autumn of 1932. His fury at what he regarded as poaching on his own reserve knew no bounds and he decided to use this 'incriminating' photograph in order to discredit his rivals and show that he was smarter than they! Accordingly, a year after the photograph had been taken, and shortly before the findings of the Hope–Rayleigh series were due to be published in the *Proceedings* of the SPR,[28] he published an article in the *Sunday Dispatch* denouncing Rudi as a fraud as well as issuing 'Bulletin IV' of his National Laboratory, covering the series he had conducted with Rudi, which included the contentious photograph. The fact that it was quite irrelevant to the many phenomena observed during the 27 sittings of the Hope–Rayleigh series, mostly movements of objects, and the fact that this series was attended by no less than 47 different sitters, many of them persons of high academic distinction and none of whom expressed any doubts or reservations about what they had witnessed, did not matter. The sceptics, of course, were only too happy to take Price's word for it and to conclude that yet another physical medium had bitten the dust!

Rudi was to produce little of any interest thereafter and was probably relieved to revert to obscurity and to a normal life. His career illustrates, more clearly perhaps than any other, the desperate obstacles that beset the courageous few who, in the face of ridicule and every kind of practical difficulty, persisted in trying to get at the truth about physical mediumship. What made them do it? Perhaps Anita Gregory put her finger on it when, at the conclusion of her monograph (Gregory, 1985, p.425) she writes:

These phenomena are, in the most profound sense of that word, scandalous. They are both signs and symbols of a spectre that haunts the strongholds of science: The spectre of the direct power of mind and imagination to transform the real world.

Margery

A so-called 'spirit-control', such as 'Olga', who serves as a kind of compère at seances with trance mediums, is usually some fanciful character thought to be a figment of the medium's unconscious. In the case of Mina Crandon (née Stinson, but known to the literature as 'Margery') however, it was her beloved brother, Walter Stinson, who had been killed in a railway accident in 1911 at the age of 28 (she was then 23), who assumed this role and, for her supporters, the focus was as much on the attempts by this *soi-disant* Walter to demonstrate his continued survival as it was on the bizarre physical phenomena which he ostensibly enabled her to produce. At certain seances, for example, Walter's voice is reported as being heard directly while Margery's mouth was held shut or was filled with liquid or marbles. 'Walter', so it seems, was even able on one occasion to penetrate a sound-proof box so as to activate a microphone which it enclosed, whence his voice was relayed to sitters in another room.

In 1918 Mina married Dr LeRoi G. Crandon, a successful Boston surgeon and a respected member of the Harvard Medical School. She was by then a divorcee and a mother; he had been married twice before. His interest in spiritualism began around 1923 after attending a lecture by Sir Oliver Lodge, and he was further inspired to undertake his own investigation by reading the works of W.J. Crawford. In May of that year he held his first seance with friends as sitters at their house at 10 Lime Street. It was on that occasion that Margery's mediumship first became apparent. From that time on, the psychical research enthusiasts gave her no peace and the exertions to which she was driven may, in the end, have undermined her health and her sanity. When she died in 1941 she had become (like the Fox sisters before her) a helpless alcoholic. One might have thought that her husband, a medical man, would have protected her from such exertions, for he remained throughout master of ceremonies. It was he who decided who was or was not to be admitted to a seance, what conditions could be allowed, and usually he acted as one of her controllers. If there was any hanky-panky going on it is hard to imagine that he was not a party to it. But if so, to what end or from what motive no one, however cynical, has been able to suggest.[29]

Before long Margery was attracting the attention of several Harvard academics, notably William McDougall, the British psychologist then head of the Department of Psychology at Harvard, and Gardner Murphy, then a lecturer in psychology at Columbia but also a Research Fellow at Harvard. A prize of $5,000 had been offered by the journal *Scientific American* for anyone who could produce any 'visible psychic manifestation'. Margery made a bid and a committee was set up with J.M. Bird, Associate Editor of *Scientific American*, as its Secretary. He, in turn, appointed a committee consisting of McDougall, Dr D.F. Comstock, a noted physicist and inventor on the staff of the Massachusetts Institute of Technology, the psychical researchers W.F. Prince, Hereward Carrington and Harry Houdini.

Testing began in April 1924. A stout wooden cabinet was used in which Margery was seated, with Crandon on one side and Bird on the other. At one seance in June of that year the side of the cabinet next to Bird was ripped off, screws and all, after the cabinet itself, with its occupants, had been dragged around the room![30] It was the most violent manifestation that Margery had produced and, in due course, Bird duly wrote up an enthusiastic report on her mediumship for *Scientific American*. It was then, to protect her and her husband from publicity, that he used the name 'Margery' which thereafter stuck.

Not all the committee, however, agreed with Bird. Prince, its chairman, was not satisfied that trickery could be ruled out; neither was McDougall. Carrington was convinced that he had witnessed genuine phenomena but Comstock would say no more than that the case deserved further investigation. As for Houdini, ever the doughty foe of the paranormal, he insisted that, at those seances which he had attended he had witnessed nothing but deliberate and conscious fraud. All this despite the fact that, when Margery had been secured inside a cabinet which he himself had designed and certified, a bell-box placed on the seance table in front of her, that could be activated only by closing an electric circuit, was heard to ring![31] In November 1924, the *Scientific American* reported the diverse opinions of the committee. No prize was awarded and the following year the competition was declared closed.

Yet, despite this setback, the Margery mediumship continued to expand and to attract increasing attention from psychical researchers both in the USA and in Britain.[32] Dingwall, on behalf of the SPR, attended sittings and was initially most enthusiastic, although later he became disillusioned as suspicion gained the upper hand. But in July 1926 a new development was initiated that was to have fateful consequences for Margery's reputation. It was decided to try, on the lines of Geley's experiments with Kluski, to obtain Walter's fingerprints in soft wax. Her dentist, Frederick Caldwell, who had participated with startling effect at some of her very earliest seances, was duly consulted and offered her some dental wax of the brand which he recommended. In December 1929 the Crandons were again in London and gave sittings at the SPR in the course of which 'Walter' produced samples of his thumbprints.

Then a bombshell exploded in 1931. E.E. Dudley, then research officer for the ASPR, wanted to check whether these thumbprints might correspond with those of anyone who had *ever* sat with Margery – if only to rule out the possibility of collusion. To his and everyone's consternation he found that these same thumbprints, both left and right, corresponded minutely with those of Caldwell, her dentist. This was confirmed by 'five competent and unprejudiced experts' and Dudley duly published his report in the *Bulletin* of the Boston SPR in October 1932. This discovery did not explain, of course, how Margery could have produced wax prints of *any* description while she was supposed to have been controlled, but, whatever one is to make of this incident, it cast a permanent shadow over her mediumship.

And yet, not only did the seances continue throughout the 1930s but some of the most striking phenomena were yet to come. I refer, in particular, to her 'linked rings'. Her chief investigators at this time were W.H. Button, then President of the ASPR, B.K. Thorogood, a retired engineer, and Mark W. Richardson, a physician. The aim of this endeavour was to get 'Walter', in the course of a seance, to link a pair of stout wooden rings. The rings had been made by a carpenter using two different kinds of timber. Most of them were six inches in outer diameter and three-quarters of an inch in cross-section. The earliest occurrence of this topological miracle occurred during the first half of 1932 at a small private sitting presided over by Thorogood who held the rings, one in each hand. After that many such linkages are reported to have taken place at sittings at the Crandons' house in Lime Street, at which usually a second medium, Sarah Litzelman, officiated besides Margery.[33]

Had any of these linkages survived, the subsequent history of parapsychology might have been very different. For, in the face of such a permanent paranormal object (PPO), the onus shifts to the sceptic to explain how it could have been fabricated in any known way. It is here that we encounter what is perhaps the most baffling aspect of this whole episode. According to Mark Richardson, 'Walter' had warned that, once the linkage had been removed from the vicinity of the two mediums, they would become unstable. Sure enough, a pair which Crandon sent to Oliver Lodge in London, though carefully packed, arrived broken. Another pair, however, was sent to the ASPR in New York where it was said to have been put on exhibition on 24 February 1934 (although no record of the fact can now be traced). All we now have, therefore, is written testimony and a photograph. But

on one occasion a pair of rings were sent to an X-ray specialist, W.K. Coffin, whose testimony that an X-ray examination
had revealed no flaw in the rings was duly published. Yet
neither this pair of rings nor the X-ray photograph could be
found when a search was made for them at No.10 Lime Street
in 1944.

APPENDIX

In this appendix I shall review the lives of two famous mediums whose careers
between them span the entire period that we have covered in this chapter. The
contrast between them could scarcely have been more pronounced but what they
do have in common – something that has been so rare since then – is that, for almost
their entire careers, they put themselves unstintingly at the service of dedicated
psychical researchers.

Eusapia Palladino (1854–1918)[34]

As with many notable mediums, her manifestations commence in childhood, she
then comes to the attention of the spiritualist community and in due course certain
scientists, some of them initially avowed sceptics, feel sufficiently challenged to
undertake their own investigation.

She was born in the province of Bari but her mother died soon after her birth
and her father is said to have been murdered by brigands when she was only 12 years
old. She then moved to Naples where she found lodgings with a number of different
families who took her in. It was then that her mediumistic propensities began to
attract attention. One of the earliest accounts is in a letter written by G. Damiani
in 1872. A keen spiritualist, he had married an English woman and was then living
in England, but he and his wife had heard that there was a good medium in Naples
and they had gone there to investigate. The next step occurred in 1888 by which time
she was already 34 years old. A certain Ercole Chiaia, who had become her principal
admirer, wrote an open letter to Cesare Lombroso (Professor of Forensic Medicine
at the University of Turin who today is best remembered as a pioneer of criminol-
ogy) which was published in a Rome newspaper. He there describes an assortment
of marvels and appeals to Lombroso, who was known as an outspoken materialist,
to undertake his own investigation and express his own opinion.

Lombroso did not respond directly to that appeal, but two years later he duly
went to Naples where two seances were held in the hotel room where he stayed.
Although nothing like as spectacular as that which Chiaia had described, they were
sufficiently intriguing to whet his appetite. Accordingly, in 1891, he organized 17
seances in Milan at the house of a trusted collaborator, G. Finzi, at which seven
other researchers besides Finzi participated, including the Russian, Aksakov, the
German, Carl Du Prel, Charles Richet, the astronomer G. Schiaparelli of the Milan
Observatory and three other Italians, two of them physicists. They sat around a

table with the medium at one end in front of a curtained recess (the cabinet). An electric light stood on the table 'with red glass sides'. One particularly bizarre phenomenon that was reported was the appearance of a hand which issued from the curtained recess above the medium's head. The room, of course, had been secured against the infiltration of an accomplice. 'It is impossible to state' writes Lombroso

> the number of times that this hand appeared and was touched by us. Suffice it to say that no doubt was any longer possible. It was actually a living human hand that we saw and touched, while at the same time the entire bust and the arms of the medium remained in sight and her hands were continually held by her neighbours on each side.[35]

Whatever the explanation of Lombroso's conversion it transformed the situation with regard to Eusapia. From then on everyone in the business wanted to get in on the act. One of those who had occasion to sit with Palladino in Italy was Julijan Ochorowicz, lecturer in psychology and the philosophy of science at the University of Lemberg and a co-director of the Institut Général Psychologique of Paris. He brought her to Warsaw where, between November 1893 and January 1894, he held 40 sittings with her. For some reason spiritualism thrived in Poland and, in its wake, a number of truly remarkable mediums arose, two of whom we have already discussed above. Another such was Stanislawa Tomczyk who was discovered by Ochorowicz and who later married the distinguished English psychical researcher, the Hon. Everard Feilding, a key figure, as we shall see, in the story of Eusapia.

Although Ochorowicz was duly impressed, not all the witnesses were satisfied that the possibility of cheating had been completely ruled out. The fact is that Eusapia was, in a quite literal sense, a slippery customer. She would engage in much wriggling or squirming during a seance in the course of which she would sometimes free an arm or a leg from her controller. She was adept, moreover, at substituting one arm for the other so that both her controllers on either side of her would find themselves holding on to the same arm! When taxed with this irregular behaviour she would round on her investigators for failing to control her properly, pleading that she could not be held responsible for what she might do while in a trance! That she indulged in trickery in this way was never in doubt and was acknowledged by all who studied her. The pertinent question was always how to explain those phenomena that could *not* conceivably have been produced in this way.

The next important move brought her to France. Charles Richet owned a small cottage on the little island of Roubaud (Ribaud)[36] in addition to his château at Carqueiranne, near Toulon. Since the cottage was the only building on the island apart from a lighthouse, one could at least be reasonably sure that no accomplice was lurking in the vicinity. Richet was anxious to get the SPR involved in the case of Palladino, and both Myers and Lodge were, at his invitation, present at the four sittings that were held on the island in the summer of 1894. The other sitter, besides Richet himself, was Ochorowicz. A feature of these seances, which later became standard practice with her, was to have continuous note-taking. Here the note-taker, who sat outside an open window of the ground-floor room where the action took place, with a lamp at his side, was Richet's secretary, Monsieur Bellier. The sittings, which were held late in the evenings, usually began in good illumination but, as they proceeded, and as the phenomena became ever more amazing, moonlight and the note-taker's lamp shining through the window provided the only sources of illumination. Yet we are assured that everyone's hands were at all times visible and, certainly, the official report written by Lodge and published later that year in the *Journal of the S.P.R.*,[37] does not suggest that visibility was ever a problem.

What went on strains credulity. At the fourth and final sitting, at which Ochorowicz replaced Bellier (who had left) as the official note-taker, the following incidents were recorded in addition to the by-now routine levitations of the table or billowing inwards of the window curtains: hammer-like blows on the table – of an intensity to make the sitters fearful for their own hands; Richet being clutched by a large alien hand while holding both the medium's hands; Myers being seized from behind and vigorously pulled and shaken; a decanter of water, which stood on the top shelf of the nearby buffet, arriving on the table and the medium drinking from it as it was brought to her lips as if by invisible hands; and five plates and a loaf of bread being likewise transported from the buffet.

Could it be that the sitters, Richet, Myers and Lodge were all three hallucinated? Sceptics have not hesitated to suggest as much. Yet it is difficult not to sympathize with Lodge who, in the official report, writes:

> However the facts are to be explained, the possibility of the facts I am constrained to admit. There is no further room in my mind for doubt. Any person without invincible prejudice who had had the same experience, would have come to the same broad conclusion, *viz*. That things hitherto held impossible do actually occur

a conclusion to which Myers assented.

The ultimate challenge, however, was to get the Sidgwicks, whose suspicious attitude to physical mediumship was notorious, to acknowledge Eusapia's phenomena. Richet now invited them to join him at his château at Carqueiranne for further seances and, grudgingly, they came. They were joined by Ochorowicz and, among others, by Schrenck-Notzing (whom we have already met) as well as by a Dr C. Segard, Chief Medical Officer of the French Mediterannean fleet. Some six further seances were held.

These were not as spectacular as the earlier ones on the island, and the illumination was even more subdued. Nevertheless, incidents occurred while the medium appeared to be securely held that could not easily be ignored: for example a large and stalkless melon weighing over 7 kilos was transported from a chair placed behind Eusapia to the table at which the observers sat. At all events, the Sidgwicks duly capitulated to the extent of admitting that they had witnessed phenomena for which they could offer no explanation. Hodgson, on the other hand, when news reached him in America of the French sittings, was far from satisfied. Indeed he tried hard to prevent publication of the report in the *Journal*. Richet, he complained, knew nothing about methods of trickery and the others had doubtless been taken in once again by Eusapia's well-known trick of freeing an arm or leg at an opportune moment. In vain did Myers protest that, with his experience, he was perfectly capable of knowing when he had control of a medium's limbs; the obvious next move would be to bring Eusapia to England, the home of psychical research, and to invite Hodgson to witness events for himself. Arrangements were duly put in train for Eusapia to stay with the Myerses at their home, Leckhampton House, Cambridge.

She arrived in Cambridge on 30 July 1895 and soon got down to business. Some 20 sittings in all were held, but Hodgson did not arrive until the 13th sitting. The SPR was represented by the Sidgwicks, Myers and Alice Johnson and other observers included eminent scientists like Francis Darwin, Lord Rayleigh and J.J. Thomson, as well as J.N. Maskelyne, the celebrated conjuror, and his son. What exactly transpired at these Cambridge sittings is still a matter of speculation and argument but it is generally agreed that the phenomena were much less impressive than they had been with Richet in the south of France and there is no question that Eusapia fell back on cheating. Indeed Hodgson would deliberately free a hand to see what she would do and, for whatever reason, she duly fell into his trap.[38]

Henry Sidgwick was appalled. He retracted his previous endorsement and even forbade publication of a full report on these sittings on the grounds that the Society ought not to give publicity to a fraudulent medium. He reaffirmed the policy of the Society not to test mediums once they had been caught cheating. No doubt he had the interests of the Society at heart although some may think it shows a poor understanding of the psychology of mediumship. Dingwall, himself no stranger to the wiles of mediums, has this to say about the Cambridge fiasco:

> There was something wholly unreal about the Cambridge sittings. It is difficult to convey the impression to persons without a long experience of the seance room, but I have the feeling that Eusapia knew that in that atmosphere she could never let go, but had to fall back on all those clever little tricks which she had found so useful during so many years. After all, they were nothing new; and she still might be able to bring off something to satisfy this serious circle of staid and unexcitable observers.[39]

Not that Mrs Sidgwick did not try her hardest to make Eusapia feel at home in Cambridge but the contrast between this peasant woman 'vital vulgar, amorous *and* a cheat', as Dingwall[39] puts it, (his italics) and these fastidious and high-minded academics could hardly have made for a congenial atmosphere.

Her career, however, was not by any means halted by this setback. She returned to France where various sittings were held during the next two years. Richet, for one, was not at all satisfied with the conduct of the Cambridge investigation and, in November 1898, he attended a number of sittings with her in Paris at the home of Camille Flammarion, the astronomer and fellow psychical researcher. He was sufficiently impressed by what he had observed there to arrange sittings for her at his own house in Paris and he decided again to invite Myers, who by now was in a fine state of perplexity, to join him. Myers duly attended two sittings on 1 and 3 December 1898 at which the most notable effects involved the antics of a zither. He returned to England, his lingering doubts having been duly dispelled. Indeed, in a letter to the spiritualist journal *Light*, he declared that the phenomena were even more striking than on the Ile Roubaud. Certainly the illumination at these Paris sittings was superior. Hodgson, however, was upset. As the then Editor of the SPR *Journal* and *Proceedings*, he refused to publish an account of them. One of the sitters on that occasion, however, was the distinguished psychologist, Theodore Flournoy, of the University of Geneva. He has described what took place in his book *Esprits et Mediums*, published in Geneva in 1911.[40]

Thus, by the time she returned to her native Italy, Eusapia was at the height of her fame and much in demand among the Italian scientific community. It was the 'Minerva' group of Genoa who first took advantage of her services. Some 20 sittings were held during 1901 and 1902 plus a further six in the winter of 1906–7. The most notable member of this circle was Enrico Morselli, Director of the Clinic for Nervous and Mental Diseases of Genoa. At some of these sessions Eusapia was securely strapped onto a camp bed and yet the phenomena persisted. Morselli provides a full account of these investigations in his two-volume *Psicologia e Spiritismo*, published in Turin in 1908. While recognizing that Eusapia was capable of ingenious fraud, he was convinced that at least three-quarters of the phenomena he had witnessed were indeed genuine, including some impressive materializations. Morselli did not, however, regard these as proof of spirit intervention but, saw them rather as bizarre indications of the mind's extended powers. Eleanor Sidgwick (who was fluent in Italian as well as French and German) had the task of reviewing his book for the SPR *Proceedings*.[41] She contrasts his experiences with her own at Cambridge but, while still reluctant to agree that genuine phenomena had at last been demonstrated, she concedes that Morselli was a 'good and careful observer' and expresses the hope that his initiative would be duly followed up.

In fact this had already been done. Philippe Botazzi, head of the Physiological Institute of the University of Naples and initially a sceptic, tested her in his own laboratory in 1907 and pronounced her genuine. In the same year, Lombroso returned to the fray and organized a series of sittings in the Department of Psychiatry at the University of Turin that was attended by a number of medical men and this was followed by a further series under the direction of Pio Foa, Professor of Pathological Anatomy and General Secretary of the Academy of Sciences. One incident that occurred during this latter series involved the complete destruction of a solid whitewood table in 'very good red light' and this followed an announcement by the medium herself of her intention to bring this about! No wonder that the committee confessed that: 'Without the objective irrefutable documents which remained we would have doubted our sense and intelligence'.[42]

One further Continental investigation worth mentioning here is that which was undertaken by the Institut Général Psychologique of Paris. It lasted from 1905 to 1907 and involved no less than 43 sittings. Among the sitters we find here the names of Pierre and Marie Curie and that of the philosopher, Henri Bergson.[43] The official report appeared in 1908 under the authorship of Jules Courtier, a Professor of Psychology at the Sorbonne. It is very guarded as far as committing itself to any definite conclusion.[44]

By this time Eusapia was 54 years of age and her powers were waning. Everard Feilding was then Honorary Secretary of the SPR. He had spent much of his career tracking down physical mediums but invariably they turned out to be hoaxers, and he had sadly come to doubt whether there were indeed any genuine cases.

Hereward Carrington, the American researcher who in 1907 had published his *The Physical Phenomena of Spiritualism*, which was largely an exposé of fraudulent practices, was likewise disillusioned, but he decided nevertheless to approach Feilding to urge him to get the SPR to have one final crack at Palladino before it was too late. The Council agreed and, early in 1908, the two men set out for Naples, later to be joined by W.W. Baggally, a Council member and expert on trickery who had already sat with Eusapia without being convinced. It was this trio who made up the Naples Committee. Unlike most of the earlier committees that had reported on Palladino, which had consisted mainly of scientists, the present trio were all experienced, not to say jaded, psychical researchers with considerable practical knowledge of conjuring. Conjurors, from J.N. Maskelyne to James Randi, have always maintained that scientists are the easiest people to hoodwink if only because they are too high-minded to fathom the mentality of a trickster. Whatever truth there may be in this argument, it was not an objection that could be raised against the Naples Committee.

Eleven sittings in all were held between 21 November and 19 December 1908 at the Hotel Victoria, Naples. Eusapia would arrive late in the evening at their rooms on the fifth floor, and she would be stripped and searched before and after the sitting. On some occasions certain outsiders were invited to attend. A professional stenographer was employed throughout to record the minutes of each sitting. The electric light used was at all times adequate to observe what was going on. And yet the full panoply of her phenomena was elicited at these sittings, including her rudimentary materializations. Gradually, but ineluctably, all three investigators came to the conclusion that she could, beyond any possibility of a doubt, produce genuinely paranormal phenomena. Already, at the very first sitting, we find Feilding saying:

> It is unthinkable to us that, for two hours, two reasonably intelligent and active men [Baggally did not arrive until the the fifth sitting] both fairly well posted in the tricks of mediums, closely clinging with arms and legs about this elderly lady, could be baffled by mere methods of substitution of feet and hands, for which they were constantly on the look out.[45]

But it was not until after the sixth sitting that Feilding finally cast off whatever lingering vestiges of doubt still persisted:

> For the first time I have the absolute conviction that our observation is not mistaken. I realize, as an appreciable fact of life, that, from an empty cabinet I have seen hands and heads come forth, that from behind the curtain of that empty cabinet I have been seized by living fingers, the existence and position of the very nails of which could be felt. I have seen this extraordinary woman sitting visible outside the curtain, held hand and foot by my colleagues, … while some entity within the curtain has over and over again pressed my hand in a position clearly beyond her reach. I refuse to entertain the possibility of a doubt that we were the victims of an hallucination.[46]

The 'Feilding Report', written by Feilding but endorsed by all three, appeared in the *Proceedings of the S.P.R.* for November 1909 with a brief preface by Eleanor Sidgwick herself explaining why, in this case, the Council had been willing to overrule their principle of boycotting mediums who had been convicted of fraud. Did this document, which Gauld has described as 'without doubt the most interesting record of its kind ever published',[47] finally convince the doubters? By no means, for such is never the case in psychical research. Podmore, for one, at once challenged these findings[48] and does so again in his book, *The Newer Spiritualism*, published the following year. Again he harps on the possibilities of the medium using an arm or leg she has contrived to free. His critique, however, was answered at length by Baggally and it made no impression on those who had been present.[49] Thereafter, the Feilding Report remained one of the mainstays of the case for the paranormal and a stumbling-block for sceptics. Just recently, however, Richard Wiseman (psychologist and conjuror) has reopened the case by speculating on the possibility that an accomplice might have infiltrated the seance room through a previously loosened panel in the door and then have operated from behind the curtain of the cabinet.[50]

Even so, the career of Eusapia Palladino would look very different today had it culminated in the Feilding Report. Carrington, however, encouraged by what he had seen in Naples, arranged for Eusapia to visit the United States. It was a move he lived to regret. She arrived in New York on the 10 November 1909, where at once she became the focus of press attentions. In all some 30 or 40 sittings were held during her visit, mostly in New York, four at Columbia University. Her investigators included some eminent psychologists, like Hugo Muensterberg of Harvard or Joseph Jastrow of Wisconsin, as well as some professional debunkers like Joseph Rinn, the conjuror. But few of her American investigators had any serious interest in, or understanding of, mediums; their aim was simply to expose her. She, in turn, felt alienated and, to her own undoing, reverted to her bad old ways. They set traps for her and she duly fell into them. By the time she left America on 18 June of the following year she was thoroughly discredited.[51]

It is by no means clear, however, that nothing of a paranormal nature occurred at these sittings. One well-known professional magician, Howard Thurston, was sufficiently impressed by what he had seen to advertise in the *New York Times* his offer of a thousand dollars to charity if any conjuror could show how she did it – there were no takers.[52] Carrington, certainly, never relinquished his belief that she could produce genuine phenomena, neither did Feilding nor Baggally. Yet, when Feilding went again to Naples in 1910 and sat with her together with three others from the SPR, they could elicit nothing but spurious phenomena.[53] On 16 May 1918 she died. One could say that no other medium has ever been investigated so relentlessly and so widely. But Dingwall's remark makes a fitting epitaph: 'It looked almost as if some malign influence had so arranged things that the truth was always just out of reach'.[54]

Gladys Osborne Leonard (1882–1968)[55]

It would be hard to imagine a more salient contrast than that between La Palladino and Mrs Leonard: the former a coarse, illiterate Neapolitan peasant, the latter a refined and educated English lady of well-to-do parents. Eusapia, as we have seen, was thoroughly devious; no taint of suspicion ever clouded the reputation of Gladys Osborne. The phenomena of these two mediums moreover could hardly be more different. Eusapia was sought after for her physical phenomena; Mrs Leonard, like Mrs Piper before her, eschewed physical phenomena and confined her mediumship to conveying messages purporting to emanate from deceased individuals. Indeed she produced some of the most telling evidence we have for the belief in survival. Finally, we may note that, while Eusapia Palladino became an international celebrity – she was, as we have seen, tested in five different countries spanning two continents – Mrs Leonard passed her whole career in Britain, where she was tested by researchers belonging to the SPR or, on occasion, to the American SPR.

Gladys Osborne, like Mrs Piper, seems to have had some unusual psychical experiences as a child, but she pursued a career in the theatre and the man she married, Frank Leonard, was a fellow actor. It was by chance that she became involved with spiritualism when she and two of the other actresses took to holding table-tipping seances to while away the time when they were not required on stage. It was in this way that she encountered the spirit, Feda, who was to be her regular control throughout her career as a trance medium. There was a tradition in the Osborne family that one of Gladys' ancestors had married a Hindu girl, around the year 1800, who then died in childbirth a year later at the tender age of 14. Feda claimed *to be* that ancestor. Whether she was, as some surmised, a figment of Mrs Leonard's unconscious of the kind one comes across in cases of multiple personality, or whether she had any kind of independent existence is not a question that need concern us here. The point is, however, that Feda, whatever we may make of her, was a salient feature of the Leonard mediumship and was, moreover, much more of a personality in her own right than Mrs Piper's 'Phinuit' or than the ubiquitous 'John King' who served as Eusapia's control. In the vast majority of cases, all the messages that purported to come from the other side were conveyed by Feda, speaking in her characteristic childish way, through the lips of the entranced Mrs Leonard. Only very rarely did the deceased communicators themselves appear to take control of Mrs Leonard's vocal apparatus so as to deliver their message in *propria persona.*

According to Mrs Leonard herself, it was in the spring of 1914 that Feda announced that something 'big and terrible was going to happen in the world' and that, through Mrs Leonard, she would have to help many people. At all events, after war broke out, Mrs Leonard was much in demand by those who had lost their loved ones on the battlefield. What, however, made Mrs Leonard famous was the publication, in 1916, of the book *Raymond* by Sir Oliver Lodge. Lodge's son, Raymond, had been killed at the front in September 1915. At a subsequent sitting with Mrs Leonard, Raymond, via Feda, appeared to communicate and spoke at some length about some group photographs that had been taken of his company. At that point Lodge had not yet received copies of such photographs but, when they arrived, they confirmed certain details to which the 'Raymond communicator' had drawn to his attention.

The importance of Mrs Leonard in the history of psychical research is due in large measure to the calibre of those who undertook to investigate her and to the detail and quality of their extensive reports, most of which are to be found in the

Proceedings of the SPR. Among the more notable of these sitters we may mention the Reverend Charles Drayton Thomas – he believed that he communicated, via Mrs Leonard, with his late father the Reverend John Drayton Thomas, a Methodist minister (see Thomas, 1922); the psychiatrist Dr William Brown (Wilde Reader in Mental Philosophy at Oxford); the writer Margaerite Radclyffe-Hall, in collaboration with her friend and posthumous biographer, Una Vicenzo (Lady) Troubridge. There was also the Reverend W.S. Irving who sought to communicate with his late wife, Dora. Finally, we may mention Mr and Mrs W.H. Salter who not only acted as sitters themselves but did so much to collate and assess the findings of the various sitters.[56]

The Leonard output falls into a number of distinct categories. There is, first of all, the regular sittings in which the sitter, him or her self, is related to the deceased communicator. Secondly there are the so-called *proxy* sittings in which the sitter is merely acting *on behalf of* a relative or friend of the communicator. The proxy sitting was an attempt to counter the suggestion that the information purporting to come from the communicator was actually information derived telepathically by the mind of the medium from the mind of the sitter. The proxy sitting was also a safeguard against the possibility of 'fishing' by the medium, i.e. deriving hints from the reactions of the sitter, a well-known mediumistic ploy. This approach was first adopted by Nea Walker who, for many years, had been Sir Oliver Lodge's secretary.

Next come the so-called 'book tests', perhaps the most distinctive achievement of the Leonard mediumship. What happens in such a test is that the ostensible communicator offers some impressions relating to a passage in some book, specified usually by means of a page reference and the position of the book on a particular shelf of someone's library. The book tests were pioneered by Drayton Thomas but many other sitters were involved. We know that in no case was Mrs Leonard herself familiar with the house where the book in question was situated, still less with its position in the layout of the shelf or library, even if the book itself had been known to her which, given the obscurity of most of the volumes involved, seems most unlikely. The book test is, of course, yet a further attempt to obtain evidence of survival inasmuch as it was thought to exceed the medium's own telepathic or clairvoyant powers – although why anyone, deceased or living, should be supposed to possess such powers, remains a mystery. Not all those who studied the matter, however, were willing to adopt Thomas' own survivalist interpretation. Nevertheless, even the most hard-headed of them had to admit that the evidence could not be dismissed as a fluke of chance.

Finally, there are the 'newspaper tests', another innovation we owe to Thomas. In this case, the target is a copy of a newspaper (normally *The Times*) which had not yet been printed at the time of the sitting. Feda, or whoever it might be, tries to describe items that will be found in tomorrow's paper on a particular page and on a particular part of a given column. Copies of *The Times* for other days provide a ready-made control in assessing the probability of a given hit being due to chance. If chance cannot accommodate the results, precognitive clairvoyance must be added to the powers attributed to the intelligence responsible.

Two distinct questions arise from the evidence obtained in these ways:

(*a*) Can they be assigned a normal explanation by invoking the laws of chance?
(*b*) Do they constitute proof, or at any rate, evidence for the survival of personality?

The first of these questions is, of course, relatively straightforward. Indeed, had the procedure adopted been slightly modified a definitive answer would be possible which would eliminate any subjective factor. In the actual Leonard book tests, the investigator knew what passage had been specified. Hence the only way of demonstrating that something more than chance was involved was to compare the designated passage with other passages selected at random. This, however, leaves open the possibility that more will be read into the correspondence in the case of the designated passage than in the case of these control passages selected at random. If the experiment were being conducted today we would now want to make sure that the person who assesses the correspondence in question does so blind, that is, in ignorance as to whether the passage in question was the target or a control passage. Of course, as with any such free-response test, the probability derived from such a calculation cannot do justice to whatever qualitative resemblance there may be between guess and target but it can tell us, at least, the minimum odds against the result being due to chance.

What is remarkable is how much effort was put into the attempt to answer the question whether the Leonard book tests could be due to the normal play of chance factors. Thus Eleanor Sidgwick makes a brave attempt to classify a large number of such book tests drawn from the records of 34 different sittings spanning 146 sittings. Of the 532 items thus obtained she rated 92 as 'successful', 100 as 'approximately successful', 40 as 'nearly complete failures', 96 as 'dubious' and no less than 204 as 'complete failures'. Combining the first two categories this gives us approximately 36 per cent hits or near-hits. Could these results have been achieved by pure guesswork on the part of the medium? Eleanor Sidgwick for all her cautiousness did not think so. Indeed 'It is impossible to doubt', she declared, 'that Mrs Leonard in trance has supernormal powers'.[57] Likewise Theodore Besterman, a notoriously critical researcher who had, nevertheless, carried out some remarkably successful book tests with the Rev. R.S. Irving as the key sitter,[58] went on to carry out a series of controlled tests with volumes drawn at random from his own library. On the basis of these he concluded that: 'all the control experiments in booktests so far devised strongly indicate the presence of some extra-chance factor in the booktests given by Mrs Leonard'[59]

To clinch the question of chance, the SPR, in 1923, invited 60 individuals to choose ten books at random. They were only then to open an envelope in which they would find three different clues each with its appropriate page reference. Thus the first clue was: 'A passage which is particularly relevant to your father ... top quarter of p.60 in each book'. The second clue was: 'An allusion to circles of some kind ... bottom half of p.35 of each book'. The third clue was: 'Frost and snow or a passage conveying that idea ... the top ten lines of p.84 in each book'. They were then asked to rate these *pseudo* book-tests as 'success' 'partial success' or 'nil' and, for the first two categories, to add remarks justifying their rating. In this way some 1,800 pseudo book tests could be evaluated. Col. C.E. Baddeley was put in charge of this experiment and compiled the report.[60] He found that only 4.7 per cent of the matchings were considered either successful or partially successful, obviously a much lower figure than the 36 per cent of hits or near-hits which Eleanor Sidgwick had found in the real tests as carried out with Mrs Leonard.

The question as to the *source* of the messages is, of course, a far more problematical, not to say insoluble, issue. The difficulty here is twofold. In the first place, how are we to judge the accuracy of the information given to the sitter when it concerns someone whom he or she knew intimately but is unknown to us? How far might even the most conscientious sitter be inclined to stretch a point to bolster his or her willingness to believe that contact has been made with the loved person? There can, in the nature of the case, be no definitive answer to such questions but neither can there by any justification for ignoring the views of those who, while well aware of the pitfalls, were nevertheless convinced that the communications could only have emanated from the person to whom they are attributed. After discussing all the alternative interpretations, Thomas (1922), at any rate, had no doubt that he was indeed communicating with his deceased father. For example, so many of the items that emerged in the Leonard sittings could only be verified by consulting his father's private diaries or by checking with his mother who was still alive. Equally, Radclyffe-Hall and Troubridge who had numerous sittings with Mrs Leonard from August 1916 onwards became convinced that they *were* indeed dealing with their lost friend 'A.V.B.' Yet their approach was that of the wary psychical researcher and they even went to the extent of employing a detective agency to spy on Mrs Leonard. Even so, the plethora of evidence that was forthcoming, including information unknown to them at the time but subsequently confirmed by others, pointed to something more than could be atttributed to the medium's own psychic powers.[61]

In the last resort, however, the question of survival must, of necessity, remain an open one. No matter how impressive the communications from the other side and no matter how puny the known psychic abilities of the living, the fact is that we can never be in a position to rule out conclusively the latter. If survival *is* a reality it is one that can be known with certainty only by those who survive and hence are, by definition, no longer in a position to testify at first hand. Some psychical researchers, without wanting to belittle the best of the mediumistic evidence, regarded the idea of a post-mortem existence as so inherently implausible that it justified, where necessary, ascribing unlimited powers to the living medium however far-fetched this may strike us. At all events, what came to be known as the Survival versus Super-Psi controversy has remained a permanent feature of subsequent parapsychological history.[62]

CHAPTER 5

The Rhine revolution

If we turn aside to consider the history of psychology as such, we would take note of the fact that its origin, as a science, is twofold, embracing as it does both the clinic and the laboratory. Clinical psychology stems from the work of the French pioneers such as Charcot, Bernheim, Janet and, later, from that of Freud and his followers in Vienna which spawned the numerous diverse schools of depth psychology, abnormal psychology and psychotherapy that sprang up in their wake. What is common to this type of psychology, whatever conceptual differences might distinguish one school from another, is that it focuses on the individual case history. Experimental psychology, on the other hand, bases itself on a statistical analysis of experimental data from which it seeks to draw conclusions about certain universal properties of mind, more especially of its perceptual, cognitive and perceptuo-motor functions. Like its clinical counterpart, it is a late nineteenth-century development closely linked with contemporary advances in the study of the brain and nervous system. Helmholtz was a key figure in its development as was the eccentric Fechner – as much metaphysician as scientist. But credit for the founding of the first psychological laboratory goes, by common consent, to Wilhelm Wundt, whose laboratory at Leipzig was set up in 1879. It was soon followed by similar institutions at other German universities, notably at Gottingen and Wurzburg, whence, before long, experimental psychology found its way to the United States, often conveyed thither by Americans who had made the pilgrimage to Leipzig to gain a doctoral degree under the renowned Wundt himself.

Psychical research had never eschewed the experimental approach. Card guessing and other simple tests that lent themselves to straightforward evaluation were, as we have seen, adopted by Gurney and others in the very earliest days of the SPR and, already in the 1880s, Richet was discussing how probability theory could be brought to bear on such tests.[1] But, overwhelmingly, the main thrust of psychical research, as was made clear in the two previous chapters, was to study the particular case and the particularly gifted individual. It was thus closer in its approach to clinical psychology than to the new experimental psychology.

Two factors may account for the comparatively late arrival of a serious experimental parapsychology. First, the necessary statistical apparatus was not forthcoming until about the 1920s when the work of R.A. Fisher and other pioneer statisticians provided a sound basis for evaluating the appropriate experiments. Statistics, after all, have always been a more critical aspect of experimental parapsychology than they have been for psychophysics or experimental psychology precisely because the results were more likely to be challenged. There is, indeed, some evidence that parapsychology acted as a spur to statisticians in developing their own discipline and in elaborating the concept of randomness. Secondly, psychical research, unlike psychology proper, lacked an academic base without which the laborious systematic research that was needed was unlikely to be cultivated. Psychical researchers, we must remember, were nearly all amateurs and it is hardly surprising if they succumbed to the allure of the spectacular one-off case rather than submit to the repetitive grind of laboratory testing. Had psychical research been embraced by the universities, as experimental psychology soon came to be (albeit grudgingly by the more conservative ones) the situation would have been very different. But the implications of acknowledging paranormal phenomena, in whatever shape or form, were truly shattering, whereas nothing much more was at stake in acknowledging the innocuous findings of psychophysics and experimental psychology than the challenge it represented to philosophers who had previously enjoyed a monopoly as authorities on the nature of mind.

What we are here calling 'the Rhine revolution' involved three main objectives. There was, first, the attempt to introduce a progressive programme of experimental research into the study of the paranormal, one based on a sound methodology where, hopefully, one problem would follow upon another to create an ever-expanding sphere of knowledge. The second, which presupposed the first, was the attempt to gain for the field academic status and scientific recognition. J.B. Rhine was not, by any means, the first to pursue experimental psychical research, or 'parapsychology' (as he now preferred to call it)[2] at a university. Psychologists both in Europe and the United States had completed parapsychological projects with varying degrees of success during the 1920s. But the Duke University Laboratory, which Rhine helped to found and thereafter to direct, was the first long-term university laboratory to be devoted exclusively to parapsychological research. The third objective was to show, if possible, that psychic ability was not the preserve of exceptional beings but was widespread and perhaps potentially present in everyone.[3]

In retrospect we know that none of these objectives were realized. There is still no consensus as to the most promising path to pursue and the crucial problem, how to generate reliable phenomena, though there has been progress, remains as yet unsolved; parapsychology still lacks scientific recognition and a firm base in academia; and it is still a matter of dispute whether psi ability is distributed widely in the population or is an idiosyncrasy of the freakish few. But, from the fact that the Rhine revolution proved abortive, it does not follow that it accomplished nothing or that it was of no consequence. In this chapter we shall be discussing Rhine's achievements and his legacy. First, however, let us take a look at the man and at his career.

Joseph Banks Rhine 1895–1980[4]

Rhine had a rural upbringing but his father, who was a schoolteacher as well as a farmer, made sure that he received a decent education. His mother was keen that he should go into the Church and his first incursion into higher education, at Wooster College, Ohio, was seen as a preparation for his becoming a Methodist minister. However, his fervent fundamentalist faith did not long survive the intellectual challenges that it encountered and thereafter science or the scientific method became his new god. After serving in the Marine Corps during the First World War, he went to the University of Chicago where he graduated in plant physiology in 1922 and gained a PhD in 1925. Prior to that, in 1920, he had married Louisa Weckesser, a companion of his boyhood days and now his fellow student of botany at Chicago. The marriage was to become a lifelong professional partnership in which Louisa was to make her own substantial contribution to the new science.

Rhine's first academic appointment was as a botanist at the University of West Virginia in 1924 and he seemed all set for a successful career in this field.[5] However, like so many others before him who had lost their religious faith, he could not readily become reconciled to the reductionist world view which the exact sciences seemed to demand. Accordingly, like Sidgwick or Myers before him, he turned to psychical research as a possible way of challenging this bleak outlook without sacrificing an impeccably scientific approach. But, how was he to go about it? Already he was convinced that the future of psychical research lay in the universities as opposed to the amateur societies as hitherto. But, although there were indeed bequests at several of the American universities, notably Harvard and Stanford, for the pursuit of such research and, indeed, a number of projects had already been carried out, there were as yet no regular jobs or tenured appointments in this deviant field.

A key event at this juncture was his encounter with William McDougall whom he first met in Boston in the summer of 1926. McDougall was then 55, Rhine was 31. When McDougall had left Oxford in 1920 to take up a post at Harvard, he was, by far, the most eminent of the pioneer British academic psychologists and had been instrumental in founding the British Psychological Society and the *British Journal of Psychology*. At the same time he was not typical of the academic psychologists of that era. He was out of sympathy with some of the prevailing trends in experimental psychology. He laid much stress on the idea of purpose as a factor in the behaviour of organisms and propounded his own doctrine of 'hormic psychology' in pointed opposition to the behaviourist doctrine which J.B. Watson had been promulgating in America with much bravado and, indeed, much success. Even more provocatively McDougall made no secret of his interest in the paranormal and in his book, *Body and Mind* (1911), a defence of a radical dualism (which he there calls 'animism'), he cites evidence from psychical research to make its point. McDougall was more akin to James than to his own contemporaries and, like James, he, too, eventually abandoned experimental research in favour of philosophical and polemical tracts.

It was partly under the influence of McDougall that Rhine resigned his position at West Virginia in order to try and retool himself academically by going to Harvard to take courses in psychology and philosophy and to sit at the feet of his mentor, McDougall. Ironically, in view of what happened, Rhine was also keen to get to Boston on account of the medium Margery (whom we met in our last chapter). Tantalizing reports about her had already reached his ears for he was by now a member of the American SPR. That society had, in fact, been hijacked by the Margery faction led by Frederick Edwards and Malcolm Bird, thereby precipitating the rift that led to the separate formation of the Boston SPR under W.F. Prince. McDougall aligned himself with Prince but, as yet, Rhine knew little about these behind-the-scene struggles.

At all events, on July 1926, the two Rhines were granted an appointment with the medium and, along with six other regular sitters, were treated to a typical seance at the Crandons' home on Lime Street. It was, for Rhine, a devastating let-down. He came away convinced that all that he had witnessed in that darkened room was just shameless trickery. Furthermore, he was confident that he understood just *how* those tricks had been perpetrated. He at once circulated a letter to this effect to the trustees of the ASPR and an article he then wrote about the sitting duly appeared in the *Journal of Abnormal and Social Psychology* for January 1927.[6] All, this, it seems, made little impression on the leaders of the ASPR, who dismissed him as an insolent upstart, but it earned Rhine the respect of McDougall who congratulated him on his perspicuity. The upshot of this episode was to confirm Rhine in his distrust of spontaneous and mediumistic phenomena in general and to strengthen his predilection for an experimental approach that would allow the experimenter, rather than the subject, to dictate what conditions are to prevail.

In the summer of 1927, McDougall, who had been feeling somewhat frustrated in the Harvard milieu, succumbed to an offer from William Few, President of Duke University, to head their Department of Psychology. The university had been established only in 1924 at the instigation of Few himself. He had been the head of Trinity College, a Methodist seminary in Durham, North Carolina, which then became the nucleus of the new university. The necessary money was forthcoming from the Duke brothers of the American Tobacco Company. But its motto, 'Religio et Eruditio', reflected a concern to uphold Christian values in academic life and, in selecting McDougall to run the psychology, Few felt that Duke would be safe, at any rate, from the influence of behaviourists and materialists. In due course McDougall recruited a staff who, while broadly sympathetic to his ideas, were reputable experimental psychologists in their own right.

Rhine abandoned Harvard that year and moved to Duke in September 1927. Oddly enough, however, it was not at the behest of McDougall that he did so. Rather, it was at the prompting of a schools inspector, John F. Thomas, whose wife had recently died and who had been attempting to communicate with her postmortem self via a number of mediums (these included Mrs Minnie Soule of Boston and the Mrs Leonard of London whom we have already met). Thomas, who was willing to pay for the service, urged Rhine to become his supervisor while he, Thomas, worked on this material as a graduate student of McDougall's at Duke. Thus it came about that Rhine's first position at Duke was as a postdoctoral fellow who, despite his recent disillusionment with mediums, found himself once again caught up in conventional psychical research. In 1928, however, Rhine was offered an appointment on the staff at Duke which involved spending half his time helping McDougall with his research and the other half giving courses in psychology.

McDougall was at that time engaged on his celebrated attempt to vindicate the Lamarkian hypothesis using evidence derived from learning experiments with rats. Essentially, these rats were immersed in a tank of water from which they could escape only in one of two ways: either via a brightly lit gangway that was mildly electrified or via a dimly lit gangway that was safe from shock. The question he thereby sought to answer was whether the descendents of the rats who had been taught to select the *safe* exit would learn more rapidly than the offspring of the untaught rats. By 1928, when Rhine was brought into the project, some 13 generations had been tested and a marked *decrease* in errors had duly been observed. Rhine continued with this work until 1933 and, independently, confirmed McDougall's findings. It was understandable that McDougall, the apostle of purpose as a characteristic of living things, should have been attracted to the Lamarkian position. He pointed out, quite rightly, that Lamarkism had not been rejected by biologists for lack of evidence but, rather, because no one had come forward with any *mechanism* to explain how an acquired characteristic *could* be transmitted from parent to offspring. If, however, some immaterial process like extrasensory perception was responsible, then Lamarkian inheritance need no longer be automatically discounted. One can thus see how germane these experiments were to the growing parapsychological concerns of both McDougall and Rhine. In the event, these Lamarkian experiments failed to make the desired impact on subsequent biological thinking, it being tacitly assumed (as has ever since been the case with parapsychological experiments) that some methodological flaw must have been responsible for the positive outcome.[7]

In 1929 the well-known American writer, Upton Sinclair,had given McDougall a copy of the manuscript of his book, *Mental Radio*, in which he describes at length the series of experiments he had conducted on his gifted wife, Mary Craig, involving the transmission of drawings. It was a technique that had already been used extensively and to good effect by René Warcollier in France who had even collaborated with Gardner Murphy in a transatlantic experiment of this nature.[8] In the Sinclair series the trials are mostly so self-evidently successful that, assuming there was no flaw in the procedure, one could hardly avoid positing an extrasensory process. McDougall, at any rate, was much impressed, especially when he found that Mrs Sinclair was also able to perform when he was himself the agent. Even Prince was impressed and duly issued a detailed report on the Sinclair tests in his *Bulletin of the Boston S.P.R.* for April 1932. The book itself was published in 1930 and carried an introduction by McDougall and, curiously, a brief preface (in German) by Albert Einstein![9] It has become a classic in the field and a persistent irritant to sceptics.

It is, however, awkward to try and build a workaday science on the basis of a talent as rare as that of Mrs Sinclair. Rhine was looking for tests that he could apply to large numbers of ordinary people. G.H. Estabrooks, one of McDougall's graduate students at Harvard, had carried out a research project, drawing on the Hodgson Fund, in which he had used playing-cards and the results had been encouraging. In the summer of 1930 he came to Duke to teach at the summer school and would certainly have met Rhine. Not everyone, however, had been as successful as Estabrooks. Gardner Murphy, another beneficiary of the Hodgson Fund, had earlier carried out similar tests at Harvard with scant success, and there had been J.E. Coover's massive project at Stanford University, completed in 1917, that had proved to be almost entirely barren.[10] Rhine's initial efforts, using numerals in sealed envelopes, yielded little to encourage further probing, but he was not easily deterred for, unlike Coover, his attitude to the paranormal was strongly positive.

One of the psychologists whom McDougall had recruited at Duke was Karl Zener, an authority on the psychology of perception. Rhine invited Zener to design a set of cards with symbols that would be easy to visualize and remember and would be as distinctive, one from another, as possible. The upshot was what, for a long time thereafter, was popularly known as the 'Zener cards'.[11] The standard 5 × 5 deck, in which the five different symbols – circle, square, star, cross and wavy-lines – are each repeated five times, simplified the statistical analysis. For, if chance alone operated, one could expect a mean score of around 20 per cent correct. However, in the 800 preliminary trials which Rhine and Zener carried out during the winter and spring semesters of 1930–1, some 207 (nearly 26 per cent) were guessed correctly as against a mean chance expectation of 160 (a score in excess of four times the standard deviation above the chance baseline). It was a modest enough start but, from then on, Rhine never looked back. It was the first foray using the new card-guessing research paradigm that was to culminate so triumphantly in 1934 with the publication of Rhine's monograph *Extra-Sensory Perception.*

What happened next, which today, in retrospect, strikes us as so miraculous (or suspicious, depending on our bias) was the sudden emergence on campus of a number of successful card-guessers. For Rhine this was the confirmation of his long-held belief that ESP was not, after all, so uncommon, in spite of so many earlier failures both in Britain and in the United States to detect it. What finally convinced Rhine that this was at last the real thing was the way in which levels of scoring yielded to systematic differences in the conditions of testing, be they psychological or physiological. With regard to the latter some experiments were tried using drugs. It was found, for example, that a depressant, like sodium amytal, *de*creased the level of scoring whereas a stimulant, like caffeine, *in*creased it.[12] Likewise, changes in the test procedure, or even the introduction of an outsider as observer, produced a temporary depression in the scoring which would only pick up again when the subject had become acclimatized to the new conditions.

At all events, encouraged by this new-found flow of good scorers, Rhine and his helpers set about devising the various test procedures that became for a long time thereafter standard practice. Such, for example, was the 'Down-Through' (DT) technique whereby the subject is required to call all 25 cards of a shuffled deck before *anyone* yet knows the order of the cards. A variant on this was the BT (Basic Technique) where, after each call, the top card of the deck is removed, though not as yet inspected by anyone. At this period Rhine was specially concerned to discriminate between the two main manifestations of ESP: telepathy and clairvoyance. The DT or BT type test was taken as a strict measure of clairvoyance. A test for pure telepathy was inevitably more problematic since, whatever the target, it must be anchored to something that has physical existence if the test is to be objective but, at this stage, what was meant by a PT or Pure Telepathy test was that the tester had simply to *think* of each successive symbol, using a coded numerical association. Rhine introduced the term GESP (General ESP) to cover those cases where the process could be either telepathic *or* clairvoyant, but in practice this designation applied to most of the test situations and so adds little to the basic term ESP. Soon it became standard practice at the Duke laboratory to dispense with an agent.

Rhine was also fortunate at this juncture in recruiting two very able graduate students at Duke to act as his research assistants: Charles Stuart and Gaither Pratt. Stuart was a mathematics student who was later able to make a useful contribution to the statistical problems that arose from the research. Pratt was initially a divinity student, as Rhine himself had been, but, like Rhine, abandoned religion in favour of science. Stuart's career was unfortunately cut short by his premature death in 1947; Pratt, who eventually parted company with Rhine, became one of the acknowledged leaders of American parapsychology and was active right up to his death in 1979.[13] Stuart figured briefly during this initial period as one of Rhine's celebrated 'high-scorers'; Pratt, as far as is known, had no ESP ability.

Rhine himself considered that his activities at this stage were not primarily aimed at demonstrating the mere fact that ESP exists, but rather at devising a paradigmatic methodology for studying its special properties as a natural phenomenon. In other words he thought of himself, from the beginning, as engaged in what later came to be known as 'process-oriented' as opposed to 'proof-oriented' research. To the world at large, however, which was not yet ready to embrace ESP, by far the most striking aspect of the early Duke research was the fact that, among Rhine's immediate entourage, there were in all some eight 'high-scorers' (the term 'high-scorer' in this connection, must, of course, be understood in a relative sense, it meant in practice the capacity to maintain an average of, say, 7, 8 or even 9 hits over a large number of runs). The very first such high-scorer to show up was an undergraduate psychology student, Adam Linzmayer. His testing began in the spring of 1931 and, by the end of the year, after completing some 600 tests involving 32,247 trials, his average score per run was found to be a fabulous 9.9 hits, giving odds against chance so astronomical as to be unfathomable.

Between 1931 and 1933 Linzmayer participated in a further 2,000 trials, but his score had fallen to a mere 5.6 per run – still highly significant in conventional terms but a marked drop. Thereafter he disappears from view as a high-scorer. Ina Jephson, in her pioneering work on card-guessing for the SPR in the early 1920s, had already drawn attention to the pervasive presence of a 'decline effect' and, indeed, it was to recur again and again in the careers of other high-scorers.[14] In addition to this long-term decline effect, Jephson had also noted, and Rhine rediscovered, that there were short-term decline effects such that scoring tended to be highest at the *start* of a run with, perhaps, an upturn at the tail end. Such effects make some sense in terms of motivational psychology.

Rhine did not have long to wait before an even more talented subject emerged in the person of a divinity student named Hubert Pearce. Pearce's career lasted longer and he survived more varied and more stringent tests of his ESP ability than any other high-scorer. At his preliminary test sessions he attained scoring rates of over 10 hits per run! His scoring held up and, during the spring of 1932, Pearce was averaging 9.7 hits per run in some 90 consecutive runs

(Rhine, 1934/1964/1973 chap.7). Such a promising start clearly called for a follow-up that would be evidentially decisive, that is to say a set-up that would exclude every conceivable possibility of a normal or artefactual explanation. Accordingly, Pratt was duly asked to conduct a long-distance experiment with Pearce in which he, Pratt, as the tester, would be in one building of the Duke campus while Pearce, the subject or 'percipient', would be in another (about 100 yards away in one series, 250 yards away in another).

In all, some 37 sessions were held between August 1933 and March 1934 divided into four subseries. In the final subseries Rhine was present with Pratt as an observer. The technique adopted was BT (Basic Technique) where each card was removed from the shuffled target pack every minute but without being inspected. The percipient, with a synchronized clock, recorded each guess onto his call-sheet. A second run followed before the session was then terminated. Both Pearce, the percipient, and Pratt, the tester, made a practice of making a duplicate copy of, respectively, the call-sheet and the target-sheet, which they then individually handed over to Rhine in a sealed envelope before meeting one another to check the results of that session.

In this way some 1,850 trials were completed, of which 558 were scored as hits as compared with a mean chance expectation of only 370 hits, the result having a significance of over 10^{22} to one. Was this, then the definitive proof of ESP that it purported to be? Over the years, parapsychologists have become cynical about talk of a 'definitive experiment' if only because, with sufficient ingenuity, one can always think up *some* counter-explanation that would vitiate such a claim. In this instance, the English critic, Mark Hansel, who in 1966 published his much heralded exposé of experimental parapsychology (Hansel, 1966), pointed out that Rhine and Pratt had failed to assign an invigilator for Pearce. Hence it was conceivable, he argued, that Pearce could have made his way to the place where Pratt was situated, peered through a glass window or transom and watched Pratt as he turned over the cards while compiling the target-sheet. Only *then* would he complete his own call-sheet. A debate rumbled on in the literature for many years without either side conceding defeat, but Hansel's scenario has become a measure of the lengths to which the critic must be prepared to go if the ESP hypothesis is to be discounted.[15]

The five remaining high-scorers who figure in *Extra-Sensory Perception*, where they are dealt with as a group, comprised two graduate assistants in psychology, George Zirkle and his fiancée, Sarah Ownbey, whom he later married, and three undergraduate psychology students, May Turner, June Bailey and T. Coleman Cooper. Zirkle, it seems, succeeded initially only with the PT (Pure Telepathy) condition but with this he was unsurpassed. Rhine says of him 'He has several times scored 22 correct in 25. Once, in calling 50 in a series, 26 were found correct in unbroken succession.'[16] Zirkle also responded differentially, in the predicted direction, to the intake of drugs, i.e. sodium amytal versus caffeine, even though apparently blind, as to which was which. What Rhine could *not* have known, of course, when he completed his report in 1933 and sent it to Prince for publication as a monograph of the Boston Society, was that *never again* would he have the opportunity to work with comparable subjects in his own laboratory. Nor could he have imagined the impact which this hastily concocted report was about to have on world opinion and the consequences that would ensue both for parapsychology and for him personally.

Indeed, Prince himself did not yet realize what a hot property he was handling, for the edition which his Boston SPR brought out in April 1934 was limited to a mere 900 copies. In the event, the demand was such that, the following year, a new edition was launched onto the market by Bruce Humphries of Boston. It would be no exaggeration to say that no other publication in the whole history of psychical research enjoyed such widespread acclaim. The acronym, 'ESP' now became a word in the English language and Rhine himself became something of a folk hero. In Europe, where the psychical research tradition was more firmly established, it made less of an impact than it did in the United States but, everywhere, it was greeted as the start of a new era. In Departments of Psychology at various American universities ESP testing became, for a time, an acceptable topic for research, and science journalists wrote enthusiastic pieces in the national press.

At Duke, Rhine was soon able to make himself independent of the Department of Psychology and establish a laboratory of his own with funds which he managed to coax from wealthy American men and women. He added to his staff some capable graduate students, notably Burke Smith, Margaret Pegram, Margaret Price and Joseph Woodruff. A few years later, Rhine and McDougall decided that a specialist journal was needed to cope with the proliferating research and so, in March 1937, the *Journal of Parapsychology* (which has been going ever since) was founded. An editorial introduction written by McDougall (but unsigned) explained that the word 'parapsychology' was here being used to denote the strictly experimental area within psychical research and he expressed the hope that the universities would soon find room for this new field of endeavour.

Rhine followed up the success of *Extra-Sensory Perception* by writing three further volumes designed to bring home to the general public the wider implications of the new science: *New Frontiers of the Mind* (1937); *The Reach of the Mind* (1947); and *New World of the Mind* (1953) (see bibliography). At the same time, to answer his academic critics who had become increasingly vociferous as it became clear that others were unable to achieve the sort of results reported in *Extra-Sensory Perception* and did not hesitate to suggest every conceivable pitfall that might have vitiated the original

Duke findings,[17] Rhine and his colleagues published *Extra-Sensory Perception After Sixty Years* (Rhine *et al.* 1940/1966) in which they discuss in some detail the original work that had been so sketchily covered in the earlier book and attempt to rebut the diverse counter-hypotheses which the critics had suggested. The phrase 'after sixty years' was a reference to 1882, the year when the original SPR had been founded, the implication being that psychical research had now at last come of age.[18]

Soon the scope of experimental parapsychology was to be enlarged by research on two other phenomena, 'precognition' and 'psychokinesis' or PK. Foreknowledge was, of course, a traditional attribute of seers since ancient times but the standard card-guessing technique lent itself nicely to an experimental approach. All that was required was for the subject to register his or her calls *before* the cards were shuffled instead of afterwards as when testing for the other modes of ESP. ESP, which was already believed to be independent of space and unaffected by material obstacles, was now to be shown as indifferent to the arrow of time. The evidence for precognition has never been comparable to that for the contemporaneous modes of ESP but, over the years, it mounted up so that, much as the idea of foreknowledge upset many theorists who sought to account for it in other ways, the evidence could not as such be dismissed without incurring a charge of inconsistency. For Rhine himself, precognition became the preferred mode in ESP testing and this for two reasons. First, it reinforced his conviction that ESP was non-physical, a property of mind rather than of brain. Secondly, a test for precognition is, in the nature of the case, the most *secure* of the standard tests for ESP, since it is immune to the possibility of sensory cueing. The target does not exist until the responses have been safely recorded.

Just as card-guessing represented the standard method of studying the statistical, as opposed to the qualitative, manifestation of paranormal cognition, so the attempt to influence the fall of dice became the standard method of studying the statistical, as opposed to the observable, manifestation of paranormal action. It was, of course, a far cry from the sort of thing that was associated with physical mediums or with poltergeists, just as card-guessing of the forced-choice variety was a far cry from the sort of thing associated with mental mediums and clairvoyants, but it was, at least, something in which everyone could participate with some hope of success. The distinction is now often made between 'micro-PK' as opposed to 'macro-PK' or between 'PK-on-random-systems' as opposed to 'PK-on-stable-systems'.

The idea is said to have been suggested to Rhine by a young man, a student, who was a keen gambler. Work was begun in 1934 and the methodology progressively improved with the introduction of mechanical dice-throwers and other such refinements. It was not, however, until 1943 that an account of these experiments was made public with a report in the *Journal of Parapsychology*.[19] The honeymoon period that followed the publication of *Extra-Sensory Perception* was short-lived and critics were soon busy casting doubt on just about everything connected with the Duke experiments. In this atmosphere, Rhine was fearful of jeopardizing the reputation of the laboratory by committing it to something as provocative as PK with dice. Yet, as Rhine himself came to realize: 'ESP and PK are so unified logically and experimentally that we can now think of both mind-matter interactions as one single fundamental two-way process'[20] It was, however, the British psychologist, R.H. Thouless, the first to attempt dice experiments in Britain, who in 1942 proposed the term 'psi' as a generic term embracing both ESP and PK. 'Psi' has remained very much part of the vocabulary of present-day parapsychology, and 'psi-research' is now often used as the modern variant for 'psychical research'. Moreover, as it gradually became clear, the distinctions between the various modes of ESP, or between ESP and PK, are rarely clear-cut except in purely operational terms. The term 'psi' is thus the least question-begging of the various terms used to denote some paranormal function.

The level of scoring in PK experiments was much more modest than those attained in the ESP work. No high-scorer like Hubert Pearce emerged in the PK domain. Indeed, by far the most impressive extra-chance results to emerge from these dice experiments was not an excess of hits, i.e. of target faces falling uppermost, but a decline effect within the run. This effect, which had already been noted in the ESP tests, proved to be even more pronounced in these PK tests where the standard run consisted of 24 throws. Thus when, in 1944, Rhine and Humphrey published their examination of the scoring pattern in the first 18 PK experiments at Duke, comprising some 27,000 standard runs, they found that, comparing the number of hits obtained in the first six trials of the run with that obtained in the last six trials, the odds against the difference being due to chance exceeded 100 million to one. Moreover, the fact that the effect was unexpected at the time when the experiments were being run made it even less likely that it could have been due to any falsification of the data.[21]

With the disappearance of high-scorers at Duke and the increasing scarcity of them elsewhere, ESP research took a new tack more suitable for work with ordinary subjects. The connection found between personality and scoring bias in ESP tests proved to be one such approach. In 1946 Betty Humphrey, who had been granted a doctorate at Duke on the strength of her parapsychological work, carried out an elaborate pioneer experiment in which subjects were asked to try and reproduce clairvoyantly drawings presented in sealed envelopes. These were then scored according to a system of preferential matching. The subjects were next divided into two groups according to the size of their drawings: 'expansives' and 'compressives'. Sure enough, it transpired that the 41 'expansives' had scored *above* chance with odds of 1,000 to one against chance, while the 55 'compressives' had scored *below* chance, the difference between the two groups corresponding to odds of 2,500 to one against chance.[22]

In 1945 Gertrude Schmeidler, who had taken her PhD in psychology at Harvard in 1935 but had become interested in parapsychology in 1942 as a result of meeting Gardner Murphy at Harvard, published a seminal paper in the *Journal of the American S. P. R.* with the title 'Separating the sheep from the goats'. What she found, briefly, was that believers in ESP ('sheep') tended to score *above* chance while disbelievers ('goats') tended to score *below* chance, both groups deviating significantly from chance.[23] Not all the many subsequent sheep–goat experiments have panned out as neatly as in her original study; nevertheless, one can say that the 'sheep–goat' effect has remained one of the stand-bys of parapsychological research. Schmeidler herself, who joined the staff of City College, New York, in 1945, went on to become one of the acknowledged leaders in the field. The discovery of this 'bidirectionality' of psi, the fact that ESP may function in either a positive or a negative mode depending on the personality of the subject or, indeed, on the conditions under which the test was conducted, was itself a remarkable innovation and one that could only have been achieved using an experimental approach. It may be regarded as the experimental analogue of what, in real life, we would call an accident-prone or ill-fated individual. At all events, it provided a theme that was to engage the Duke laboratory for many years.

Attempts to professionalize parapsychology continued to concern Rhine. By 1954, Rhine had left the Department of Psychology and was running his own independent laboratory. In 1957 he and Pratt brought out a general textbook of parapsychology for students (Rhine and Pratt, 1957) and, the same year, he helped to found the Parapsychological Association, a professional body that, unlike the various societies for psychical research, admitted only those who had published in refereed journals and had actively contributed to the field. Its first President was Robert McConnell, a physicist and biophysicist at the University of Pittsburg who, in 1955, had published the definitive experiment on PK using dice[24] and who, in 1958, was co-author with Schmeidler of the book *ESP and Personality Patterns.*[25] The new Association met for annual conferences but never numbered more than about 300 members world wide. Its acceptance, in 1969, as an affiliate member of the American Association for the Advancement of Science, in the teeth of much opposition, represents perhaps the furthest that parapsychology has yet managed to penetrate the portals of official science. Murphy, it is true, had been elected President of the American Psychological Association in 1945, but it was for his services to psychology, not to parapsychology, that he was so honoured.

When Rhine reached retirement in 1965 he was still by far the best-known representative of parapsychology. However, resentment at the publicity accorded to his laboratory by his colleagues in the Department of Psychology had been smouldering and, with McDougall no longer there as his patron (he had died in 1938), the authorities decided that the time had come for Duke to sever its ties with parapsychology. By then, however, Rhine had accumulated sufficient funds to set up an independent research institute. The Foundation for Research into the Nature of Man (to give it its somewhat grandiose but very Rhinean title) was originally intended to embrace a number of separate institutes. In the event, the Institute for Parapsychology, situated just outside the campus area, has remained its only component, albeit one which became one of the main centres for parapsychological research ever since. But, given the original McDougall–Rhine policy of infiltrating the universities, it represents a retreat. During his 'nonretirement' (as his wife called it[26]) although he appointed a director of research to supervise the day-to-day running of the laboratory, Rhine remained the head of the Foundation and continued with Louisa to direct its policy.[27]

Then, in 1974, a disaster erupted which very nearly wrecked the Institute and sadly clouded Rhine's remaining years. A few years earlier, a keen young medical student, Walter J. Levy, had become so interested in parapsychology that he took up a position at the Institute while still completing his MD at the University of Georgia. Levy developed what had hitherto been a backwater in parapsychology, namely the study of psi ability in animals: what, in the technical vocabulary, become known as 'anpsi'.[28] He soon showed his extraordinary skill and ingenuity by devising novel set-ups in which his jirds (a type of gerbil) and other species were tested for precognitive or PK ability. The beauty of these experiments was that, since they were largely automated, they required a minimum of human intervention. But what specially endeared him to Rhine was his extraordinary success in achieving positive results. Article after article appeared in the *Journal of Parapsychology*, under his name as senior author, which amazed the entire parapsychological community by an unprecedented consistency in their positive results. Indeed, it began to look as if parapsychologists had been wasting their time all this while testing temperamental human beings when the repeatable experiment was there for the asking using lowlier species. Nor was Levy just a backroom boffin. His enthusiasm combined with his organizing abilities were such that, young as he was, Rhine appointed him Director of Research. This position has been held since 1969 by the physicist, Helmut Schmidt, who then took over a privately funded laboratory in San Antonio, Texas, to become one of the leading lights of modern parapsychology.

Given that his experiments were supposed to be fully automated, Levy's colleagues became suspicious when they noticed that he was spending unnecessary time near the computer. Accordingly, they arranged for the responses to be recorded independently and secretly on a separate event-recorder. In this way they were able to demonstrate that Levy had indeed been tampering with the record in order to gain spurious additional hits. Summoned by Rhine he confessed, and, although he pleaded that it was only this once that he had yielded to temptation,[29] he was, of course, dismissed and all his previous findings declared suspect.[30] He never showed his face again in parapsychological circles and, if his name is ever mentioned in the literature, it is as a cautionary tale.

Then in 1978 another disaster struck which, though not in Rhine's own bailiwick, was an even greater blow to the good name of experimental parapsychology. By a curious irony, the culprit in this instance was a man who had been among Rhine's severest critics. Samuel Soal, a mathematics lecturer at London University, had been the most assiduous exponent of the card-guessing technique in Britain. However, his repeated failure over the years to obtain significant results, despite the large number of tests he carried out, had made him very cynical about the claims coming out of North Carolina. Meanwhile, however, Whately Carington, another prominent British investigator, had completed a successful remote ESP experiment using a set of drawings as his targets (a different target drawing was pinned up in his study each week.[31] In this experiment he had been struck by the fact that often the response drawing corresponded, not with the target then on display, but with another in the set that had not *yet* been selected or had *already* been used on a previous trail (the now familiar phenomenon of time-displacement in ESP). In the light of his experience he urged Soal to look again at his own results and check whether any significant scoring might emerge if the guess was compared with, say, the card one ahead or one behind the actual target. Sure enough, two such subjects were located who had displayed this tendency: Basil Shackleton, a photographer by profession, and Gloria Stewart, a housewife. Soal duly went back to the job and began experimenting anew with these two special subjects.[32]

His protracted work with Shackleton in wartime London, that was witnessed by almost everyone of importance in British psychical research (including C.D. Broad, the well-known Cambridge philosopher), was soon to become a beacon in the general case for the existence of ESP, both on account of the hugely non-chance nature of the scoring, the apparent rigour of the test situation, and the formidable reputation of his co-worker, Mollie Goldney. Later, his work with Gloria Stewart confirmed Soal's new-found reputation as a successful practitioner as opposed to the sour critic of yesteryear.[33]

Suspicions, of course, *were* voiced, as always with all successful ESP experiments, but when Soal died in 1975 he was still revered as one who had provided bedrock evidence for the reality of ESP. Alas, his reputation did not long survive his demise. Curiously, even while his investigation of Shackleton was still in progress, one of his collaborators had accused him of altering figures on the score-sheet, but he promptly silenced her with threats of legal action. Then in 1974 Scott and Haskell published a paper in *Nature* showing that the pattern of scoring in certain sessions was indeed consonant with his having made certain alterations to the target sequence.[34] However, it could not account for all the facts and it was not until 1978, with the publication of a paper in the *Proceedings of the S.P.R.* by Betty Markwick,[35] that it became impossible to doubt any longer that Soal *had* indeed been tampering with the target figures. Curiously, this discovery was only possible because Soal had been in the habit of re-using the sequence of random numbers that determined the sequence of targets (in those days there *were* as yet no published tables of random numbers,let alone any computers). Markwick was able to carry out a computer search from which it transpired that every time a new digit was found to be interpolated into the re-used random sequence, it was invariably such as to correspond to the subject's call for that trial, thus providing Soal with a spurious extra hit!

Thus did the Rhines live to witness these two major scandals wreaking havoc in a cause to which they had tirelessly devoted their long and active careers. Yet parapsychology survived even these setbacks, as we shall see. Rhine died in 1980. Unlike that earlier pioneer of psychical research, Frederic Myers, Rhine died without any firm conviction that he was destined to enjoy a postmortem existence. He had never lost interest in the problem of survival but felt that parapsychology had, in fact, made its resolution all the harder since, so long as we know no limits to the scope of ESP among the living, it would remain a matter of arbitrary choice which interpretation of the evidence we adopt.[36] This debate between survivalists and supporters of the so-called 'Super-Psi hypothesis' has indeed persisted ever since with no end in sight.[37]

Louisa's death followed in 1983. Her most notable contributions to the parapsychological literature were the collections she made of spontaneous cases compiled from the ample postbag of the Duke laboratory. But no special effort was made to check on the authenticity of such testimony, as had been done in the case of earlier collections such as *Phantasms of the Living*; the idea, rather, was that, viewed collectively, they might give clues as to the nature of ESP that could be subsequently tested in the laboratory.[38] Gaither Pratt, Rhine's faithful lieutenant up to the time when he fell out with Rhine after the break with Duke University, had died in 1979, but we shall have more to say of him in the next chapter. Many others who have carried the torch for parapsychology in America during the past few decades had their initiation at the hands of J.B. Rhine.[39]

Aftermath of the revolution

Rhine always maintained that he and his team had proved the existence of psi so that, in future, parapsychology would be able to concentrate on exploring its peculiar characteristics. In other words, proof-oriented research could now give way to process-oriented research. Unfortunately, in the empirical sciences, unlike mathematics or logic, it is not clear what constitutes proof other than the consensus of expert opinion. This, alas, was *never* forthcoming. Resistance was, of course, to be expected. The very fact that parapsychology, by definition, deals with the 'paranormal' means that it is not compatible with the scientific outlook as currently understood. Even so, this would not have mattered in the long run, for science can change, if only the evidence had been more reliable. But, as Rhine himself came to recognize, one cannot expect to get results simply by following mechanically the instructions. Success may depend on a number of intangible factors including the personality of the experimenter, the motivation of the subject and the atmosphere prevailing in the test situation.

Thus when Rhine came to write an introduction to the 1964 edition of his *Extra-Sensory Perception*, by which time high-scorers had long since vanished, he says:

> It seems clear to me at least, and all the more so from a re-reading, that we had in those early years at Duke a very special situation and it was largely responsible for the unusual and unequalled production of results in ESP experiments. Where has there ever been such teamwork, a comparable spirit, a similar atmosphere?

That says it all. Today the notion of an 'experimenter effect' has become a commonplace of parapsychological thinking, as has the idea of a 'field effect' – for it has become more and more problematic who, or what, is the effective *psi source* in a given case. No wonder that parapsychology has earned the name of 'the elusive science', to borrow the phrase used by Mauskopf and McVaugh (1980) as the title of their book. Unfortunately, it was the experimental psychologists, to whom it was most germane, who were the most reluctant to embrace it. There have, of course, been individual academic psychologists who have pursued such research at universities, both in America and in Europe, but, in general, the most ambitious projects are still those that are undertaken at privately endowed research institutes.

That being said, it would be agreed, I think, even by Rhine's detractors, that he established what henceforth became the dominant approach to the study of putatively paranormal abilities. Card-guessing, as such, might prove to be of transient interest or utility and dice-throwing was anyway soon to be superseded by electronic random-event generators, but, whatever techniques might in future be introduced, they would, in this post-Rhine era, have to meet the exacting standards of experimental science where conditions must be precisely specified and results evaluated statistically in relation to chance expectation. And this was to remain the case even when the so-called 'forced-choice' tests for ESP, where the subject knows beforehand the range of alternative responses from among which the guess is to be made, gave way to 'free-response' tests where, as in traditional tests of clairvoyance or psychometry, the subject has no prior clue about the target object. In the latter case, the precise accuracy of the qualitative resemblance between the percipient's descriptive protocol and the target object or scene cannot be assessed objectively but, using matching techniques, whereby the set of protocols are matched blind against the set of targets, an exact figure can be arrived at regarding the significance of the overall score.

It has latterly become commonplace to decry the sterility of the Rhine paradigm and its presumption in assuming that psi can be boxed into the confines of the laboratory. But, as the century wore on and the older spiritualism gave way to new forms of occultism and New Age beliefs, parapsychology might well have degenerated into becoming just another popular cult had it not been for the efforts of Rhine and his followers to uphold rigorous standards. Yet even this did not make it proof against attack and, during the 1970s, organizations like the Committee for the Scientific Investigation of Claims of the Paranormal (CSICOP) provided powerful rallying grounds for scientists, academics and sceptics in general who felt threatened or affronted by parapsychological claims. They reacted by treating parapsychology as little more than the respectable face of popular superstition. Yet, if the Rhine revolution can be summed up in a word, 'respectability' might best express it. It achieved little in the way of theoretical advances. Psi had still to be characterized by its negative aspects, that is to say by its transcendence of the material conditions that constrain normal physical phenomena. Moreover, while ESP shared some of the features of normal psychological functions, Rhine insisted that it was, inescapably, an 'unconscious' process which meant, for him, that it was futile even to attempt to bring it under conscious control or to expect that it could ever be elicited on demand.

We must remember, however, that McDougall had introduced parapsychology as just the *experimental* branch of general psychical research although at the present time, as the title of this book implies, 'parapsychology' may be used as a synonym of psychical research. Much that has happened in the post-Rhine period, however, has been a reversion to, and a reaffirmation of, the classic psychical research tradition, albeit with a distinct post-modernist flavour. At the same time, the advent of electronic automation has given a new impetus to the Rhinean paradigm by eliminating so much of the donkey-work that went with traditional manual testing. Furthermore, the existence of computers has opened up fresh possibilities for psi testing such as Rhine could not have imagined.

CHAPTER 6

Recent developments

EXPERIMENTAL PARAPSYCHOLOGY

The geography of parapsychology

From the time that Rhine established his laboratory at Duke University, experimental parapsychology remained a preeminently American science. Psychical research, which had arisen in the wake of the world-wide spiritualist movement, continued as before to attract a following in almost every civilized country, but it still concerned itself mainly with the testing of psychics and mediums, the collecting and assessing of spontaneous cases, or the investigation of sporadic poltergeist disturbances which continued cropping up from time to time as they had done over the centuries (Gauld and Cornell, 1979). The strict experimental approach, however, which sought to model itself on experimental psychology, remained primarily an American enterprise even though it acquired some keen followers in Europe and elsewhere, most notably, perhaps, among the British and the Dutch. The Parapsychological Association, a floating organization of predominantly American composition, which held annual conferences whose proceedings in due course were published, represented the academic approach.

Another notable support organization was the Parapsychological Foundation of New York which was founded in 1952. This was the creation of Eileen Garrett, a remarkable woman of Irish origin who made her name and her fortune as a medium but who, unlike most mediums, became more interested in what the scientists could make of her special gifts than in their spiritualist implications. Then, when she came into money, she decided to devote the rest of her life to supporting serious research.[1] After her death in 1970 her daughter, Eileen Coly, took over the running of the Foundation. It sought to bring parapsychology to the attention of prominent scientists and academics by organizing invited conferences on selected topics, usually in Europe. It published the *International Journal of Parapsychology* and the *Parapsychology Review* (both now defunct) and it provided research grants and scholarships for aspiring researchers.

An outstanding figure in European parapsychology after the Second World War was Hans Bender (1907–1991). Bender was already involved in ESP-type experiments in 1933 while working for his PhD at the University of Bonn. He discovered one exceptional subject, a student of philosophy, who convinced him that she possessed clairvoyant ability.[2] At that time he was still ignorant of Rhine's work but soon after he was sent a copy of Rhine's *Extra-Sensory Perception* which he reviewed favourably for the *Zeitschrift für Psychologie*. Rhine was delighted and the two thereafter became firm friends. Eventually, in 1950, Bender managed, with the help of private funding, to set up an institute in his native town of Freiburg im Breisgau dedicated to *Grenzgebiete der Psychologie und Psychohygiene*. Then, in 1954, a Chair in these 'Border Areas of Psychology and Mental Health' was inaugurated at the University of Freiburg which he duly occupied until his retirement in 1975. Although some card guessing experiments were conducted at the Freiburg Institute, using Rhine's ESP cards, Bender, unlike Rhine, was always much more interested in the strong phenomena associated with exceptional subjects or with poltergeist cases.[3] The Institute published a quarterly journal, the *Zeitschrift für Parapsychologie*, now edited by Eberhard Bauer.

Another European parapsychologist who acquired university status was W.H.C. Tenhaeff (1894–1981). For his doctorate in psychology at the University of Utrecht in 1933 he submitted a thesis on 'Clairvoyance and empathy', the first such thesis on a parapsychological topic at a Dutch university. In 1953 he set up his own institute for parapsychology in Utrecht which was affiliated to the university (although financed by the Dutch SPR) and he was accorded the title of Professor. Like Bender, with whom he often collaborated, his interest lay more with the study of special sensitives ('paragnosts' he called them) than with experimentation. He is now mainly remembered for his association with the internationally celebrated clairvoyant, Gerard Croiset, who specialized in the recovery of missing persons.[4]

A new chapter in the relationship between parapsychology and the University of Utrecht began in 1974 with the establishment of a Chair of Parapsychology within the Department of Psychology. A Swedish psychologist, Martin Johnson, was appointed to the post. Unlike Tenhaeff, he was very much in the mainstream experimental tradition. Together with Sybo Schouten, a Dutch psychologist, plus various associates and visiting fellows, the Utrecht Chair produced a steady output of reputable parapsychological work until 1988 when it fell victim to the cut-backs at the Dutch universities and was forthwith wound up. It also published a journal in the English language, the *European Journal of Parapsychology*. Johnson himself, is best remembered for his discovery of a relationship between the psychological trait of 'defensiveness', as measured by the so-called Defense Mechanism Test or DMT, and ESP ability as measured in card guessing tests. There have since been some dozen attempts to test this relationship which has proved to be one of the more repeatable findings in experimental parapsychology.[5]

With the closure of the Chairs at Utrecht and at Freiburg, the sole European Chair at present is that at the University of Edinburgh. It was established within the Department of Psychology in 1985 following the demise of the writer, Arthur Koestler, who had bequeathed his entire estate for this purpose.[6] Robert Morris, a much respected experimental parapsychologist from the United States, who had originally learned his trade under Rhine, was duly appointed the first Koestler Professor. Since then, he has, with his associates and his PhD students, pursued a programme of research that has included topics such as the devising of a training schedule for ESP, volitional factors in PK on random systems using a computer game,[7] the psychology of deception, defensiveness and ESP, and the application of sports psychology to improve PK performance. *The European Journal of Parapsychology*, previously edited by Martin Johnson at Utrecht, is now published annually from Edinburgh.

Perhaps the fact that all educated Dutch know English made it easier for American-style parapsychology to permeate the Netherlands. There has never been any lack of enthusiasts in Italy, France and Spain but I think it would be fair to say that little has emerged from these countries during the past decades that one would call 'state of the art' parapsychology. Among the French exponents, by far the best-known has been Rémy Chauvin, of the Sorbonne, a noted authority on animal behaviour. He has persevered in private doing a great many original and ingenious experiments, mainly on animals but sometimes with himself as subject. However, in France, more perhaps than would be the case elsewhere, he has had to contend with prejudice and opposition from the academic establishment.[8]

The geography of parapsychology would be incomplete without some mention of what has been going on in the Soviet Union and Eastern Europe. In the early days of the

Revolution, there were a number of distinguished scientists who were eager to do research on telepathy and kindred phenomena including the well-known psychiatrist/reflexologist, V.M. Bekhterev, the neurologist K.I. Platonov of the University of Kharkov and, above all, L.L. Vasiliev of the Leningrad Institute of Brain Research. As a result, the then Commissar for Education, A.V. Lunacharsky took the initiative of forming a Soviet Committee for Psychical Research. However, the Stalinist regime could not tolerate any kind of unorthodoxy, let alone one that, to a Marxist-materialist, must have sounded dangerously 'idealistic'. At all events, from the late 1930s to the early 1950s, all periodicals and papers dealing with parapsychological topics that were sent to the Soviet Union were returned to their senders.[9] Then, in 1959, a French magazine published a report (which turned out to be quite spurious!) that the Americans had been using telepathy to communicate with the crew of the Nautilus, their atomic submarine, at such times as it was submerged beneath the ice-cap and so was shielded from any form of radio communication. The Soviet authorities took the report seriously enough to decide that such possibilities should not go uninvestigated. As a result, Vasiliev was given permission to publish his own findings which for so long had been kept under wraps and to set up his own parapsychological laboratory at the University of Leningrad – the first such in the Soviet Union.

The type of telepathic communication with which Vasiliev had been principally concerned was that of hypnosis at a distance, a phenomenon that had aroused serious interest in late nineteenth-century France.[10] In his experiments he attempted to convey telepathically to his subjects the command to wake up or to go to sleep at a designated time. Vasiliev was specially concerned to test an hypothesis, put forward by the Italian physiologist, F. Cazzammali, based on an electromagnetic interpretation of telepathy. Accordingly, Vasiliev varied both the distance between himself and the subject (in some cases the latter might be thousands of miles away!) and the screening of the subject which could be designed to eliminate electromagnetic radiation. When he found that he could obtain significant results, irrespective of distance or screening, he rejected the Cazzamalli hypothesis which, initially, he had hoped to vindicate (Vasiliev, 1962/76).

It cannot be said that Soviet involvement in parapsychology did much to advance the field, and it was handicapped by the fact that there was no official organization to which aspiring parapsychologists could belong, nor was there an official organ that could act as their mouthpiece. Nevertheless, once it was no longer forbidden, there were no lack of enthusiasts. Soon, rumours reached the West of sensational developments and it was widely believed that the Soviet military were engaging in advanced parapsychological projects. Then, in 1970, two American women journalists, L. Schroeder and S. Ostrander, published their book, *Psychic Discoveries Behind the Iron Curtain* where they recount various stories they had picked up during their visit to the Soviet Union. It became something of a best-seller in the West but the Soviet authorities took strong exception to it; they especially resented the expression 'Iron Curtain' in the title. Edouard Naumov, the chief publicist for Soviet parapsychology at that time, who had acted as host for the two American women and for other Western visitors, was sent for some years to a penal labour camp. However, in 1973, an article appeared in the prestigious journal *Questions of Philosophy* by four Soviet psychologists (of whom A.R. Luria, was by far the best known internationally) which offered some guarded support for parapsychology so long as its research was conducted under proper conventional scientific auspices.[11]

Perhaps the most significant outcome of Soviet parapsychology of this period was the discovery of two outstanding subjects who attracted international attention, Nina

Kulagina and Rosa Kuleshova, about whom we shall have more to say later. It also gave rise to a new phenomenon that came to be known as Kirlian photography, after its discoverers Semyon and Valentina Kirlian of Alma Ata, in Kazakhstan. Basically, a Kirlian photograph is obtained by placing a given object between electrodes and subjecting it to a high-frequency electrical discharge. The resulting photograph then reveals the object surrounded by a peculiar corona or aura. In fact there is nothing paranormal in the phenomenon as such, but it was said by its practitioners to exemplify 'non-physical energies', 'bioplasmic bodies', etc., and was even associated with the acupuncture points. It was practised mainly in connection with psychic healing; the idea being that the healer's powers or, alternatively, the patient's condition, would show up in a Kirlian photograph of their hands. At all events it became something of a cult during the 1970s and especially in Eastern Europe.[12]

Whereas, in the West, parapsychology had been largely driven by the desire to confound materialism or reductionism, Soviet and East European parapsychology seems to have been inspired by the hope of finding new kinds of matter and/or energy that would extend, rather than challenge, the existing scientific world view. Indeed, the very word 'parapsychology' was discarded by these countries in favour of the term 'psychotronics' (whatever that might mean). Psychotronic conferences, organized by groups in Eastern Europe, became a regular feature of this period but, to many in the West, much that went on under this aegis seemed suspiciously pseudoscientific.

One Czech researcher, however, who belongs with Western parapsychology rather than with Eastern psychotronics was Milan Ryzl who sought to develop his subject's ESP using hypnosis. He is now remembered, however, for his discovery of one particular subject, Pavel Stepanek, who, though he soon ceased to be hypnotizable, showed a remarkable staying power as a card guesser. The task at which he excelled involved a binary choice, to guess which side of a concealed coloured card, the green or the white, was upper-most inside an opaque envelope. Stepanek was soon attracting parapsychologists from all over the world and was eventually taken up in a big way by J.G. Pratt who not only tested him in Prague but later brought him over to the University of Virginia for additional testing.[13]

We must, perforce, skip over the remainder of the globe: South America, South Africa, India, Japan etc., pausing only to note that, in every continent and in most countries, one could find a nucleus of keen researchers.[14] But I do not think it would be belittling their efforts if one were to describe them as satellites of the American initiative rather than as auton-omous centres capable of breaking new ground. The one supreme exception is the People's Republic of China. Chinese Marxists had, of course, the same difficulties in coming to terms with parapsychology as had their fellow Soviet idealogues and, during the clamp-down known as the Cultural Revolution, say from 1966 to 1976, it was firmly denounced as a decadent Western legacy. Then things began to change very rapidly. In 1978 a group of scientists tested a 12-year-old boy who convinced them that he had what we would call psi ability. A few years later, in 1981, a documen-tary dealing with this topic was shown in cinemas and on television screens across the country as a result of which hundreds of children emerged who appeared to possess sim-ilar ability. Research was undertaken at more than a hundred different centres, and reports were duly published mainly in *Nature Journal* (a popular science periodical). Some esti-mates claimed that as many as 50 per cent of 10-year-olds had some such exceptional ability, it being specially marked in girls, although few children of either sex were said to retain the ability much after puberty.[15]

The most common phenomenon in this connection was what we would call clairvoyance – in this case the capacity to ascertain inscriptions or pictures when the target-sheet is concealed from view – although the occasional psychokinetic ability was also noted. The Chinese, however, repudiated Western terminology with its pointed distinction between normal and paranormal and designated all such abilities by the phrase 'Exceptional Human Body Function (EHFB)'.[16] This was seen as a special kind of physical phenomenon that had yet to be understood and so, whereas in the West most parapsychologists were psychologists by training, in China it was mainly physicists who took up the cudgels. Although the bulk of those who were studied were children, there were a few adult males who were credited with demonstrating certain bizarre physical phenomena of a strength far exceeding anything now known in the West. Some of these, like Zhang Baosheng, were studied at such important national organizations as the Institute of Space Medico-Engineering (ISME) in Beijing.

Perhaps one reason why parapsychology flourished in this way in China, once it was permitted, is that it had strong roots in traditional Chinese teachings. In particular, the concept of *qi*, a kind of universal elusive energy, not unlike the subtle fluid of the mesmerists, afforded a familiar handle for dealing with the phenomena. Moreover, *qi-gong*, a kind of Chinese version of yoga, permeated both traditional Chinese medicine and the Chinese martial arts and it was often the *qi-gong* masters themselves who produced the phenomena studied by Chinese parapsychologists. Unhappily for parapsychology in general, China still remains a largely closed society. Hence, although some Westerners went to China to try and find out what was going on and a few Chinese were allowed to go to the West and meet Western parapsychologists, such exchanges were never enough to allow a fully satisfactory assessment of what was going on there and what credence could be given to the amazing reports which (in translation) percolated to the West. If, one day, the Communist regime is dismantled, as it has been in Russia, and genuine cooperation between East and West becomes possible, only then shall we be in a position to judge the true extent of the Chinese contribution – but it may yet profoundly alter the course of parapsychological history.

Free response ESP

By the 1960s, behaviourism was losing its hold on American academic psychology. Humanistic psychology was one of several new movements which were challenging the strictly objective approach, laying emphasis on states of mind, altered states of consciousness, peak experiences, creativity and other such aspects of mental life which behaviourism had sedulously avoided. This was, moreover, the decade of the counter-culture with all that that implies in terms of the search for new modes of experience and new forms of self-expression. Against this background the dry routine of card guessing, now no longer a novelty, began to seem boring and trivial. In this climate, new and more exciting ways of evoking ESP were eagerly sought after. In a so-called *free-response* test, the target, be it a picture, an inscription, an object or a real-life scene, has no predetermined range, as is the case with a forced-choice test. Hence what, in a free-response test, constitutes a hit is when the percipient's description of the target matches it sufficiently for a judge, who is of course blind as to which target is used on which trial, to assign it to that target. The procedure is, of course, very time consuming as compared with that involved in forced-choice guessing, but it is much closer to what happens in reports of spontaneous ESP as well as to traditional tests for clairvoyance. However, when it comes to estimating the statistical significance of the given overall score, the qualitative correspondences are ignored and the calculations are as objective as for a forced-choice technique. Below we shall describe three types of free-response test that have figured prominently in the post-Rhine era.

The Maimonides Dream Laboratory[17]

The possibility of awakening a sleeper immediately after he or she has been dreaming was a consequence of a discovery published in 1953 by two psychophysiologists, Aserinsky and Kleitman, who demonstrated that a period of rapid eye movements (REMs) regularly accompanied a dream phase as subsequently described by the awakened subject. Normally five or six such phases may be expected in the course of a normal sleep cycle. This discovery gave a big impetus to the psychological study of sleeping and dreaming but it was the psychiatrist, Montague Ullman, of the Maimonides Medical Centre, Brooklyn, New York, with his long-standing interest in parapsychology,[18] who first saw the possibility of exploiting these developments in sleep research for *para*psychological ends.

Dreams, had, of course, always figured prominently in the study of spontaneous ESP and more especially in cases of spontaneous precognition. J.W. Dunne's *An Experiment with Time*, based on his dream diary, evoked enormous popular interest when it first appeared in 1927. But the idea of experimenting with dreams, and of attempting to modify the dream narrative using extrasensory means, was an altogether new departure. To this end what Ullman now needed was a suitably equipped sleep laboratory and a willing and, hopefully, sensitive subject. In the event, none other than Eileen Garrett herself came to his aid and put at his disposal not only the facilities of her own laboratory at the Foundation and the services of the two researchers whom she then employed,[19] but offered herself as the subject for his first pilot experiment which was duly carried out in 1960. In terms of the qualitative resemblances between dream content and target picture it was strikingly successful; many of the items of her protocol were 'bang on'. At all events, two years later, funding was obtained to set up a laboratory at the Maimonides Hospital where systematic research began in 1964 after Stanley Krippner had joined the project as its research director.

The standard procedure was as follows. The subject was put to sleep in a sound-proof room after being wired up to an electroencepholograph (EEG) which monitors his/her brain-waves during sleep. In another sound-proof room in the hospital an 'agent' spent the night ready, when given the signal, to look at, and preferably to think about, the target picture (art postcards served as the standard target). The target for that particular night was selected beforehand from a large pool using a table of random numbers. When the EEG polygraph showed that the subject had *entered* a dream phase (REM period) the experimenter who monitored the instrument would duly signal the agent to take appropriate action. Then, later, when the EEG indicated that the subject had *emerged* from that dream phase, he/she would be awakened via the intercom and would record his/her impressions of the preceding dream onto a tape-recorder. Normally we would forget our dreams very quickly but in this way they could be captured while still fresh in memory. The procedure would then be repeated with each ensuing dream phase; the same target was generally used throughout any one night. Dreams that occur in the course of a single sleep cycle are, it would appear, often thematically related so using the same target made good sense.

On awakening next morning the subject would be shown a set of pictures (usually eight or a dozen), including the actual target, and was required to rate each picture on a scale from 1 to 100 expressing his/her degree of confidence that that picture was indeed the target (the experimenter in charge of the subject was, of course, kept ignorant during this procedure as to the identity of the actual target). In making these judgements the subject was free to utilize the tape-recordings from the previous night. A complete experiment along these lines might last a month or more, but each night would correspond to just a single trial. At the close of the experiment copies of all the dream protocols from each nocturnal session were sent to two or more judges specially selected for their expertise. They were, of course, blind as to the actual targets and their job was to compare each set of transcripts with each of the pictures and rank them for closeness of resemblance. An appropriate statistical evaluation could then be carried out, both on the subjects' ratings and on the judges' ratings, and the result compared with the mean chance expectation.

Between 1964 and 1972 some fifteen formal studies were completed and duly published in accredited journals using the procedure described or some variation on it. Of these, only seven produced a significant outcome, using either measure, but considering the small number of trials involved in each experiment this was, in fact, very remarkable. Moreover many striking qualitative resemblances were noted although, as is inevitable in a free-response design, one cannot assign these a definite numerical value. What *does* stand out from these results is that the most impressive scores were due to three subjects in particular, each of whom completed at least one series of eight nights at the laboratory: William Erwin, Robert Van de Castle and Malcolm Bessent. Erwin was a young psychologist who, as a practising analyst, was interested in dream processes. Van de Castle was himself the Director of a Sleep and Dream Laboratory at the University of Virginia who, as a subject, showed a remarkable capacity for dream recall (his transcripts were twice as long as those of most other subjects). Bessent was a well-known psychic who had shown willingness to cooperate with parapsychologists. The variant used for the two Bessent series introduced a precognitive factor: that is to say, the target was not selected until the next morning when selection was made on a random basis and, of course, in ignorance of what dreams had been recorded the previous night.

Subsequent attempts to replicate the Maimonides findings at other sleep laboratories in the USA met with little or no success and, as always happens after a sufficient lapse of time, critics have sought to belittle them as best they can and not always too scrupulously.[20] For the history of parapsychology, however, the importance of Ullman's initiative lies not so much in the new data that it produced as in the fact that *(a)* it introduced parapsychology into research on the psychophysiology of sleep – at that time a focus of widespread interest, *(b)* it became the first important new centre for parapsychological research since Rhine established his laboratory and, from that vantage point, was able to challenge the monopoly of the Rhinean paradigm, and *(c)* it popularized the free-response technique that was used to such good effect in the later ganzfeld and remote-viewing research which we discuss below. As a methodology, however, it was of very limited utility for how many researchers, after all, are dedicated enough to sacrifice an entire night for the sake of completing one single trial?

The ganzfeld
One junior member of the Maimonides team was a young man who, having fallen out with Rhine, was seeking new opportunities to pursue a parapsychological career. Charles Honorton joined the Maimonides project in October 1967 and remained there until the summer of 1979, becoming Director of Research when Krippner left in 1974. He became, in due course, the leading exponent of free-response ESP testing using altered states of consciousness *other* than the dream state.[21]

A critical question posed by the Maimonides project was whether the successes it achieved were due to the fact that the subject was asleep and dreaming or whether the nocturnal dream is simply one of a number of possible states of mind that are distinguished by the fact that they exclude external sources of stimulation. Three such states, after all, had already yielded evidence of their psi-conducive potential: hypnosis, relaxation and meditation.

Hypnosis, with its roots in mesmerism, was traditionally thought to be psi-conducive, hence the so-called 'higher phenomena' of hypnosis. In experimental parapsychology there had been a number of studies during the 1960s and '70s using hypnosis with both the forced choice and the free-response paradigm. Relaxation is suggested by the accounts of successful sensitives of their technique for inducing a requisite state of receptivity. Experiments during the 1970s by Braud and Braud and by others used progressive relaxation exercises to good effect. Finally, as regards meditation, this has even older associations with the paranormal if we include under this heading the techniques of yoga with their reputed *siddhis*. Gertrude Schmeidler was the first to use meditation in the context of an ESP guessing task but her lead was soon followed by Dukhan and Rao and then even extended to PK tasks by Schmidt, Pantas and others. In the case of meditation, however, testing has to take place *after* rather than *during* the altered state in which all activity, mental and physical, is suspended.

Sensory deprivation produces the nearest thing to sleep. It is well known that there is a twilight zone before we enter the stage of actual sleep characterized by enhanced imagery known technically as 'hypnagogic imagery'.[22] The 'ganzfeld' technique is so called because it exploits the effects of exposing the subject to a uniform visual field or ganzfeld. The simplest way of producing the effect is to make the subject wear translucent goggles (half ping-pong balls make a convenient device) through which a light can be shone. To complete the total absence of perceptual patterning, earphones should be worn into which a white noise (something like the shushing sound of waves breaking) can be fed while, to obviate tactile and somatic sensations, the body should be relaxed and cocooned with ample cushioning. The first ganzfeld experiment was that by Honorton and Harper published in 1974. In a typical ganzfeld experiment the target is selected at random from among four different pictures. After ten minutes or so in the ganzfeld, the subject's imagery should start to become enhanced and, hopefully, to reflect the objects depicted on the target picture. When, after a lapse of, say, half an hour, the subject is aroused from this condition, he or she is presented with all four potential targets by an experimenter (who is, of course, ignorant as to the identity of the actual target) and has to rank them according to the degree to which they correspond with the images experienced during the ganzfeld.

Experiments using the ganzfeld technique have been going on steadily since 1974 and Honorton himself has progressively refined its methodology by automating as much of it as possible. In 1979 Honorton founded his own laboratory in the Princeton area, the so-called Psychophysical Research Laboratories, which became the main centre for ganzfeld studies up to its closure ten years later in 1989.[23] In 1985, in an article responding to a critic of the ganzfeld evidence, Honorton included a meta-analysis of all the ganzfeld experiments to date which had appeared in accredited journals. These included some 42 such studies from a variety of American laboratories plus a few from Britain. Then five years later another article examining the automated experiments appeared. Although there were some hiccups in some of the studies – some experimenters, for example, have admittedly been guilty of multiple of *post-hoc* analyses in their search for significant effects – one would need a very strong prior conviction about the non-existence of the paranormal to dismiss entirely the evidence from the ganzfeld work.[24, 24a, 24b]

Remote viewing

In most of the research that used a free-response technique the subject was intended to function in a special state of consciousness. This was not the case, however, with what came to be known as 'remote viewing'. Another feature of this approach is that the target is, normally, an actual real-life scene or object, not a mere representation or a symbol, making it closer, therefore, to real life psi as reported in spontaneous cases. The idea, of course, was not new: it had its roots in the 'travelling clairvoyance' of the early nineteenth-century mesmerists or in the 'psychometry' of clairvoyants who, on the basis of some token-object, purport to describe some distant location with which it is connected. However, in a remote-viewing experiment, the subject is given no props but is merely asked to describe what impressions he or she gets and, whenever possible, to make rough sketches of his or her mental images.

Interestingly, it was a gifted subject who provided the idea for what then became the standard remote-viewing test. The subject in question was a retired American-Irish police commissioner, Patrick H. Price, who insisted that he made use of just such a faculty in his daily professional life. The experimenters whom he contacted in this connection were two young physicists, Russell Targ and Hal Puthoff, who were then at the Stanford Research Institute (SRI), a high-power science laboratory at Menlo Park not far from San Francisco. Targ was already by then a keen parapsychologist and had carried out similar kinds of experiments with one well-known professional psychic, Ingo Swann, who not only, like many of his predecessors, appeared capable of describing remote locations, but did this sometimes, we are told, on the basis of nothing more than the coordinates on a map![25]

In a standard remote-viewing test, as originally devised to accommodate Pat Price, the outbound experimenter who will act as agent drives to a location in the vicinity, one of 100 such that had been selected as potential targets the actual target having been randomly assigned by an administrator at SRI. Meanwhile another experimenter who is, of course, ignorant as to which location was the target for that trial, remains with the subject who is encouraged to pay attention to whatever passes through his or her mind. At the end of a series of such trials, the transcripts from each session, including any sketches which the subject may have drawn, are sent to one or more independent judges who are required to rank each of the sites, from 1 to *n*, against each transcript, where 1 signifies the most resemblance and *n* the least resemblance. In the initial experiment with Pat Price, in June 1973, no less than 7 out of the 9 sessions gained a rank of 1, signifying a direct hit. Indeed, in one instance, the Hoover Tower in Stanford, the target site, was named as such. The overall score was, of course, hugely significant.[26]

To a much greater extent than with the ganzfeld technique, remote viewing has relied on outstanding subjects. Pat Price died in 1975 but a new star subject soon entered the arena in the person of Hella Hamid, a professional photographer, who has demonstrated her ability many times since then. In her first experiment, carried out shortly after the Pat Price experiment and using a similar design, her overall scoring was even more significant than his. Another successful remote viewing subject was Duane Elgin, a research analyst at SRI.[27] But many casual visitors to SRI achieved some success in single trial attempts. Russell Targ once told me that he liked to work with individuals who had made good in whatever walk of life as such persons were accustomed to succeeding in what they set out to do!

Not surprisingly, the initial successes of the SRI project provoked an even more strenuous critical backlash than had the ganzfeld experiments. At the spearhead of this attack were two psychologists from the University of Otago, New Zealand, David Marks and Richard Kammann. They discovered a procedural flaw in the Pat Price experiment whereby certain incidental information had crept into the protocols which could have influenced the judge in making his matchings.[28] They even, in due course, visited SRI to argue their case. However, Charles Tart, an independent and much respected parapsychologist of the University of California at Davis, decided to submit the transcripts in question, *purged of these tell-tale cues*, to another judge who knew nothing about the particulars of the original experiment. The outcome was no less significant than before![29, 29a]

A remote-viewing experiment is not difficult to do and, not surprisingly, given the importance of the special subject, many attempted replications ended in failure. However, since the initial experiments of Targ and Puthoff, there has been a sizeable body of remote-viewing experiments that support the claims for this technique which, like the ganzfeld technique, can also be performed in the precognitive mode, where the target site is not selected until *after* the subject has completed his/her protocol.[30] Two of those who achieved success as remote-viewing subjects, Brenda Dunne and Marilyn Schlitz, are best known as distinguished researchers in their own right. Of particular interest is the transcontinental remote-viewing experiment in which the agent, Elmar Gruber (a German parapsychologist, then at the University of Freiburg) was in Rome while the subject, Marilyn Schlitz (of the Mind Science Foundation, of San Antonio, Texas) was in Detroit, Michigan. For this experiment, some 40 potential target sites in Rome were selected by Gruber in consultation with an Italian colleague from which 10 were actually used during the 10 consecutive days of testing. The transcripts were then submitted to five judges who duly visited all ten sites before ranking and rating all ten transcripts. A statistical analysis of these data yielded odds against chance of the order of a million to one.

This striking result did not escape the attention of the critics and it was pointed out that the agent, Elmar Gruber, was also responsible for translating the transcripts into Italian and so could have biassed the outcome, even though his translations had been passed as accurate by a professional translator. Furthermore, the agent's personal impressions of the site were included in the material sent to the judges and this, it was suggested, might, in some undefined way, have been a source of illicit information. Accordingly, a year later, the same set of transcripts were submitted to two *new* judges in a such a way that the results were not open to these objections. The scores on this occasion were not as significant as on the first occasion yet, even so, the odds against chance were still of the order of a thousand to one.[31]

Micro-PK:
The intentional biassing of random systems

The Micro-PK is a term which parapsychologists use to distinguish it from macro-PK where observable effects of a gross kind are produced, as in seances with physical mediums or in poltergeist disturbances. Micro-PK is detectable only by due statistical analysis covering a large number of trials, as in Rhine's dice-tossing tests or, in modern automated tests, with electronic random-event generators or REGs. The contrast between such micro-PK and traditional macro-PK is so stark that doubt has been expressed as to whether it is the same faculty that is involved in the two cases. Be that as it may, operationally speaking, both come under the umbrella term 'PK' inasmuch as both exemplify the fulfilment of one's wishes or intentions without recourse to normal muscular action. With ESP, one is dealing with a transfer of *information* rather than a physical *effect* but, with both ESP and PK, it is the automatic *realization of an intention*, be it conscious or unconscious, that is the essential property of psi.

The outstanding exponent of modern micro-PK techniques is Helmut Schmidt, a German physicist who, after obtaining his doctorate from the University of Cologne, settled in the United States where, from 1965 to 1969, he served as senior research scientist at the Boeing research laboratory in Seattle. Since then, however, he has been fully committed to parapsychological research, first as Research Director of Rhine's Institute for Parapsychology at Durham, North Carolina from 1969 to 1972, and then at the Mind Science Foundation of San Antonio, Texas. His major contribution to the field has been his introduction of automated electronic testing devices. In his original 'Schmidt machine', which he used to test ESP or more specifically precognition, beta emissions from a radioactive source of strontium 90, striking a geiger counter, served to trigger the selection of a target lamp which would then light up to provide immediate feedback. The subject's task was to predict which of four lamps the machine would select by pressing the appropriate key. The beauty of such a set-up, from the point of view of a physicist like Schmidt, was that the rate of radioactive decay, which here determines target selection, is *theoretically* unpredictable and yet, as the results showed, highly significant scores were forthcoming from a few specially selected subjects.

Given such an automated device, the transition from ESP to PK testing was no real problem. Indeed, one could not be completely sure that the successful subjects in his first experiment were not in fact using their PK ability to *make* the machine conform to their chosen response rather than simply *predicting* which target the machine would choose. However, for his designated PK tests, Schmidt used a binary REG coupled with a display such that while, in the ordinary way, a point of light on the screen would execute a random to-and-fro walk, by exerting a PK effect the subject could make the same point of light veer significantly in a designated, say clockwise, direction. Using an analagous auditory display with headphones a subject could be instructed to increase the number of clicks fed into, say, the right ear as against those fed into the left ear. Although the absolute deviation from chance in such PK experiments was small, say 51 per cent against the theoretical expectation of 50 per cent, the huge number of trials that could be run during quite a brief space of time with such a set-up allowed for highly significant results, in some cases reaching an order of millions to one against chance.[32]

Schmidt is, perhaps, the nearest thing to a genius which the science of experimental parapsychology has yet produced. His work has, moreover, been suffused with a theoretical orientation that has appealed to many fellow experimenters. Briefly, he sees PK (which he regards as the fundamental psi ability) not as any kind of force or energy acting on the apparatus in question, but rather as a goal-oriented power analogous to the observer effect in quantum theory. For, according to the orthodox Copenhagen interpretation of quantum mechanics, a given quantum event remains indeterminate up to the point where a measurement is made – whereupon there follows what is called the 'collapse of the state vector'. Where Schmidt's theory *diverges* from accepted physics is that, for the latter, the observer is powerless to influence the particular value of the observed event whereas, according to Schmidt, an individual who can function as a 'psi source' *can* bias the outcome of the event being observed and in such a way as to facilitate the attainment of a goal.[33] To illustrate the point, Schmidt carried out successful experiments using various animal subjects who were rewarded when his REG selected one binary outcome as opposed to the other – for example a lamp would come on, thereby warming his pet cat that he was using as subject. Even more disturbing to conventional thinking, Schmidt was able to demonstrate that PK was possible using '*pre*-recorded random numbers' to govern the output of the REG instead of an ongoing random source. For this seems to imply that PK can be retroactive in its effect. However, this was not so anomalous from the standpoint of the theory which Schmidt had espoused, since it would then follow that all PK is, in the last resort, *retro*active – that is, if we grant the premise of the so-called Observational Theory, that we influence events in the very act of observing them.

Despite striking successes, Schmidt's achievement fell short of discovering a readily repeatable experiment which could, at a blow, have relieved parapsychology of the stigma of purveying unrepeatable claims. Schmidt took a lot of trouble before commencing a formal experiment, selecting his subjects with care and training them appropriately.

Consequently his published output was small and the fact that he worked on his own, and that few could emulate his results, lessened the impact which his work might otherwise have made. Fortunately a laboratory at Princeton University, founded by Robert Jahn, Dean of the School of engineering, in the spring of 1979, and calling itself the Princeton Engineering Anomalies Research (PEAR) laboratory, undertook an extensive programme of PK research using a REG. Unlike Schmidt, Jahn made a point of accepting as subjects anyone who was willing to put in the necessary time, including members of the laboratory, and no training was introduced. The upshot was that, by the time he published a book on the work of the laboratory (Jahn and Dunne, 1987), some 47 subjects had contributed to the data bank covering a combined total of 2.5 million trials.[34]

Comparisons were made, moreover, not just between cumulative total and mean chance expectation but also between scores from three alternating conditions: where the subject was aiming for a high score (PK+), where the subject was aiming for a low score (PK-) and where the subject was trying *not* to interfere with the spontaneous behaviour of the REG (BL = Baseline). Plotting the cumulative deviation of all subjects over some 250,000 trials, it transpired that the PK+ condition attained a positive deviation significant at the 1 per cent level, the PK-condition attained a negative deviation, likewise significant at the 1 per cent level, while the BL condition remained consistently within the limits defined by the 5 per cent level of confidence although, be it noted, its variance was significantly restricted.

Of course, for such a huge output the significance levels thus attained are very meagre. They represent something like just one extra hit in the desired direction for every thousand bits generated by the REG. Nevertheless, the conclusion to be drawn is clear enough. We must also bear in mind that it was a matter of policy with this laboratory to accept all comers. As always, however, individual differences soon asserted themselves. Thus an analysis of Operator 10 on his/her own [35] showed that the difference between the PK+ condition and the PK- condition following 5,000 trials on each was significant with odds of approximately 10 million to one although, with an idiosyncrasy typical of this set-up, the PK- scores were far more significant than the PK+ scores.

Having demonstrated PK with their REG, the Jahn team then constructed a mechanical cascade as a basis for testing PK. Normally, when balls are fed into this contrivance they fall via the rows of pins into the columns provided along the base of the apparatus in accordance with the familiar binomial distribution. From this baseline attempts can be made to influence the distribution by skewing it to the right (the PK + condition) or to the left (the PK- condition). Although the total number of trials run with the random cascade was only a fraction of those using the REG, significant scores were obtained here, too (even though, for whatever reason, only the PK- condition proved significant). That broadly similar results can be obtained with either an electronic *or* a mechanical system nicely illustrates the goal-oriented nature of PK which can thus transcend the particular physical process required to attain the desired result. What is, however, disconcerting for the attempt to arrive at any kind of coherent understanding of what is involved in testing for PK is that significant results were *still* forthcoming when a *pseudo*-random series of numbers was used to control the REG, as opposed to a truly random ongoing process. Such a series can be produced by a computer on the basis of a given algorithm so that it is determined at the outset and should not, therefore, be open to *any* sort of extraneous influence whether we call it PK or whatever.[36]

The work of pioneers like Schmidt and Jahn, along with that of the many other researchers who have worked on this problem has reinforced the conclusions suggested by the earlier work with dice that micro-PK is a phenomenon with which we have to reckon.[37] What is unfortunate from the standpoint of research is that, unlike all known physical forces, PK influences do not seem to be cumulative. Using many subjects to influence the target system produces no improvement on using one successful subject. This, too, would suggest that the analogy with a physical force is mistaken but, whatever the explanation, it certainly increases the difficulty of establishing the reality of this mysterious and elusive phenomenon to the satisfaction of all concerned.

Bio-PK: PK on living systems

Although the bulk of the evidence for the existence of PK comes from the sort of experiments that we have been discussing, using mechanical and electronic target systems, it would be surprising if, granted that we possess such a faculty, its operations were confined to such artificial situations. If, however, it could be shown that PK can somehow affect or influence animate targets, this could have far-reaching implications for a variety of phenomena which have hitherto defied satisfactory explanation. Of particular relevance here is the healing process. Today medicine freely recognizes the importance of mental (psychosomatic) factors in the recovery from illness. Indeed no drug, these days, is ever tested without recourse to a placebo group – so potent is mere expectation and confidence for the success of a given treatment.

Another example of psychosomatic medicine can be found in the biofeedback technique which has been used to enable patients to gain control over certain physiological functions such as blood-pressure or pulse rate which are not normally susceptible to voluntary control. What happens here is that such processes, of which normally we are unaware, are made visible to the patient as a continuous fluctuating line on a screen.

Any positive modification which the patient can then induce, by dint of some kind of striving, immediately becomes apparent and a learning process is set up – much as when people learn to wiggle their ears by watching themselves in a mirror. Of course, in orthodox medicine, a 'psychosomatic' factor is regarded as being actually a 'cerebro-somatic' factor, even if we are not in a position to spell out exactly which brain mechanisms are activated in the process. For the parapsychologist, on the other hand, for whom PK is a reality, such examples of self-healing inevitably raise the question as to whether PK might be involved here, too. If so, might it not be possible to direct it onto organisms *other* than one's own in order to cure an affliction?

Once *this* question is posed, a mass of suggestive historical and anthropological evidence calls for consideration. Down the ages, and in many different societies, we find that certain individuals have been credited with the power to heal others, using nothing more than just their touch – the 'laying on of hands', to use the traditional expression. Almost certainly mesmerism, as originally practised by Mesmer himself, and before it became inextricably confused with hypnotism, was little more than a new-fangled version of this age-old laying on of hands. Mesmerism contrived to make it more palatable to the outlook of the time by introducing the concept of animal magnetism or the magnetic fluid, magnetism itself being then still fraught with mysteries, but essentially it involved what nowadays we would call 'therapeutic touch'.

From the point of view of the experimental parapsychologist, however, healing, as traditionally practised, is a messy business inasmuch as it does not permit us to distinguish its effects from those of ordinary suggestion. As a result, if one wants to isolate a specific psi effect in healing, one must resort either to the practice of distant healing, where the patient does not know that any healing is taking place, or devise elaborate control conditions that can obviate the suggestibility factor. In the event, most of the work that has so far been done to demonstrate PK on living systems has used animals or plants as targets for healing.

The undoubted pioneer in this connection was Bernard Grad, a Canadian biochemist at McGill University, Montreal. Grad had already developed unorthodox ideas about healing through his association with Wilhelm Reich, inventor of the so-called 'orgone accumulator'. Then in 1957, the year when Reich died,[38] Grad met an Hungarian emigré healer by the name of Oskar Estabany. Estabany, the first practitioner of the laying on of hands whom Grad had met, was persuaded to collaborate with Grad on an experimental investigation of this phenomenon using animals and plants as targets.[39] For his first experiment, Grad decided to study the effects of such treatment on wound healing in mice. In the critical experiment, Estabany would hold between his hands a cage of mice, on each one of which a small skin wound had been surgically inflicted beforehand, for a period of 15 minutes. He did this twice daily for the 20 days of the experiment with a five-hour interval between treatments. Results showed that the wounds of the animals thus treated by Estabany were significantly smaller than were those of the animals whose cages had been similarly held by volunteer medical students acting as controls or were those of animals that had received no treatment of any kind. Naturally, the measurement of the wounds was made by staff who were blind as to whether the animals in question had been drawn from the experimental or the control groups. The absolute effect observed here was slight but the design of this experiment, on which Grad collaborated with a physiologist and a statistician, was such that any normal counter-explanation does appear to be ruled out.[40]

Grad now shifted his attention to plants. Preliminary testing suggested that Estabany's powers extended to plant life but that the effect was most pronounced when the plants in question (he used barley seedlings) were grown under suboptimal conditions. It was as if Estabany's healing powers could be used to greatest effect when the seedlings were exposed to adverse conditions such as being kept rather dry and watered with a saline solution. Moreover, it was found to be unnecessary for Estabany to hold the pots with the seedlings in his hands: it was sufficient for him to hold the flask of water that would be used to water them. Accordingly, for the critical experiment, Estabany was duly told to hold between his hands a flask which contained a 1 per cent saline solution for a period of 15 minutes per day for fourteen days. The assistant who did the watering did not know, of course, whether or not the water had been thus treated nor which of the seedlings had been designated targets and which controls.

Three measures were used in ascertaining the outcome: (1) the overall number of seeds per group which had germinated, (2) the mean height of the seedlings per group on the 14th day, including the seeds which had not germinated and so had zero height, and (3) the mean 'yield' which took into account only those seedlings in each group which had germinated. Results showed clearly that the target seedlings were significantly taller than the control seedlings on both measures (2) and (3) but there was no overall difference in the number of seeds that had germinated as given by measure (1). In a further experiment along these lines Grad used a ground glass stopper on the flask instead of leaving it open to preclude the possibility of some chemical getting into the water but, as before, the target seedlings were significantly taller than the control seedlings.[41]

Such a finding raises the question as to whether the water that is 'treated' in this way undergoes some subtle physical change that could be detected by spectroscopic analysis. Grad himself was unable to detect any such change, whether using visible, infra-red or ultra violet light. Douglas Dean, however, working mainly with the American healer, Olga Worrall, and using an advanced type of spectrophotometer, has claimed to detect a difference.[42] There have also been a large number of experiments, mostly with ordinary subjects, in which the aim has been to facilitate the growth of plants merely by willing that the target plants flourish more than the control plants and some success has been achieved in reputable research.[43] There has also been a successful attempt to *inhibit* the growth of a noxious fungus by PK alone.[44]

Grad himself made few further contributions to research in this area after these striking initial successes but there have since then been various confirmatory studies by others bearing on both the PK healing of animals and the PK facilitation of growth in plants.[45, 46] There was also a striking confirmation of Estabany's peculiar powers in an experiment where he was required to modify the activity of an *in vitro* sample of the enzyme trypsin.[47]

But, if Grad was the pioneer of this field, William Braud has been its most active exponent thereafter and, indeed, it is to him that we owe the term 'bio-PK'.[48] Braud joined Helmut Schmidt at the Mind Science Foundation of San Antonio, Texas, in 1975 and has since then specialized in the study of PK using live target systems. In some of his early experiments he used animals that were naturally very mobile and active, in one case a species of electric fish, in another a gerbil (a small rodent). The task here was to try, mentally, either to *in*crease or to *de*crease the activity of the target animal during certain set periods according to a prearranged schedule. He also, however, experimented extensively with humans to see whether it was possible for one human being to influence the physiological activity of another human being otherwise than through the known mechanisms of sensorimotor communication. The particular physiological activity he chose as the target system was that which physiologists call 'electrodermal activity'. It is a well-known fact that the skin's resistance to a mild electric current will vary from one moment to the next depending mainly on the degree of moisture of the skin in question. The fact has been exploited psychologically in the so-called 'lie detector', the idea being that one will respond to an emotive stimulus by sweating, however minimally, thereby lowering the skin's electrical resistance. In the particular experiment I shall describe,[49] an attempt was made to increase or decrease the target person's electrodermal activity, using only a volitional effort on the part of the subject who sat watching a screen on which appeared a continuous recording of that other person's electrodermal output. The set-up was thus very similar to that used in biofeedback therapy except, of course, that the output came from another organism, – hence the term 'allobiofeedback'.

Thanks to the highly automated set-up that existed at the Mind Science Foundation, it was legitimate for the researchers themselves to act as their own subjects. In this experiment both Braud and his co-experimenter, Marilyn Schlitz, took turns to act as 'influencer'. Their pool of 32 target-persons was obtained by advertising for those worried about headaches, high blood-pressure, ulcers or other such symptoms of stress, the idea being that such persons might respond more readily to a calming influence, albeit a paranormal one! However, they predicted that those who, on a preliminary test, showed a higher level of electrodermal activity (the 'active' group) would respond more to such an influence than those who had shown a lower level of arousal (the 'inactive' group). The influencing process took place during preset periods of 30 seconds, randomly interspersed among equivalent control periods. Of course, the target-person knew nothing of what was going on in this connection; he or she sat in a separate room and was just told to relax.

Results were impressive if somewhat surprising. For the 16 so-called 'inactive' target-persons, the effect was nil. For the 16 'active' target-persons, on the other hand, there was a significant drop in their electrodermal output amounting to a drop of about 10 per cent as compared with the control periods. It certainly looked, therefore, as if bio-PK was operating. But at this point we touch upon a curious ambiguity which is probably unresolvable. Perhaps the calming influence which here seems to have been involved might have been due to a straightforward telepathic rapport between influencer and influencee. If telepathy is, indeed, conceptualized as direct mind-to-mind communication, then we would not need, presumably, to invoke PK. Opinions differ, however, as to what is actually involved in a given case of telepathy. On one prevalent view, the sender is exercising his/her PK to influence the brain of the receiver, thereby transmitting the relevant message.[50] At all events, taking the biofeedback analogy, it would be plausible to assume that Braud and Schlitz were using Bio-PK to influence those centres of the other person's brain that normally control their electrodermal activity.

SOME PSYCHIC VIRTUOSI OF THE 1960s AND '70s

The phenomena we have discussed in the first part of this chapter constituted the staple fare of the parapsychological laboratory. A history of this period would be deficient, however, if we failed to take note of certain cases that attracted much wider publicity. I am here using the word 'psychic' noncommitally to refer to any individual purporting to possess mysterious powers. In what follows we shall look at the careers of four such individuals whose problematic abilities made them the focus of world-wide interest and speculation. They include a pair of Russian women whom we shall discuss first; an American psychic-photographer (or 'thoughtographer' as he came to be called) and, thirdly – and best known of them all, perhaps the only psychic this century to become a veritable household name – Uri Geller.

Nina Kulagina and Rosa Kuleshova[51]

The idea that vision might not be confined exclusively to the eyes but could be present to some degree in the skin – with the exciting corollary that blind persons might be able to acquire some rudimentary vision using their fingertips – has cropped up in various places and at various times. There was a flurry of interest following the publication of a book, in 1924, by the well-known French novelist, Jules Romains, in which he claims to have taught himself and others to use this ability.[52] In its most elementary form it involves distinguishing between objects of different colour; at a more advanced level it involves the reading of a printed text. Romains called the ability 'extra-retinal vision' but, today, in the West, it is usually referred to as skin vision or, more technically, as 'dermo-optical perception' (DOP). Romains, however, failed to convince his scientific contemporaries that anything more unusual was involved than self-deception and, as it seemed to make no sense physiologically, interest in the phenomenon subsided.

It cropped up next, in a big way, in the Soviet Union, following the claims of a young woman who, in 1962, told her doctor that, using her fingertips alone, she could distinguish different coloured papers and even read print. This was Rosa Kuleshova of Nizhniy Tagil, in the Urals, where she worked as a schoolteacher. Being partially blind herself and having a number of blind relatives, she had taught herself to read braille. Thus, from the outset, she saw her discovery as a new means of helping the blind. It was while she was being treated for epilepsy at the local City Hospital that she demonstrated her peculiar ability for the benefit of her doctor, I.M. Goldberg. After satisfying himself that she was genuine, he invited colleagues to witness her performance and sought to bring her to the attention of others in Nishniy Tagil who might be interested.

From then on there was no looking back. A neurologist, Shaefer, invited her to a psychiatric clinic in Sverdlovsk for a six-week investigation; then, back in Nizhniy Tagil, she was studied by A.S. Novomeisky of the Pedagogical Institute where, among other tests, she was required to identify the colour and shape of curves projected onto an oscillograph screen; her next appointment was in Moscow at the Biophysics Institute of the Soviet Academy of Sciences which issued a positive report on her in 1965. Meanwhile, Novomeisky started training others to do similar tasks, as did Larissa Vilenskaya, an engineer by profession but a leading activist of the Moscow group of parapsychologists (Vilenskaya eventually emigrated to the United States where she has since done her best to build bridges between American and Russian parapsychologists).

Unfortunately, Rosa was never a very stable character and her success was her eventual undoing. Her performances deteriorated, she took to cheating and, at a demonstration she gave at the Moscow offices of *Literaturnaya Gazetta*, she was caught cheating and denounced as a fraud. Her reputation never recovered. Her health, never robust, deteriorated; she became increasingly irrational; and she died prematurely in Sverdlovsk, in 1978 at the age of 38. Her active career had lasted only some six years.

What is one to make of it all? All the normal explanations, e.g. differential textural or even thermal effects, were soon ruled out. For example, targets were placed under glass or, in some instances, beneath opaque paper sheets. Could it all have been a question of inadequate blindfolding? This, too, seems incredible if the reports can be trusted, as she was often said to operate from behind a screen. At all events, A.R. Luria, Russia's most eminent psychologist and no friend of parapsychology, was convinced that Rosa *was* indeed genuine, although he consoled himself with the belief that a physiological explanation would, in time, be forthcoming.[53] And what, finally, are we to make of all the 'mini-Kuleshovas' who flourished in her wake but have since, alas, disappeared?

There has, since her demise, been some desultory research in this area in the West but it was low key and, considering its potential utility with respect to the blind, the results are disappointing.[54] Most of those who have concerned themselves with the phenomenon still persist in regarding it as border-line sensory, rather than extrasensory. For Kuleshova herself it is understandable that she should take this line, given the ideological constraints within which she had to operate. However, pending some explanation that would satisfy conventional scientists, it is surely both more logical and more parsimonious to treat the phenomenon, if it is to be accepted at face value, as just another species of clairvoyance, what our mesmeric forebears would have called a transposition of the senses.

Kulagina (recently deceased) is now remembered as a woman who could demonstrate directly observable PK with small target objects. Yet she too began as an exponent of skin vision in emulation of Rosa. She claimed to have discovered her own gift while convalescing in hospital, in 1964, following a nervous breakdown. While doing embroidery she discovered that she could find the right coloured threads without using her eyes. Eventually she was brought to the attention of L.L. Vasiliev, whom we have already encountered as Russia's foremost pioneer of parapsychology and who was then Professor of Physiology at the University of Leningrad. That same year a positive report on her abilities was published by a group of scientists whom Vasiliev had invited to participate in her investigation.

She discovered her PK abilities almost accidentally while engaged on her skin vision exercises when she noticed small movements of objects in her vicinity. Vasiliev, *without warning*, got her to try influencing the needle of a compass and when, by holding her hands over the compass she got the needle turning, her career as a PK subject was launched, and from then on it became the focus of interest. Her principal investigator was G.A. Sergeyev, a neurophysiologist and EEG expert at the Utomsky Institute of Physiology in Leningrad. Sergeyev was specially interested in the physiological changes that could be observed in Kulagina's brain and body while she concentrated on trying to move some target object.

It was said that the sheer effort she had to make to achieve even some quite small effect seriously affected her health. It is tempting to contrast her performance with that of the physical mediums of an earlier period who, so far as one can now judge, could produce much larger effects with apparent ease, usually in a trance. At all events, at an international parapsychological conference in Moscow, in June 1968, Sergeyev showed a film of Kulagina in action which much impressed the foreign delegates.

Very few foreign visitors got round to testing Kuleshova while she was active[55] but a concerted effort was now made by a number of foreign parapsychologists (not only from America and Britain but also from Finland and Czechoslovakia) to get to grips with this new and challenging phenomenon. Unfortunately the regime at that time (it was the year that Russia invaded Czechoslovakia) was very much in two minds as to the advisability of encouraging parapsychology, and all requests from foreigners (even those that had official backing from American or West German authorities) to be allowed to carry out their own investigations of her were met with the icy retort that 'parapsychology is not studied in the Soviet Union'. Nothing daunted, the foreign visitors, among whom J.G. Pratt was, perhaps, the most assiduous, [56] persisted in visiting Leningrad where Kulagina was duly brought to their hotel rooms which then had to serve as improvised laboratories. There Kulagina would perform feats such as making small objects move across a table or depressing the heavier of two pans of a balance. A peculiarity first noted by Pratt was that cigarettes would be propelled along a table in the *vertical* position even when on a textured cloth! Attempts to achieve the same effect by sticking a pin into the cigarette and using a magnet would invariably cause the cigarette to topple. There is also evidence that Kulagina could produce a burn mark on a person's arm simply by touching them – it would then take some hours to heal – and that she could occasionally produce patterns on photosensitive material.

No serious evidence that Kulagina used trickery was ever forthcoming, although she was inevitably a focus for suspicion both in the Soviet Union and in the West. Unfortunately, Kulagina had few successors. Mention should be made, however, of Alla Vinogradova, a psychologist who worked at a Pedagogical Institute in Moscow. She was the wife of Viktor Adamenko, a physicist, who, after Naumov had been sent to a labour camp for being a nuisance to the authorities, became the leader of the Moscow parapsychologists. Like Kulagina, she too found that she could move lightweight objects in this unaccountable way. Moreover, she could do this without suffering the exhaustion that afflicted Kulagina. In March 1977, in what proved to be Kulagina's last public appearance, the two women joined forces in Moscow to demonstrate their abilities in front of the camera.[57]. In the West I know of only two claimants who arose in the wake of Kulagina[58] and their careers were short lived. Now that the barriers between Eastern Europe and the West have fallen, we can expect much closer collaboration between parapsychologists on either side, but what phenomena will be forthcoming remains to be seen.

<u>Ted Serios</u>[59]

Psychic photography entered the spiritualist movement during the 1860s as an added token from the deceased, and there were mediums who specialized in portraits of the sitter with 'spirit extras' appearing as an inset when a print was developed. However, it was even more open to suspicion than most mediumistic activities, as plates could easily be switched in the dark-room and other tricks used to fake the effects. Thoughtography, however, which has no bearing on the survival problem, must not be confused with psychic photography of the traditional spiritualist kind. The concept was introduced in the early years of this century by a Professor of Psychology at the Imperial University of Tokyo, Tomokichi Fukurai, who came upon the phenomenon while carrying out experiments in clairvoyance with a number of mainly female amateur sensitives. He discovered, at first by accident, that the target Japanese characters which they were attempting to ascertain clairvoyantly somehow became imprinted onto sensitive photographic plates. His findings, however, produced such a furore among his sceptical scientific colleagues that, in the end, he was forced to resign his post at the university and to discontinue his research. His book, describing his experiments, appeared in English in 1931.[60] Its title, *Clairvoyance and Thoughtography*, represents the first appearance of that word in the English language.

The next case of thoughtography in the history of parapsychology came about through the unlikely agency of a Chicago bellhop of no intellectual pretensions, one Ted Serios. He, together with a fellow bellhop, had taken to using hypnosis in the hope of conjuring up an image of lost treasure which they might then try to discover. Somehow a camera was brought into the proceedings and it was then that Ted, ostensibly under hypnosis, produced his first thoughtographs. Although these activities began to attract the attention of a number of fringe groups, and although Ted was even given a going-over at the Polaroid Corporation of Chicago, his career might well have petered out had not Freda Morris, a graduate psychology student of the Illinois Institute of Technology, brought him, in March 1964, to the attention of Jule Eisenbud. Eisenbud, a psychiatrist at the University of Colorado, Denver, was already well known for his interest in the paranormal.[61] For the next three years the Eisenbud household became Serios' home and one of the strangest episodes in the whole of parapsychological history was played out against a background of swelling publicity and fierce controversy.

This was the age of Polaroid photography which meant that one stage in the processing of conventional photographs, that involving the dark-room, one that had bedevilled traditional psychic photography, could now be eliminated. The set-up with Serios was as follows. The camera was loaded and held by Eisenbud (or whoever might be invited to act as experimenter on a given trial). Serios would sit peering into the lens and, when he was ready, would signal to the experimenter to trip the shutter. If, as so often happened, nothing out of the ordinary transpired, the result would be a photograph of Ted's face. What constituted a hit was the appearance on the photograph of something that could *not* be explained in straightforward optical terms. In the case of Serios, this usually amounted to a blurred but recognizable picture of buildings that were usually identifiable. Often these were located in the Chicago area but sometimes an internationally famous building, such as Westminster Abbey, would appear on the print. Occasionally figures, too, could be discerned but these were rare. Sometimes a target would be selected beforehand by Eisenbud as a theme for the ensuing thoughtograph, usually without informing Serios as to its nature, but the ensuing correspondence was seldom close. Ted, though good natured and willing, had a wayward personality that made him awkward to handle. Thus, in order to get him to perform at all, he had to be plied with drink, and sessions with Ted tended to become protracted and disorderly affairs.

However, in the course of his brief career, Serios performed on some several thousand trials in the course of which he produced about a thousand of these anomalous pictures in the presence of at least a hundred different observers who had been invited to act as witnesses.[62] Most of these were scientists and academics, some had expertise in conjuring, one was a professional magician. While most of the formal testing was done in Denver, at the Medical School of the University of Colorado, Serios accepted an invitation from Ian Stevenson and Gaither Pratt of the University of Virginia to visit them in Charlottesville. There he underwent investigation in the spring of 1967 with some positive results and returned for a further round of testing, but with less success, in 1968.[63]

When a psychic develops bad habits, should these be corrected even at the risk of putting him off his stroke? Even before he met Eisenbud, Serios had got into the habit of using a short tube through which to peer into the lens before giving the order for the shutter to be released. He told Eisenbud that he would not insist on using it but it made him feel more comfortable. As he could see no harm in it, Eisenbud decided to humour him and let him have his way.[64] It was a decision he lived to rue. Critics fastened on this 'gismo', as it soon came to be called, as the weak point in the chain. It was known that an image can be projected onto film from a small optical device, incorporating a lens and a microfilm or transparency, if held directly in front of the camera lens, and that such a device could produce results similar to those that Serios was producing. Could it be that Ted's gismo was indeed concealing just such an optical device? The fact that he never refused to be searched, or that the gismo was usually kept by another experimenter up to the moment when he needed it, did not suffice to allay suspicion. Unfortunately, the one test that would have proved conclusive, had the outcome been positive, namely placing secretly an opaque cover *behind* the camera lens, was *never* tried – which is odd seeing that the sensitive plates onto which Fukurai's subjects projected *their* images were securely wrapped.

There were, all the same, some formidable objections to this counter-explanation (the only serious counter-explanation ever to be mooted) which Eisenbud duly spelt out. As he puts it:

the question of whether or not Ted could have used a gimmick of some sort to produce his effects is largely academic, since more than three dozen pictures were obtained with Ted at varying distances from the cameras and gismos operated by others. These were obtained at nine different locations on twelve occasions over a period of about fifteen months from March 4, 1965 to May 25, 1966. Besides myself thirteen persons other than Ted held and triggered the camera on these occasions.[65]

It can easily be shown that, for such an optical device to be effective, it must be held in close proximity to the lens.

However, the idea that 'thoughtography' might be a reality was not something which the sceptical community could readily tolerate and no effort was spared to discredit Eisenbud and to demolish Serios. Nemesis arrived on 3 June 1967, in the shape of a weekend visit from the staff of *Popular Photography*.[66] David Eisendrath and Charles Reynolds were professional photographers and amateur conjurors and (though no mention was made of it in the article they subsequently published) they were accompanied by a distinguished academic, Persi Diaconis, a statistician who was also an expert conjuror and well known as an opponent of belief in the paranormal. Very little of a paranormal nature transpired that weekend, although a few puzzling photographs were produced. However, the visitors succeeded in goading Serios sufficiently so that, at one point, just before the team were about to depart, he refused to hand over his gismo arguing, not without logic, that since he had not been producing anything paranormal, there was no need to do so. Eventually, Eisenbud persuaded him not to let his momentary cussedness ruin his career, but it was too late. By then his inquisitors declared that they were no longer interested. Yet, however trivial the incident, it was all that *Popular Photography* needed to publish a report suggesting that Serios was hiding a device in his pocket,[67] even though they acknowledged that they had failed during their visit to detect any evidence of fraud on Ted's part. It was enough, however, to give the sceptical community what they needed. Word went round that Serios had been found out and piles of copies of Eisenbud's now discredited book were duly returned to the publishers for pulping from booksellers all over the United States.

Even so, Ted's self-destructive behaviour would not have mattered in the long run had he been able to continue producing images on film. Two weeks later, however, on 15 June, Serios produced what was to prove his final 'thoughtograph' (at any rate the last unambiguous result to be produced under proper conditions). It was, fittingly enough, an image of curtains! After that, although Serios would still occasionally produce anomalous effects, e.g. 'whities' (where the print comes out white all over) or 'blackies' (where the print comes out all black all over) the power to produce discernible images had deserted him.

It was widely assumed by the general public that Serios never recovered from the humiliation of the *Popular Photography* weekend. According to Eisenbud, however, some private disappointment in his love-life which just happened to coincide with that event was the real cause of Ted's decline. Whatever the explanation, with Ted out of the running, conjurors like James Randi were free to boast with impunity that they could do everything that Serios had done. [68] Soon Serios was forgotten by the public, like any pop-star who has had his day, but, for those who had studied the case, the mystery remained. Unhappily, Serios had no successors. The few claimants who did surface in his wake never persevered long enough to establish their claims[69] and so, gradually, thoughtography dropped out of the parapsychological agenda.

Uri Geller[70]

It is not easy to write factually about Geller inasmuch as with no other psychic of modern times is it harder to separate fact from fiction or to decide whether to treat him as an ingenious entertainer or as a genuine purveyor of the paranormal.

Moreover, Geller himself seems to relish this ambiguity. Indeed, the strongest argument for doubting his powers is not that some conjurors can perform similar feats but that, if he is what he claims to be, it would be relatively simple to put the matter beyond all reasonable doubt were he to submit to a sustained programme of research.[71]

As with all 'miracle workers', stories about their childhood are best disregarded. Geller was born in Tel Aviv in 1946; he is reputed to have served in a paratroop regiment during the Six Day War of 1967; but his entry into parapsychological history starts when an American, Andrija Puharich, went to Israel in August 1972 to meet Geller who was then making his début as an entertainer. Puharich was an inventor who had a number of patents to his credit in the field of medical aids including a miniaturized hearing-aid. But he was one of those who are obsessed with miracles and miracle-workers. Eileen Garrett had worked with him on telepathic experiments and, later, he became fascinated by the famous Brazilian healer and psychic surgeon, José Arigo. When Arigo was then killed in a car crash, in January 1971, Puharich was devastated. It was then that Puharich recalled a letter he had received from an Israeli army officer in 1970, describing the extraordinary powers of a certain young Israeli, and he duly decided that the time had come for him to act. The trouble with Puharich was that, not only had he embraced the paranormal long before he ever met Geller, but he was also a firm believer in current extraterrestrial mythology. The biography of Geller which he published in 1974 is an unabashed attempt to present Uri as some kind of new messiah specially selected by extraterrestrial intelligences to redeem mankind.[72]

Be that as it may, Puharich's decision to bring Uri to the United States, where he was duly introduced to Edgar Mitchell, the astronaut,[73] to Wernher von Braun, the rocket pioneer, and to various scientists with an interest in the paranormal, was the impetus that was soon to make Geller a media sensation. However, even before he left for the States, Geller paid a brief visit to Germany where he met and impressed Freidbert Karger, of the Max Planck Institute of plasma physics in Munich – to much attendant publicity.

Geller is by now so well *known* that it seems almost superfluous to describe what he actually *does*. In fact his repertoire covers both divisions of psi phenomena. With respect to ESP, his usual task was to try reproducing a drawing which someone else had prepared. With respect to PK, his standard task was to bend metal objects, such as cutlery, merely by stroking them. It was this latter feat that is now indelibly associated with his name. It was a novelty which had played no previous part in the history of psychical research (or in the history of conjuring for that matter) but it was soon to be copied by numerous other claimants, mostly children, and it is this phenomenon that we shall refer to, hereinafter, as 'the geller effect'.

As it happens, however, it was Geller's ESP pretensions that first induced the scientific community to pay attention to him. In August 1973 Geller visited the Stanford Research Institute at Menlo Park (SRI) where physicists Russell Targ and Harold Puthoff had been engaged in their remote-viewing studies, as discussed earlier in this chapter. In the formal experiment, Geller was put into a sound-proof isolation chamber and the target drawings were prepared elsewhere (in one instance by a computer). In all, some 13 such targets were used but in only 10 did Geller provide a response drawing. The quality of these responses varied from a perfect fidelity in one instance (the target was a bunch of grapes) to a vague correspondence in others, but, when submitted to an independent judge, whose task was to match, blind, each of Geller's drawings, or set of drawings, with one or other of the target drawings, two such judges succeeded in doing so without error (the *a priori* probability of one perfect match, corresponds to odds of approximately a million to one).

In due course, this study was published in *Nature* for 18 October 1974. It is very rare that *Nature* consents to publish parapsychological findings of any sort but, as explained in an editorial in that issue, so much publicity had already accompanied this investigation and so many unfounded claims had been made for Geller himself that, as they put it: 'The publication of this paper, with its muted claims, suggestions of a limited research programme, and modest data, is, we believe, likely to put the whole matter in more reasonable perspective.'[74] Actually, *Nature* had been pre-empted by one day by the magazine *New Scientist* which devoted most of that week's issue to a withering account of Geller in general and the SRI investigation in particular. An ingenious counter-explanation was offered: perhaps Geller, benefiting from Puharich's patent miniaturized hearing-aid, had such a device implanted in a tooth? (A subsequent dental examination to which Geller submitted revealed no such implant).[75] In due course, other suggestions were made throwing doubt upon the impregnability of the isolation chamber and raising the possibility that some member of Geller's entourage might have been able to signal to him a description of the target drawing.[76] The authors, Targ and Puthoff, never retracted their claims but it became obvious that, short of a sustained research programme to which Geller would never consent, his alleged ESP abilities would remain controversial.

In the course of the next few years, Geller visited most of the countries outside the Communist bloc and duly appeared on their television screens. Two consequences of these appearances regularly ensued: scores of viewers would phone in to say that, following his appearance, they had discovered bent cutlery in their own homes or watches and clocks which had previously refused to go had now started up (this too was part of Geller's repertoire)[77] and, secondly, scores of children, having watched Geller, found that they, too, were metal-benders! These consequences were especially notable following Geller's visit to Britain in November 1973. Two

British scientists, not previously connected with psychical research, became interested in Geller and in these 'mini-gellers' (as such children came to be known): John Taylor, Professor of Applied Mathematics at King's College, London, and John Hasted, Professor of Physics at Birkbeck College, London.

One of the tests which Taylor devised for Geller is described by him as follows:

> A brass strip about 20 cm long was taped horizontally to the platform of a balance [of the type used to weigh letters and parcels]. The major portion of the strip extended out from the platform, and Geller stroked the top surface of it while I measured, directly by reading the scale, and by using an automatic recording device, the pressure he was applying. At the end of the test the strip had acquired a bend of ten degrees although Geller had at no time applied more than half an ounce (20 gm) of pressure. It is out of the question that such a small pressure could have produced that deflection. What is more, the actual bending occurred *upward – against* the pressure of the finger [author's italics]. Earlier, another subject gave a similar result, producing, with less than an ounce of pressure, a small upward deflection (two degrees) on a strip of copper. While Geller was doing this we found it a little disconcerting, to say the least, to have the needle, which indicated the amount of pressure on the balance, also bending, as it moved, through seventy degrees.[78]

Could Geller have distracted Taylor's attention long enough to produce the upward bend of the strip or the outward bend of the dial-needle without his noticing anything amiss? And could the unnamed mini-geller have done the same? We shall now never know. Having published his best-selling *Superminds* in 1975, describing his work with Geller and with his mini-gellers, Taylor underwent a change of heart. Whether he had been got at by his fellow scientists or whether he lost interest when he discovered that electromagnetic radiation was not, after all, the answer to the mystery of PK or ESP we can only speculate. At all events, he retracted his earlier endorsement of the paranormal and, in 1980, published *Science and the Supernatural* in which he allies himself with the sceptics.[79] Sadly, he never ventures to tell us how he *now* thinks that Geller fooled him into thinking that that brass strip had bent paranormally.

John Hasted, on the other hand, never repudiated his endorsement of Geller or of the mini-gellers although it was, perforce, with the latter that he did most of his research. In 1981 Hasted published his report on the geller effect in his book, *The Metal-Benders*, in which he explains why he stuck to his guns.[80] The advent of the mini-gellers was a sharp reminder to us all that children can be as cunning and as devious as their elders. Few of the mini-gellers were successful when asked to perform under satisfactory conditions of observation and some were even caught *in flagrante* by concealed cameras.[81] Since the geller-effect usually involves stroking the metal object, one way in which Hasted sought to counter the possibility that force was being used was to use a bar made of a special alloy which, though soft and elastic in appearance, is in fact brittle and, if bent quickly, would snap. Although this ruse was kept a close secret for a long time, none of his mini-gellers contrived to break the brittle specimen.[82] Hasted's main contribution to the field, however, was his introduction of the strain-gauge to detect micro-bending in a target specimen. The advantage of this technique was that the child did not need to touch the object at all and, indeed, the effects might register while the child was playing and merely willing the target to bend. The disadvantage was the difficulty of convincing doubters that the flips seen on the polygraph recording of the strain-gauge were actually due to such micro-PK rather than to some electrical artefact in the atmosphere. The technique does however offer great scope for a new approach to the study of micro-PK that has advantages over the standard technique using REGs. The term PKMB (PK metal-bending) has now joined the parapsychological vocabulary.[83]

One country where the mini-gellers flourished was Italy. Between 1975 and 1978, Ferdinando Basani, a physicist at the University of Bologna, carried out a series of tests on a selected number of these 'gellerini' whose families had brought them to the attention of the *Bologna Centro Studi Parapsicologi*. Although a number of seemingly paranormal events were observed, Basani's main contribution to the field was to devise a method whereby the children could operate in private, using built-in safeguards which would at once reveal if there had been any cheating. Thus, metal objects would be inserted into elaborately sealed glass jars which would also contain coloured powders so that even shaking the jar would expose illicit tampering. Two professional conjurors who were consulted approved the experimental design. Yet a number of positive results were still forthcoming.[84] It seems a pity that the children were not also monitored by a video-camera (concealed if necessary) but this omission was not so much an oversight as an acknowledgement of the arcane idea of the 'camera-shy' subject.

There were only two adults who, in the wake of the Geller craze, attracted the attention of researchers: one a Parisian, Jean-Pierre Girard,[85] the other a Swiss, a resident of Berne, Silvio Meyer. Girard is described as a medical technician, Silvio (as he was known professionally) as a graphic artist. Both men are credited with conjuring skills. Girard is important mainly because he attracted the attention of a metallurgist, Charles Crussard, who worked for the large firm of Pechiney Ugine Kuhlmann of Paris. Crussard studied not only evidence of both macro- and micro-PK metal-bending but, as a metallurgist, he was also interested in comparing the micro-structure of specimens treated by

Girard with control specimens. His investigation at the Pechiney laboratories at which a number of independent witnesses had been present, including a professional conjuror, is described in a paper by Crussard and Bouvaist in the *Revue Métallurgie* for February 1978. Crussard's work has, of course, been attacked[86] but it has not been invalidated.

Silvio, whose career as a metal-bender began in 1974 after seeing Geller on TV, was never as closely studied as Girard. He was, however, investigated by Hans Bender who was duly impressed,[87] as also by Hans Betz, a Professor of Physics at the University of Munich. Silvio was, I believe, unique among metal-benders in claiming, on occasion, to be able to *coalesce* the broken pieces of a given metal object! Of course, neither Silvio nor Girard were always able to deliver the goods and, when they failed, critics were only too ready to claim that they had outsmarted them. Meanwhile Geller's own career had taken a new turn. Sir Val Duncan, Chairman of Rio Tinto Zinc, met Geller at a party in 1973 and urged him to take up dowsing for minerals. Sir Val died two years later but Geller heeded his advice and, as he began to tire of the entertainment business, he devoted himself increasingly to dowsing at the behest of industrialists who were willing to pay his sizeable fee.[88] But these commercial activities made the problem of a scientific evaluation even more remote. Geller still sometimes appears on TV, but when he does oblige with some metal-bending, it is no longer with the same flair that first made him celebrated. The geller-effect still crops up from time to time but, whether it will become a permanent feature of parapsychological research remains to be seen. For a brief period in the mid-seventies Geller succeeded in putting the paranormal squarely on the map for perhaps the first time in living memory but, as had so often happened before in the history of parapsychology, the phenomena declined, leaving a trail of question-marks as their legacy.

MODERN SURVIVAL RESEARCH

The hope that psychical research might cast some light on the age-old question of an after-life inspired the work of some of its foremost pioneers. During the second half of this century, however, survival research can no longer be considered part of the cutting-edge of parapsychology. Various reasons may be adduced for its decline. The spiritualists, for their part, were by now satisfied that their case had been made, while the parapsychologists no longer needed mediums to produce the phenomena they wished to study. Spiritualism, in any case, had lost the dynamism of its early days and good mediums had become rare. Some parapsychologists, like Rhine, argued that, until we knew more about the limits of psi, it was pointless to pursue the survival hypothesis since the possibility of a this-worldly interpretation of the relevant findings could never be excluded; 'super-psi', as it came to be known, could always be invoked to exclude 'theta psi'[89]

Yet the question persisted and there were always some enthusiasts who insisted on seeking an answer. During the 1960s and 1970s two new developments occurred which did much to revitalize the flagging corpus of survival research. The first that we shall discuss concerns those who *would* have died had they not been resuscitated, usually with the help of modern medical techniques. The accounts they give of the experiences which they underwent during this critical interval when they were adjudged clinically dead, invite the speculation that they were having a brief preview of that after-life that may awaits us all. The second development that we shall then consider concerns the possibility that the after-life might be lived out in *this*, our familiar world. Although alien to orthodox Judaeo-Christian or Moslem teachings, belief in reincarnation can be found everywhere and is, of course, a key element of the Hindu and Buddhist traditions. Yet, curiously, it was not until the 1960s that reincarnation first became a topic for serious systematic research, thanks to the efforts of one dedicated individual. The empirical evidence for the reincarnation hypothesis derived from two quite different sources: (*a*) memories of a previous life obtained from adults under hypnosis and (*b*) memories of a previous life given spontaneously by a very young child. The former are the more suspect, however, being more vulnerable to fantasy or cryptomnesia. The latter, though not unproblematic, has, in the event, provided the more impressive evidence.

There were other novel approaches to the survival problem which exploited modern technology. Enthusiasts have claimed, for example, that mysterious voices can be captured on a tape-recorder that is left running, and that such voices represent an attempt by discarnate entities to communicate with the living. More recently still, images of the deceased are said to have been spotted on a television screen. But all such claims must, for the time being, be classed as pertaining more to 'fringe parapsychology' than to mainstream parapsychological research and so will be omitted from consideration here.[90]

The near-death experience (NDE)[91]

In 1975, Raymond Moody, then a prospective psychiatrist and erstwhile philosophy lecturer, published a brief volume of case-histories which had come to his notice of persons who, having been rescued from the brink of death, described vivid experiences which they had undergone during this interval. Moreover, such experiences were, overwhelmingly, of a blissful or transcendental nature and seemed to exercise a profound influence on the patient's subsequent attitude to life. To his own and to his publishers astonishment his book, *Life after Life*, rapidly became a best-seller and, two years later, he brought out a brief sequel, *Reflections on Life after Life*. For obvious reasons it is exceedingly rare to discover, as Moody did, a new psychological phenomenon. For, although earlier accounts in the medical literature have since been noted, it would be true to say that the NDE was unknown to the public at large before Moody drew attention to it. And yet we now know that almost half of those who are resuscitated after having been declared clinically dead are able to recall such experiences and, thanks to improvements in techniques of resuscitation, there are increasing numbers of such cases. The explanation for the earlier reticence of those who underwent the experience seems to be the fear of ridicule or misunderstanding. However, once medical personnel started to show an interest in what they had to relate, accounts were forthcoming.

Moody's approach had been unashamedly anecdotal but, having made his case, it was not long before others followed on a more systematic basis. Of special importance was the work of Kenneth Ring, a Professor of Psychology at the University of Connecticut. His book, *Life at Death*, which appeared in 1980 and carries a brief introduction by Moody, is based on an interview survey of some 102 individuals who had come close to death, of whom 49 (48 percent) were able to recall an experience of some kind. On the basis of these reports, Ring was able to tabulate a succession of stages making up a complete NDE with declining numbers falling in each successive stage.

The first stage, described by Ring as one of 'peace and the sense of well-being', was experienced by nearly 60 per cent of his potential sample of 49. Here it was as if all their fears, worries and frustrations had, at a stroke, been banished. The second stage involves the out-of-body or autoscopic experience, a special kind of hallucination in which the self appears to be separated from the physical body and to be looking down on it from a point near the ceiling. There is a huge literature on the out-of-body experience (OBE) which, though it was first brought to the attention of the scientific world by psychical researchers, does not necessarily have any paranormal implications and may arise in a variety of situations that are by no means related to the near-death experience.[92] About 37 per cent of Ring's sample graduated to this stage during which they claim that their sight and hearing became exceptionally acute while, at the same time, their attitude became strangely detached, considering the dire condition of their body and the emergency it was undergoing.

Ring's third stage, which he calls 'entering the darkness', involves the much discussed tunnel-effect. Some 23 per cent of his respondents reported entering a dark tunnel or black vastness. The experience is mostly described as pleasant, and as if laden with the promise of leading them away from their earthbound miseries and towards some heavenly abode. The final stage, that of 'entering the light' was reported by only 10 per cent of his sample, but it is this aspect of the NDE that brings it closest to traditional notions of heaven. Thus we find phrases such as a 'glorious pool of light' coupled with allusions to beautiful gardens or meadows and, sometimes, enriched by an encounter with a religious figure such as Christ, or more commonly by a meeting with deceased members of the patient's family. This last feature is reminiscent of the earlier literature dealing with deathbed visions.[93] Finally Ring discusses two other common features of the NDE, (*a*) the panoramic life-review, whereby the whole of the subject's past life passes in a flash through the mind and (*b*) the decision which has to be confronted whether or not to go back into the ailing body and continue the struggle.

A still more extensive corroborative study was carried out by a cardiologist, Michael Sabom, who published his findings in 1982. Between 1976 and 1981 he interviewed some 116 individuals who were known to have experienced the NDE, although in many cases it had occurred many years earlier. They were of diverse backgrounds and covered a wide range with respect to age, occupation, religious affiliation, etc., but, though only a small minority had had any previous knowledge of the phenomenon, their accounts were remarkably similar and follow essentially the lines expounded by Ring. Their prior religious outlook seems to have made little difference to the nature of their experience. Sabom pays special attention to six cases where the NDE occurs during surgery and is struck by the circumstantial accounts which the patient, thanks to such autoscopy, was subsequently able to give of what had gone on inside the operating theatre, or even, sometimes, elsewhere.

During the 1980s interest in the NDE burgeoned. In 1982 George Gallup published the findings of a Gallup poll on some 1,500 randomly selected American adults and found that some 3.5 per cent reported having had a NDE, a much higher figure than was expected.[94] An International Association for Near Death Studies (IANDS) was founded with branches in the USA and in Britain, and its own specialist journal, *Anabiosis* (later the *Journal of Near-Death Studies*). Soon the NDE had become a springboard for far flung speculations of a metaphysical or religious nature. One consequence of all this was to remove the NDE from the agenda of mainstream parapsychology and to pass it on to the medical community who were, of course, best placed to conduct the necessary empirical investigations or to those with religious interests.

As far as survival, as such, was concerned, the NDE could not, in the nature of the case, afford anything like direct proof, for the experient is, after all, still in the body, however much the brain may be temporarily incapacitated. Nevertheless, its claim to afford some support for a survivalist position rests on two counts. First, it seems to support a dualist interpretation of the mind–brain relationship – one can say, at any rate, that no such phenomenon would ever have been predicted, let alone one as vivid or with such distinctive features, given only what we know about the brain or about the psychophysiology of comatose states. Moreover, the difficulty of providing a reductionist interpretation becomes insuperable if we are prepared to acknowledge the para-psychological aspects of the NDE although, in the nature of the case, these are difficult to prove and have been hotly contested. Secondly, there is by now overwhelming evidence to show that the NDE can be a powerful spiritual experience. Those who have undergone such an experience tend thereafter to lead more meaningful and more compassionate lives as well as losing their erstwhile fear of death. The expectations that it generates concerning another world may be only illusory but they are remarkably consistent.[95]

There were, however, some considerations which pointed to a more mundane interpretation, and attempts to explain the phenomenon along either psychological or physiological lines followed hard upon the predominantly survivalist interpretations favoured by such pioneers as Moody or Sabom. For one thing, it could be shown that the NDE may be triggered by the *expectation* of imminent death, as opposed to its *actual* imminence.[96] Foremost among the advocates of the psychological approach was Russell Noyes who saw the NDE as primarily a reaction of the ego in the face of imminent extinction. He treats it as a case of 'depersonalization'. One part of the self contrives to split itself off and become a passive observer of what is happening to the organism that is now at risk.[97] On the physiological level much has been made of the effects of oxygen starvation (anoxia) on the brain as a cause of the hallucinations but, while the NDE is indeed an hallucination, it is its special thematic *content* that is of interest, rather than its causation. However, an attempt has been made to account for the experience of the tunnel in terms of processes in the visual cortex which could be triggered by such a lack of oxygen.[98]

At present, then, there is no agreement as to whether the NDE does have paranormal features, let alone whether it provides evidence for an after-life. However, as a phenomenon it still provokes interest, and parapsychology can only gain from further efforts to penetrate its mystery.

Reincarnation

Hypnotic regression

Morey Bernstein was a Colorado businessman whose hobby was hypnotism. He also took an interest in the paranormal and had visited Rhine at Duke University. By 1952 he had, in the course of the past ten years, hypnotized some hundreds of volunteers. He had often attempted hypnotic regression to early childhood but in that year a friend drew his attention to the exciting possibility of regressing one's subject to a period *prior* to birth, if only to see whether an account would be forthcoming of a previous existence. There was, of course, nothing new in this idea: it was familiar to hypnotists and psychical researchers in the late nineteenth century.[99] Now hypnotism is a treacherous tool even when it is used to retrieve ordinary memories since, if the hypnotized person cannot reproduce a veridical account,he or she, always motivated to oblige in that condition, will tend to confabulate one – which is why evidence obtained in this way is treated as suspect in a court of law. Likewise, hypnotically induced regression to childhood is now regarded more as a case of simulation than of an actual reliving of past episodes. Even more so, then, in the light of all we know about hypnosis, must the practice of pre-birth regression be viewed as an open invitation to the subject to fantasize. Hence, only if there is exceptionally strong evidence that more is involved than just fantasy or buried memories, are we entitled to consider the possibility of a prior existence or, at any rate, of paranormal retrocognition.

Nevertheless Bernstein, undaunted, decided to have a go, using as his subject a young woman who had previously shown herself to be capable of entering a deep level of hypnosis. Mrs Virginia Tighe (née Burns), who lived with her husband in Pueblo (where the Bernsteins lived), was then aged 29. The first session at which a pre-birth regression was attempted took place on 29 November 1952, and the sixth and final session occurred on 29 August 1953. In the course of these six sessions, by dint of appropriate questioning, a life was pieced together of an Irishwoman, Bridget Kathleen Murphy, known as Bridey Murphy, who had been born in Cork in 1798 and who died, childless, in Belfast in 1864. She was, she said, the daughter of a Duncan Murphy of Cork, a lawyer and a Protestant, and at the age of 20 was married to Sean Brian Joseph McCarthy, the son of a Catholic lawyer of Cork. The couple then moved to Belfast where her husband eventually taught law at Queen's University.

Bernstein was impressed by the sheer amount of circumstantial detail he was able to elicit concerning life in nineteenth-century Ireland – seeing that Virginia herself was brought up in Chicago and never took any special interest in Irish affairs. So, although he made no attempt to verify the information he had gleaned, he decided that the case was worth publishing and the book, *The Search for Bridey Murphy*, duly appeared in January 1956 using a discrete pseudonym, 'Ruth Simmons', for its protagonist.[100] To everyone's surprise, for there was nothing exciting or colourful in the tale itself, the book proved to be a best-seller. This had two consequences. On the one hand it inspired numerous imitators, spawning a large and mostly worthless literature, on the other hand it provoked strenuous attempts to rubbish it. For the idea of reincarnation was not only a challenge to the sceptics, it was also anathema to religious orthodoxy. Indeed both Virginia's own family and that of her husband were hostile to the claims being made for her.

Even before the book appeared, some accounts of the case had appeared in magazines and, soon after its publication, the *Chicago American* ran a series of debunking articles on the case, in May and June 1956, seeking to show that there was nothing there that Virginia (alias Ruth) could not have picked up from Irish neighbours during her childhood in Chicago. Undoubtedly, in the vast majority of such cases, this 'cryptomnesia' would, indeed, be the most plausible explanation. In this instance, however, the suggestions put forward by the *Chicago American*, though they achieved wide currency, and indeed are still sometimes cited when the case comes up for consideration, turn out to be baseless.[101] At all events, the *Denver Post* decided to send its reporter William J. Barker to Ireland to see if he could track down the historical Bridey Murphy, if such there was, and, in March 1956 it duly published a twelve-page supplement under the title 'The Truth about Bridey Murphy'. It was largely thanks to the efforts of Barker that the case still has to be taken seriously. For while, on the one hand, Barker never succeeded in identifying either Bridey Murphy herself, her father or her husband (either because they never existed or because of the lack of public records in the Ireland of that period), yet he was able to verify *some* of the information she had provided. Thus she had mentioned buying provisions in Belfast from two grocers, Farr's and John Carrigan. The Belfast Chief Librarian duly discovered a directory of 1865–66 in which these names are listed as being those of two grocers. And there are many other such veridical details in the record. For example, at one point during a session Virginia has a fit of sneezing and 'Bridey' calls for 'a linen'. It transpires that, in the Belfast of that time, a handkerchief *was* commonly known as 'a linen'. Again, she mentions at one point an improbable twopenny coin and again it transpires that such a coin *was* in use in Ireland from 1797 to 1850.[102]

The fairest verdict would seem to be that, while there are no firm facts that would entitle us to conclude that there ever *was* such a person as Bridey Murphy, it certainly does look as if, in the hypnotic state, Virginia did acquire knowledge about a certain time and place in a way that defies normal reckoning. Moreover, this seems to be a regular feature of subsequent cases of this kind which crop up in the post-Bridey Murphy literature. For example, Ian Stevenson has paid particular attention to evidence of xenoglossy that may arise where the previous personality belonged to a different language community. By 'xenoglossy' here is meant the ability to speak and to understand a language which the subject had never learnt. Stevenson presents detailed evidence on three such cases which he had studied in depth, each showing knowledge of another time and place that would be difficult to explain normally. Yet in none of these cases was he able to identify, from available records, the previous personality.[103]

Britain did not escape the reincarnation vogue that followed the publication of *The Search for Bridey Murphy*. The foremost British exponent was Arnall Bloxham who had a practice in Cardiff and became President of the British Society of Hypnotherapists in 1972. His star subject was a woman to whom he gave the pseudonym Jane Evans, but whose actual identity he never revealed – a commendable clinical discretion but an unfortunate impediment to serious research. She luxuriated in no less than six past lives including a tutor's wife in Roman Britain, a Jewess in twelfth-century York and a servant to a nobleman in fifteenth-century France.[104] Subsequent research, however, has dealt harshly with most of the cases based on the Bloxham tapes and, at least in the case of the Roman episode, the particulars are so close to those of a published historical novel (*Living Wood* by Louis de Wohl) that it is impossible to doubt that the pseudonymous Jane Evans must have come across it at some point during her waking life.[105]

The most recent case of this sort to figure in the serious literature is one we owe to Linda Tarazi, a clinical psychologist of Illinois. Her subject, Laurel Dilmen (LD) had originally become interested in hypnosis during the mid-1970s as a means for controlling weight or countering headaches. But, by then, past life regressions were already in vogue and LD showed a flair for producing plausible but obviously fictitious lives pertaining to a wide variety of historical backgrounds. There was, however, one particular historical character to which she constantly reverted and which seemed more and more to obsess her, that of a Spanish woman of the late sixteenth century whom she called Antonia (Antonia Michaela Maria Ruiz de Prado). Much of Antonia's life had centred upon the town of Cuenca in Spain where she ran into some trouble with the Inquisition. This was not, however, a case of xenoglossy. Although the Spanish pronunciation was said to be good, in fact little Spanish was spoken. Furthermore, the travels and adventures she recounts as 'Antonia' are so reminiscent of popular historical romances that Tarazi could well have been forgiven had she decided not to pursue the matter further. On the other hand her subject did come up with such a wealth of detailed information about such obscure persons and places that, in the end, Tarazi's curiosity got the upper hand. She then devoted some three years to the necessary research, travelling to Spain, North Africa and the Caribbean, visiting libraries and consulting historians, as a result of which she was able to verify over 100 obscure facts or names, some of them from archival sources, and, surprisingly, uncovered no errors. The result would appear to rule out the possibility that LD could have acquired this information in any normal way. LD identified herself so strongly with her heroine that she, at any rate, was satisfied that it *was* indeed a case of reincarnation, even though the identity of Antonia herself was never established. From our point of view it looks as if we have here yet another case, like that of Bridey Murphy, where paranormally acquired knowledge is woven into the life of a presumably fictitious historical character.[106]

Before we leave the question of hypnotic regression, it is worth noting that so called 'past-life therapy' has featured to some extent in the practice of various quite reputable psychotherapists. However, the parapsychological question, whether the past life episode recounted by the patient under hypnosis is fact or fiction, is secondary to the practical therapeutic question as to whether such a reliving of experiences, be they real or imaginary, contributes significantly to the patient's recovery.[107]

Children's memories of a past life[108]

In 1960 Ian Stevenson, then Chairman of the Department of Psychiatry of the University of Virginia School of Medicine, who had already a long-standing interest in psychical research, won the prize, in an essay competition organized by the American Society for Psychical Research, for his essay, 'The evidence for survival from claimed memories of former incarnations', which was then duly published in the Society's journal.[109] He concluded his essay by suggesting that 'Further investigation of apparent memories of former incarnations may well establish reincarnation as the most probable explanation of these experiences', adding 'In mediumistic communications we have the problem of proving that someone clearly dead still lives. In evaluating apparent memories of former incarnations, the problem consists of judging whether someone clearly living once died.' At the time, however, Stevenson little thought that he himself was going to be the one who would eventually put reincarnation firmly on the parapsychological agenda.

However, his essay came to the attention of Eileen Garrett, who approached him on behalf of the Parapsychology Foundation, asking him whether he would be willing to go to India and investigate a new case like those he had discussed in his essay. So, in August 1961, Stevenson made his first trip to India, where he spent about five weeks before going on to Ceylon (as Sri Lanka was still known). He took with him the addresses of persons connected with some of the cases that had figured in his essay. In 1966, following a second visit to India to check on the details of some of his cases, the American Society published his monograph *Twenty Cases Suggestive of Reincarnation*.[110] By then Stevenson had some 600 such cases on his files of which some 200 had been personally investigated by himself or his associates. The monograph soon attracted widespread interest and has been translated into some seven foreign languages. Thereafter, Stevenson, a scholar of international repute and one of the outstanding figures of modern parapsychology, devoted much of his time and energy to expanding and refining this line of inquiry. The aim was to make us aware of the claims – made for the most part by very young children, often to the consternation of the parents – to remember events connected with the life of someone who had died before that child was born.

By 1987, when Stevenson published his book *Children Who Remember Previous Lives*, addressed to a wider readership, he had published some 65 detailed case-reports and his files contained documentation on some 2,000 cases of variable quality. He was clearly now in a position to make certain broad generalizations about the characteristics of such cases. 'A child who is going to refer to a previous life' he tells us 'nearly always does so for the first time between the ages of two and five'. Unfortunately, between the ages of five and eight the children usually stop talking about their previous lives as they become more attuned to, or accepting of, their present situation, and only a few children retain these memories intact into their adult life. Moreover, as their verbal competence increases, so their imagery weakens which further obliterates their memories of the previous life which is usually retained in the form of images. As a result, by the time an investigator gets round to examining a case, much of the information that would initially have been available has been lost. Nevertheless, in most of the cases that he had investigated, Stevenson tells us, 'the informants have remembered between five and fifty separate statements that the child had made about the previous life'.[111]

Hopefully, these separate statements suffice to identify the person or family of the 'previous personality' and the investigator, if he or she is fortunate enough, can be present when the two families meet for the first time in the course of which various tests of recognition and identification can be arranged. For, in the great majority of cases which Stevenson has brought to light, the previous personality would have died only a few years before the present personality was born[112] and would have lived not too far away. Verbal memories, however, do not exhaust the case for identifying the present and previous personalities. Often the child will reveal strong behavioural anomalies indicative of his or her previous existence.[113] Thus, in those cases where a sex-change is involved, gender identity confusion may be expected or, where a child claims to have lived as a member of a different caste, class or ethnic group, this too may become apparent in its attitudes towards its present situation and family – an attitude that may well arouse strong resentment. But perhaps the strangest sort of evidence which crops up occurs in those cases where the previous personality died a violent death where the appearance of a birthmark corresponds with the wounds inflicted in the killing of the previous personality. Such stigmata are indeed puzzling enough on any hypothesis, paranormal or otherwise, yet since violent deaths figure prominently among some well-attested rebirth cases, birthmarks now constitute an important component of the general evidence for reincarnation.[114]

Of course, in many cases the identity of the previous personality is never established, either because the information provided by the child is insufficient or because of practical difficulties or because no such person existed. Hence, many of the cases recorded in Stevenson's files have to be classed as 'unsolved cases'. As an approach to the problem of survival, children's memories of a previous life has several grave disadvantages. In the first place, most of the best cases crop up in remote parts of the world not readily accessible to Western investigators and, even if the logistical problems of the kind familiar to an anthropologist, can be overcome, there is the linguistic barrier to contend with. So often the child or the witnesses have to be interrogated via interpreters. Secondly, by the time the researcher has been alerted to a given case it may be difficult to reconstruct what exactly the child was trying to say and to discount the overlay of interpretation that the family may have imposed on the original testimony. It is also disconcerting to find that the countries that have produced the best evidence for reincarnation are precisely those countries or those communities where belief in reincarnation is a strong component of the culture. Indeed, as Stevenson himself has pointed out, even the type of case tends to reflect cultural beliefs.[115] This does not invalidate the evidence since, as the history of parapsychology has taught us, the kind of phenomena one finds at any given time or place nearly always reflects cultural and situational expectations, yet may still be paranormal. Nevertheless, the investigator has to be on his or her guard against the risk of a 'pious fraud'.

Given so many formidable pitfalls that face the intending researcher, it is not perhaps surprising that so few, so far, have been tempted to take on the task, or that most of the good evidence comes from cases that have been investigated by, or at the behest of, one exceptional individual. The fact remains, nevertheless, that as a result of the Stevensonian initiative there now exists a sizeable body of literature which, on the face of it, confronts us with the case of a child struggling to tell us about a previous life on earth. Nothing that critics have suggested so far strikes me as providing a reasonable normal counter-explanation for this fact in more than a small number of marginal cases.[116] Whether this justifies our saying that the child *is*, indeed, one and the same person as the deceased, as Stevenson himself inclines to do, is a philosophical problem to which there is no single correct answer. The question of personal identity is one which philosophers have long debated but never resolved.[117] In the ordinary way, for legal and most other purposes, corporeal identity is all that counts. From the subjective standpoint, however, it is memory that links us to our past selves and anticipation that links us to our future selves. When we are dealing, as here, with the possibility of the same mind animating more than one body, the corporeal criterion is no longer applicable and so memory alone has to decide the issue. However, the most we are strictly entitled to claim is that we have here evidence of *extra-cerebral* memory coupled with such objective signs as behavioural peculiarities or physical signs such as birthmarks. This is not to deny that reincarnation is the simplest hypothesis which covers all these facts or, indeed, that we may eventually experience for ourselves such an awakening in an another body, as if after prolonged sleep. But we should not forget that there *are* other ways of conceptualizing the evidence than that which is pertinent to the question of survival as such.[118]

PHILOSOPHICAL PERSPECTIVES

We have now completed our survey of what we may call the evidential basis of parapsychology. In this final section we shall consider briefly some of the ways in which that evidence has been conceptualized. At the one extreme, there are those who urge us to jettison this whole enterprise and relegate it to the scrap-heap of discredited ideas, as with phrenology. A more constructive, albeit sceptical, alternative that has lately come to the fore, is to assimilate the evidence to the psychology of belief, more particularly to the psychology of deception, illusion, delusion, magical-thinking or other similar cognitive anomalies.[119] But, whatever the merits of such sceptical proposals, I shall here confine myself to those approaches that accept the reality of psi as their point of departure. The myriad theories that have, over the years, been put forward in this connection, can then, for convenience, be divided into two principal categories: (*a*) the physical or quasi-physical and (*b*) the transcendental. By a 'physical theory' I imply one that is compatible with contemporary physics and by 'quasi-physical' I mean one which *would* be compatible with physics, granted some extension of, or modification to, the existing paradigm. By a 'transcendental theory' I mean one which invokes another plane of reality, be it mental, spiritual, occult or whatever, over and above that of our mundane material existence.

Physical and quasi-physical theories[120]

In the two centuries during which the Newtonian world view went virtually unchallenged, although by no means all scientists abjured the paranormal, nevertheless there was little prospect of reconciling such phenomena with physics as then understood. By the end of the nineteenth century, however, when the SPR was being established, electromagnetism and the concept of a luminiferous ether began to make it seem more plausible that telepathy, at any rate, might yield to some such physical explanation. It was certainly no accident that so many eminent physicists served on the Society's Council during its formative years.

The electromagnetic theory of ESP, in one form or another, proved extraordinarily tenacious. Indeed, it still has its adherents.[121] Yet, for all that, it was never a viable option. For not only did it transpire that ESP could operate irrespective of distance, of intervening material barriers and perhaps even of temporal direction – in that messages could be transmitted backwards in time – it ignored the fact that the problem is not just about the transmission of energy, in whatever shape or form, but, more pointedly, about how *information* could be encoded at the transmitting end and decoded at the receiving end. We know, in general terms, what goes on when we converse with someone who understands our language, but how would we encode our *thoughts* or our *mental images* in the neural networks of our own brain if we are to make them decodable by another brain? One desperate answer is to suggest that brains can simply *resonate* with one another, without requiring *any* mediating signals – simply by virtue of their basic structural similarity.[122] But, while this may get round the transmission problem, it runs foul of the selectivity problem. Why should my brain resonate only with that of the one individual with whom I am in telepathic rapport? And, anyhow, what becomes of this explanation when there is no sender or receiver but just an object which must be ascertained clairvoyantly?

Of far greater significance for contemporary parapsychology were the theories inspired by the revolutions in twentieth-century physics. The new cosmology, based on quantum theory and relativity, was vastly different from that of the clockwork universe of classical physics. It was also much more open to speculations about the nature of paranormal phenomena. In the first place, modern physics involves hypotheses that are no less counter-intuitive than anything that the parapsychologist proposes. As Arthur Koestler put it: 'the seemingly fantastic propositions of parapsychology appear less preposterous in the light of the truly fantastic concepts of modern physics'.[123] In the second place, the new physics introduces a degree of interconnectedness which makes instantaneous communication at a distance no longer, at any rate, unthinkable.[124] One could even say that it echoes, in this respect, some of the features of the pre-Newtonian universe of the hermeticists that we touched upon in our first chapter.

Of these new-style theories the most successful and important from the point of view of generating empirical tests was the so-called 'Observational Theory'. It was formulated in a variety of different models but its point of departure was the so-called 'Copenhagen Interpretation' of quantum theory. However, since it goes beyond orthodox quantum theory, it belongs, provisionally at any rate, in the category of the *quasi*-physical. If it ever *were* to become an accepted feature of standard physics, parapsychology would truly have arrived as a science and psi phenomena could, thereafter, be classed as physical phenomena of a special kind.

Now, according to the Copenhagen Interpretation, the observer plays a critical role with respect to the events that are being observed. Prior to observation, matter is said to exist in an indeterminate state whereby each particle can be described only as corresponding to a 'probability wave' in accordance with the universal Schroedinger equation. Then, once a measurement or observation has been performed, the particles in question assume a determinate value. This is what is known as the 'collapse of the state vector'. On the orthodox interpretation, however, the observer can in no way *bias* the outcome of the observation; his/her intervention is limited to making determinate, or collapsing, what previously was necessarily or theoretically *in*determinate. Observation Theory (OT) starts from the postulate that some observers, i.e. those who are to be called 'psi sources', can exert a *statistical* bias on what is observed given a series of such observations.[125]

How, then, we must now ask, does this explain ESP or PK? The explanation of PK, especially the micro-PK we associate with a binary random-event generator (REG), is the more straightforward of the two, so let us consider it first. Let us suppose that the subject, or 'psi source', is receiving feedback in the form of clicks to the right ear for every hit and clicks to the left ear for every miss. Then, depending on the given strength of the psi source (which can be expressed mathematically), the behaviour of the critical particles that would normally generate a random sequence is *retroactively* affected by the observer who is striving to increase the frequency of hits. In this way the target sequence will be biassed so as to produce an excess of hits. But what if the random behaviour of the REG is governed by a tape carrying a *prerecorded* sequence of the binary digits, 1 or 0? Surely it should then be impervious to PK *whatever* the strength of the psi source? Apparently not. The retroactive influence simply extends from the moment of observation back to whatever random process was initially used to generate that recorded sequence before the experiment had even begun. That PK *has* actually been demonstrated by Schmidt using prerecorded random digits represents, perhaps, one of the subtler and more impressive vindications of OT.[126]

What then about ESP (whether of the forced-choice or free-response variety)? Here, the Observational Theorist will say that the brain itself behaves somewhat like a REG and can thus be retroactively influenced by PK which the psi source exerts once feedback is received and the target is revealed. ESP, it thus transpires, becomes a special case of PK. At first blush, such an explanation strikes one as non-sensical. By the time the subject is given feedback, he/she will already have *had* the relevant experience, and *made* the appropriate guess, which, in turn, will have determined whether the feedback in question indicated a hit or a miss. How, then, could such feedback conceivably influence the result? Or, as Braude bluntly puts it: 'the only reason S guesses correctly is that he later made a certain PK effort; and the only reason he made *that* PK effort (and not one that would have resulted in a different guess), is that he guessed correctly'. We seem, here, to be locked into a causal loop whereby 'the subject's guess ... is explained without reference to his having access to any information about the target independently of his guess.'[127] To counter this objection, the observational theorist must insist that OT is not concerned with individual trials but only with global statistical effects involving entire sequences of trials. From that standpoint the causal loop argument need not enter into consideration.[128]

In 1973, Koestler suggested to Eileen Garrett that, for their next invited conference, the Parapsychology Foundation should discuss the possible relevance of quantum physics to parapsychology. In August 1974, just such a conference was duly convened in Geneva to which a number of physicists, plus a number of parapsychologists with a background in physics, were duly invited including Koestler himself. A range of relevant topics were discussed but, most notably, the conference included two papers which served to launch Observational Theory; the one by Evan Harris Walker, the other by Helmut Schmidt.[129] Their approach and formulations were somewhat different but their basic idea was the same. It was not, however, until 1978 that an exposition of Observational Theory was forthcoming in a non-technical language, that made it comprehensible to the wider parapsychological community, in a much quoted article by Brian Millar in the *European Journal of Parapsychology*.[130] Although Millar became a strong proponent of the theory, his exposition is cautious and guarded. He also draws attention to one of the paradoxes of the theory which later came to be known as the 'divergence problem'. Given that feedback is all important, at whose feedback are we to draw the line? At that of the subject? The experimenter? And what about the reader who may later peruse the results of the experiment? But, if all such are to be taken into consideration, can an experiment *ever* be said to end? Earnest disputations were to figure in the subsequent parapsychological literature over such esoteric points as this.

There can be no denying that Observational Theory had a stimulating effect on experimental research, evoking for some reason a specially keen response from the new generation of Dutch parapsychologists.[131] However, not even its supporters could claim that it has won the day. Although it does not readily lend itself to decisive refutation, it cannot easily be reconciled with the fact that there is, by now, increasing evidence from the literature that feedback is *not* as crucial in generating psi effects as the theory would imply. Its main success has been in connection with the sort of PK experiments for which Schmidt is justly famous, but it had little influence on contemporary ESP work whether of the ganzfeld or remote-viewing variety. Its idealist implications, moreover, though typical of many contemporary theories which likewise regarded modern physics as legitimizing such neo-idealist metaphysics,[132] made it unwelcome to those (like myself) who stoutly adhere to the traditional, commonsense, realist view of the universe as existing, in some sense, irrespective of whether or not it is observed or who observes it.

Transcendental theories

Of the numerous theories that might be included under the heading of 'transcendental' I shall limit myself to only two (i) the theory of synchronicity and (ii) radical dualism.

The theory of synchronicity

In 1952, C.G. Jung published an essay on 'Synchronicity: An acausal connecting principle'.[133] Jung had long been interested in striking coincidences, especially those he had observed in connection with his patients where some objective event in real life appeared to echo an incident in the patient's inner or dream-life.[134] Rejecting the null assumption that such a matching was just a freak coincidence, of the kind one must in the long run expect by chance alone (though it is hard to see how such a null assumption could ever be actually disproved where one is dealing with spontaneous events), he postulated a new principle in nature to which he attached the term 'synchronicity'. Then, having created this new concept, Jung, who had, of course, a long-standing interest in parapsychology and had corresponded with Rhine, proposed that psi phenomena, too, could be regarded as instances of synchronicity. This, he argued, was more consonant with the scientific world view than was the traditional view of psi as involving the interaction between mind and matter. For Jung, be it noted, did *not* regard his synchronicity as a transcendental principle, as we are treating it here, but rather as the fourth aspect of nature over and above (1) 'energy', (2) the 'space–time continuum' and (3) 'causality' (which, for Jung, be it noted, could *only* mean physical causality).

In his introduction, Jung mentions an anticipation of his idea in a treatise by Paul Kammerer (a somewhat unorthodox Austrian biologist) on 'The Law of Series' (*Das Gesetz der Serie*) published in 1919. Kammerer collected cases which appeared to indicate that odd events of daily life tend to cluster in series rather than being interspersed randomly over time (an observation which, I think, most people can confirm from their own everyday experience, whatever significance, if any, one might try to attach to it). Thus both Kammerer and Jung came to the conclusion that science was incomplete and that, in addition to a universe of causally interacting elements, there was this peculiar tendency for events to group themselves into meaningful clusters. Synchronicity or seriality could thus provide the conceptual basis for a science of meaningful coincidences.[135]

At all events, the idea proved immensely popular and it was not long before the parapsychological literature was peppered with allusions to synchronicity – even if its explanatory value remained problematical.[136] So what is one to make of this concept? Undoubtedly, meaningful coincidences make good sense with reference to a work of art or literature where the artist or author has contrived such juxtapositions for aesthetic or dramatic effect. It is much harder to see what it could mean as applied to the natural world – unless, of course, one thinks of the world as a drama contrived by deities or demons. To Jung, however, profound student of alchemy that he was, it did not seem so unthinkable that events in the real world could somehow echo events within the psyche. For just such an assumption pervades so much in astrology, alchemy and the multifarious arts of divination. Be that as it may, the term 'synchronicity' is now unlikely to disappear from the parapsychological vocabulary, if only because it fulfils a need when we are confronted by those cases which cannot easily be assimilated to 'psi' and yet suggest something more significant than 'mere coincidence'. Admittedly the concept has little to offer the experimentalist but it has already given a new impetus to the study of spontaneous phenomena.[137]

Radical dualism[138]

After Descartes and up to the end of the nineteenth century

it could more or less be taken for granted that the prime function of mind was to animate the body. That is to say that, though the body might, to some extent, be self-regulating, an act of volition would imply that the mind intervenes to ensure that one's behaviour conforms to one's intentions. During the twentieth century, however, as a result of diverse developments in philosophy, experimental psychology, the neurosciences and, latterly, artificial intelligence and the cognitive sciences, a succession of new doctrines about the mind–body relationship arose: epiphenomenalism, stimulus–response behaviourism (Watsonian or Skinnerian), linguistic behavourism (à la Ryle or Wittgenstein), materialism (e.g. mind–brain identity theory) and, most recently and now the front runner, functionalism. The upshot of all these doctrines (none of which paid any regard to the parapsychological evidence) was to reduce mind to a nullity, to eliminate it as a relic of 'folk psychology' or, somehow, to equate it with information processing in the brain.[139]

There are many sound arguments, both conceptual and empirical, for challenging this downgrading of mind that has been such a salient feature of the twentieth century outlook, without needing to go beyond conventional science.[140] However, if we take on board psi phenomena, the case for a reductionist view of mind cannot be sustained. For, once we abandon, as we must, the analogy of the brain with the transmitter and receiver of radio communication, there is nothing we know about the brain, as an organ, that could remotely justify crediting it with the capacity to exercise ESP or PK.

The most explicit statement of what we are here calling 'radical dualism' is to be found in a seminal paper of 1947 published jointly by Robert Thouless, a psychologist and a past president of the SPR, and Benjamin Wiesner, a biologist.[141] In their paper they present the diverse forms which psi may take (it was Thouless who invented 'psi' as a generic term embracing ESP and PK) as essentially extensions of the normal mind–brain interaction (which we call 'normal' only because we have come to take it for granted). The Thouless–Wiesner formulation was not by any means the only version of what we are here calling 'radical dualism' but it was an important point of departure.

As with the case of synchronicity, radical dualism has not so far inspired much in the way of empirical research, although it could be said that it tallies well with the promising new field of bio-PK research if only because influencing someone else's brain or organism could be regarded as the most natural *next step* for a given mind after influencing its own brain or organism. However, as we have seen, PK is by no means restricted to animate targets.

On the other hand, radical dualism cannot be dismissed as a purely metaphysical theory for it does possess one essential attribute of any theory that aspires to be scientific – it is clearly falsifiable. Thus, if it could be shown that information exchange without energy transfer (i.e. ESP) can occur between two entities to which we would *not* ordinarily ascribe mind or consciousness, then clearly we would need to look elsewhere for the source of psi. For example, we might search for such an effect in the communication between two suitably programmed computers. If this *were* forthcoming, we might be justified in suggesting that psi was perhaps a function of information-processing systems that have attained an appropriate level of sophistication. Alternatively, we might search for a psi effect among organisms not normally credited with minds, e.g. plants, seedlings, bacteria, or even tissue preparations of some kind.

The following hypothetical experiment might justify our attributing ESP to plants. Let us suppose that the plants could thrive by sending out roots in the direction where moisture was to be found. If, then, they were able to do this, in the absence of any physical clues, or of any human intervention, to a statistically significant extent, we would have no option but to credit the plant with a clairvoyant knowledge of the location of the water. It might not be easy to eliminate the possibility of the experimenter exerting a PK effect on the plants but, given a suitable double-blind design, it could be tried.

At one time, considerable publicity was given to the work of an American lie-detector specialist, Cleve Bakster, who claimed that, when the plants in his laboratory were wired up to his polygraph, the recording showed that the plants would respond to mere *thoughts* on the part of the experimenter, for example, the experimenter might think about burning the leaves of the target plants. In the event it took a lot of careful work and expertise to demonstrate that his results were due to artefacts and not to the existence of plant-ESP.[142] Nevertheless, plant-psi, like animal psi (anpsi), remains on the parapsychological agenda and, if the phenomenon *were* to be vindicated, this would effectively dispose of radical dualism.

But is there any way by which radical dualism could be shown conclusively to be correct? At first blush it may seem as if, were the survival hypothesis ever to be confirmed beyond all doubt, that in itself would validate it, for what, after all, could be more telling in this context than the persistence of memory and personality in the absence of corporeal continuity? The problem here is whether the survival hypothesis itself could ever be vindicated beyond reasonable doubt. As we have seen, the alternative super-psi hypothesis can always be advanced by those for whom the concept of survival is, for whatever reason, unacceptable. And, even among those who accept survival, not all are prepared to acknowledge *disembodied* survival, preferring to invoke some quasi-physical vehicle to underpin the surviving entity. In the last resort, even when we can agree about the facts (which is rare enough in parascience) theoretical positions remain optional.

Epilogue

In his essay, 'The Final Impressions of a Psychical Researcher' (which first appeared in the *American Magazine* in 1909),[1] William James writes as follows:

> Like all founders, Sidgwick hoped for a certain promptitude of result; and I heard him say the year before his death [i.e. 1899], that if anyone had told him at the outset that after twenty years he would be in the same state of doubt and balance that he started with, he would have deemed the prophecy incredible. It appeared impossible that that amount of handling evidence should bring so little finality of decision.

James then proceeds to describe his own experience:

> For twenty-five years I have been in touch with the literature of psychical research, and have acquaintance with numerous 'researchers'. I have also spent a good many hours (though far fewer than I ought to have spent) in witnessing (or trying to witness) phenomena. Yet I am theoretically no 'further' than I was at the beginning; and I confess that at times I have been tempted to believe that the Creator has eternally

intended this department of nature to remain *baffling*, to prompt our curiosities and hopes and suspicions all in equal measure, so that although ghosts and clairvoyances, and raps and messages from spirits, are always seeming to exist and can never be fully explained away, they also can never be susceptible to full corroboration.

But, on further reflection, James concludes as follows:

It is hard to believe that the Creator has really put any big array of phenomena into the world merely to defy and mock our scientific tendencies; so my deeper belief is that we psychical researchers have been too precipitate with our hopes, and that we must expect to mark progress not by quarter-centuries, but by half centuries or whole centuries.

It is now some eighty-odd years since James penned these lines which were published only a year before he himself died in 1910. What, one wonders, would he have thought had he been able to read the present volume? He would, no doubt, have noted with disappointment the virtual disappearance of the strong phenomena that had aroused such stormy controversies in his own day. On the other hand, he would, presumably, have welcomed the methodological and technological sophistication that is now to be found in state-of-the-art parapsychology and its professionalization as represented by such bodies as the Parapsychological Association. But he would, no doubt, have reiterated with regret what he said before he died: 'I am theoretically no "further" than I was at the beginning'.

But, if it comes to that, what, one wonders, would James have said had he been able to read a history of psychology written today? Freud was just coming over the horizon when James died and James was impressed by him when the two men met. But Behaviourism, Gestaltism, Cognitive Psychology and all the other numerous competing schools and incompatible doctrines, lay in the future. Presumably James would have rejoiced in the enormous expansion of the field and in its many practical applications. But would he have considered that it represented a major theoretical advance as against his own famous *The Principles of Psychology*, published in 1890?

The question is worth pondering because when we think of progress, as when we speak of a 'breakthrough', we think, normally, of advances in the exact sciences or in their associated technologies. James could not even have envisaged the advent of computers, space-travel or genetic engineering but I reckon he would soon have made himself at home with present-day psychology or parapsychology. Admittedly, psychologists, unlike parapsychologists, have long since won the battle for scientific and academic recognition. But they are not handicapped by having to call into question the dogma of physicalism. Normal mental activity can always be attributed to brain activity and the brain conceived as a natural computer with electrochemical neural circuits for its wiring. Parapsychologists, on the other hand, threaten the ontological foundations of conventional science.

What, then, might the future hold for parapsychology? On this point history can afford few firm clues. A number of different developments could lead quite rapidly to removing at least the sceptical barrier which, at present, ensures that the field will remain underfunded and, as a rule, denied entry into academia. Let us enumerate a few such scenarios.

(1) Parapsychology might forgo its paranormal pretensions, either by becoming the study of certain popular beliefs, and so merging with psychology or anthropology, or by showing that its phenomena can, after all, be derived from recognized principles of physics, so merging with the physical sciences. Personally, I cannot see much prospect for either contingency.

(2) The vanguard of experimental parapsychology may

reach a pitch where the effects become so reliable that it is no longer possible to ignore them without incurring a charge of being scientifically illiterate or incurably prejudiced.

(3) It may prove possible to train *psi* ability as we can now train athletic ability. Not every child can be trained to become an Olympic-grade athlete and it may be that even fewer could be trained to become star psychic performers. Nevertheless, a successful training programme could transform overnight the status of parapsychology.

(4) Out of the blue another 'D.D. Home' may emerge. This time however, such an individual would, thanks to the media, gain a world-wide audience. (It began to look as if such an eventuality might arise during the early 1970s with Uri Geller but it soon became apparent that he was no D.D. Home!)

(5) Some psychic might produce a permanent paranormal object (PPO) such that it could not be copied by any known technique. Such an object would be paranormal in itself irrespective of who produced it or in what conditions it was produced. There have been a few such claims in the past but I know of no such object now available.

(6) Some practical application of a paranormal kind might be found whose utility would be such as to override any sceptical doubts that it might otherwise evoke. Of course, most of the traditional psi phenomena were associated with practical applications, whether it be in the field of communication, forecasting, healing, detective work[2] or whatever. So far, however, all such claims have proved unreliable in the extreme. What I am here envisaging is an application so dependable that no one could afford to ignore it!

Any or all of these six possibilities might arise at any time, creating a radically new situation for which there is no historical precedent. Alternatively they may for ever remain in the realm of fantasy.

One truth about psi phenomena which every parapsychologist learns the hard way is that they are not just elusive, in the sense of being difficult to pin down, they are, or at any rate they seem to be, actively *evasive*. One well-known contemporary experimentalist (William Braud) has spoken of the 'self-obscuring' aspect of psi. The following historical episode and its denouement may help to illustrate the point I am trying to bring home to the reader.

In 1924, a certain Polish-American, F.W. Pawlowski, then Professor of Aeronautical Engineering at the University of Michigan, had occasion, while on a sabbatical in Europe, to participate in a few seances held in Warsaw with the famous medium, 'Franek Kluski' (whom we met in Chapter 4). He described his experience in an article which later appeared in the *Journal of the American SPR*.[3]

One of the astounding features of Kluski's seances was the large number of phantoms that invaded the seance room, many of them self-luminous. They came in all shapes and sizes, performed various antics, gabbled away in a variety of languages and eventually disappeared. Pawlowski, being a down-to-earth fellow (if that is an appropriate expression for an aeronautical engineer!), understood that the only problem that would bother a sceptic in all of this was how these pretend phantoms had managed to infiltrate the seance room. But then he realized that, on some occasions, especially if the medium was feeling weak, the phantoms would be undersized, perhaps two-thirds or even a half their normal height, although, as the 'power' increased, they would expand to normal size. What are *we* to say about such testimony? Could Pawlowski have hallucinated the whole affair? What rules that out is that it was the practice, at these Kluski seances, to request the phantoms to dip their hands into a bowl of liquid paraffin wax from which plaster casts were later produced. Many of these casts are still extant: perhaps the nearest thing we have to a permanent paranormal object. Now a remarkable fact about these objects, which supports Pawlowski's account, is that many of these casts, although having the proportions and markings of an adult hand, are in fact less than life-size!

But the most poignant aspect of Pawlowski's article, which nicely illustrates the evasiveness of the paranormal, comes at the end when he declares:

> I am perfectly convinced that we are on the threshold of a new science and probably of a new era. It is impossible for anyone to reject or to deny these phenomena, and it is impossible to explain them by clever trickery. I realize perfectly that it is difficult for anyone to accept them. To accept the possibility of creating in a few minutes live and intelligent human beings, whose bones one can feel through their flesh, and whose heartbeat one can hear and feel is beyond comprehension.. To accept them would mean to change entirely our attitude towards life and death, to be obliged to revise entirely our sciences and our philosophy.

Alas, Kluski died in 1943 and, so far from his manifestations giving rise to a 'new science' or a 'new era', nothing remotely like this was ever to be seen again (at any rate not outside Brazil![4]). By the 1940s mediumistic seances were 'old hat' and the new respectable and sanitized parapsychology that J.B. Rhine had introduced at Duke University was all set to take the academic world by storm. But Rhine's new science soon ran up against the same obstacle that had beset traditional psychical research – the evasiveness of the phenomena. The 'new era' which Pawlowski thought so imminent is still pending. Time and again since then it has looked as if parapsychology was poised to sweep away all the familiar doubts and objections, overcome all prejudice and opposition and take its rightful place in the spectrum of human knowledge but so far this aspiration remains stillborn.

What is it that makes psi so evasive? One possible answer lies in the fact that, more perhaps than any other psychological phenomenon, psi appears to be extremely sensitive to situational factors. It is more than just a question of the subject being in the right frame of mind. The whole cultural milieu in which the subject operates might influence decisively what is or is not possible for the subject to achieve.

The late Kenneth Batcheldor, a clinical psychologist by profession, devoted much of his life to an attempt to discover the underlying psychodynamics of the paranormal. He published very little, partly because he did not want to be constrained by the kind of precautions that are required if one is to satisfy the demands of a refereed journal. Working, often through the night, with a small group of his followers, he recreated the Victorian 'home circle', but without taking on board Victorian spiritualist beliefs. He argued that the main obstacle that prevents us from producing strong psi phenomena is an inherent *fear* of the paranormal that is largely unconscious. By working in 'sitter-groups' the individual could overcome his/her fear of psi since nothing that occurred need be attributed to that individual's personal powers. Moreover, Batcheldor's method did not even forbid the use of some mild cheating at the start of such sittings if this would help to 'prime the pump', as it were, and get the group into the right frame of mind.[5] On Batcheldorian principles, one can now see what an advantage it must have been to the well-known mediums of former times to be able to attribute their phenomena to the intervention of spirits rather than to their own unaided powers.

The popularity of sitter-groups has declined in recent years and not many people have the perserverence required for the Batcheldorian discipline. But it certainly looks as if some genuine results were achieved in this way, notably with the 'Philip' group of Toronto.[6] Unfortunately, once the novelty of this approach wore off, it was unlikely that it would continue to be effective.

So, where does this leave us in our attempts to explain these vicissitudes that are such a distinctive feature of parapsychological history? If, having perused this book, the reader still remains unconvinced that there are or ever were any genuine paranormal phenomena, an explanation is not hard to concoct. Some novel form of trickery starts to attract public curiosity; this trickery is, in due course, exposed or discredited; people lose interest until some new kind of deception takes its place and the sorry cycle then repeats itself once more. This is certainly the simplest hypothesis but it is not one that I can find convincing when I ponder the best of the historical cases. What, then, can I suggest if we agree to accept such cases at face value?

The best that I can do, for the time being, is to offer the reader a metaphor that may be helpful. Let us, then, think of nature as one vast immune system. Paranormal phenomena, on this metaphor, correspond to infections comparable to the intrusion of viruses or bacilli into a healthy body. A new paranormal phenomenon for which there was no precedent, say table-levitation or metal-bending, would correspond to a powerful infection of this kind. The immune system of nature would go in to action with the result that such phenomena would thereafter be eliminated. But nature would still be helpless in the face of a new infection, and so a constant search for novelty would become the *sine qua non* of successful attempts to demonstrate whatever lies outside the normal course of nature or violates the laws of physics. Pursuing this metaphor, we may say that another method that would allow us to get away with the paranormal would be to introduce it in very *dilute* doses. In that case, the immune system of nature need never be activated just as in our own immune system very minor infections, as occurs with a vaccine, need not elicit any symptoms. This, indeed, seems to be the logic of much in current experimental parapsychology, such as attempts to bias the output of a random-event generator. The drawback of that strategy, however, is the difficulty of arousing any interest in such marginal results among those who are not professional parapsychologists.

History deals with facts; futurology relies on speculation. Of one thing we can feel reasonably sure, however, parapsychology will continue to challenge our assumptions about the world, and about what can or cannot happen therein, for a long time to come.

Notes and bibliographies

List of journal abbreviations

Brit. J. Phil. Sc. *British Journal of Philosophical Science*

Brit. J. Psych. *British Journal of Psychology*

Internat. J. Parapsych. *International Journal of Parapsychology*

J. Amer. S. P. R. *Journal of the American Society for Psychical Research*

J. Parapsych. *Journal of Parapsychology*

J. S. P. R. *Journal of the Society for Psychical Research*

Proc. Amer. S. P. R. *Proceedings of the American Society for Psychical Research*

Proc. S. P. R. *Proceedings of the Society for Psychical Research*

Prologue

Notes

1. See Thomas (1971).
2. See Yates (1979).
3. See H.M. Pachter, *Magic Into Science: The Story of Paracelsus* (New York: Schuman, 1951).
4. See Giorgio de Santillana, *The Crime of Galileo* (London: Heinemann, 1961).

5. If John Bossy is right, then Bruno served as a spy for Walsingham who was intent on tracking down Catholic conspiracies to overthrow the Queen. See his *Giordano Bruno and the Embassy Affair* (New Haven: Yale University Press, 1991). But, if so, Bruno was, of course, never suspected of any such involvement in his day.

6. Charles Singer says of Gilbert: 'His book is the first major original contribution to science published in England. It earned the admiration of Galileo' (*A Short History of Scientific Ideas to 1900*, Oxford: Clarendon, 1959).

7. See Thomas (1971) p. 224.

8. See E.J. Dingwall, 'Emanuel Swedenborg: Life in two worlds', in his *Very Peculiar People* (London: Rider, n.d.?1950).

9. Cf. Thomas (1971) p.643: 'The notion that the universe was subject to immutable natural laws killed the concept of miracles, weakened the belief in the efficacy of prayer, and diminished faith in the possibility of direct divine inspiration. The Cartesian concept of matter relegated spirits, whether good or bad, to the purely mental world; conjuration ceased to be a meaningful ambition.'

   Of course there were sceptics before the Scientific Revolution during the heyday of the Renaissance. Thomas mentions in particular the Paduan school of the early sixteenth century but, as he points out, 'The inspiration of these writers was not the new science so much as the rationalist authors of antiquity: ... ' (p.646). There were also, one may add, believers *after* the revolution. Indeed, Newton himself, the most revered exponent of the new order, was in private life, as we now know, a devotee of alchemy and of biblical prophecy and exegesis.

10. The expression was coined by W.F. Prince who, in 1930, published his book *The Enchanted Boundary: Being a*

Survey of Negative Reactions to Claims of Psychic Phenomena (New York: Arno, 1975). His coinage was used by Brian and Lynne Mackenzie in their important article, 'Whence the Enchanted Boundary? Sources and significance of the parapsychological tradition', *J. Parapsych.*, 44 (1980) 125–66. They conclude: ' ... parapsychology remains tied to its historically conditioned adversary relationship with the natural sciences. Without that it has no continuing basis for identity.'

11. An excellent introduction in only 33 pages is that by P.M. Harman in his *The Scientific Revolution* (London: Methuen, 1983). A classic series of lectures by the eminent Cambridge historian, Herbert Butterfield, was published in his book *The Origins of Modern Science 1300–1800* (London: G. Bell, 1962). Another Cambridge historian, A.R. Hall, covers the topic in his *The Scientific Revolution 1500–1800: The Formation of the Modern Scientific Attitude* (London: Longmans Green, 1962). A much quoted source is E.A. Burtt's *The Metaphysical Foundations of Modern Science* (London: Kegan Paul, 1932). Burtt is plainly unhappy with the direction in which the Scientific Revolution has led us and in his conclusion he asks: 'Granted ... the legitimacy of the motives which wish to render mind material for exact prediction and control after the fashion of objects of the other sciences – were the ancients and mediaevalists entirely astray in their doctrine that mind is in some sense a privileged and superior entity in face of the vastness of physical nature?' See also, in somewhat the same vein, C.D. Broad, 'The new philosophy Bruno to Descartes', in his *Ethics and the History of Philosophy* (London: Routledge, 1952).

A similar note of doubt and dismay is sounded by Arthur Koestler in his epilogue to his *The Sleepwalkers:*

A History of Man's Changing Vision of the Universe (London: Hutchinson, 1959) where he accuses contemporary scientists of excessive conservatism in ignoring the evidence for ESP (extrasensory perception). Koestler covers the Scientific Revolution up to the publication of Newton's *Principia*, but his book is chiefly memorable for its in depth treatment of Kepler as the great transitional figure between the old and the new dispensation. Much more positive in its attitude to science is Richard Gregory's *Mind in Science* (London: Weidenfeld & Nicolson, 1981; Penguin, 1988). Gregory makes no concessions to mind as an autonomous entity. As a pioneer of artificial intelligence he seeks rather to show that mind can hopefully be understood by machine analogies and in materialist terms.

12. The ideological link between the Scientific Revolution and the Enlightenment is memorably discussed in Paul Hazard's *The European Mind (1680–1715)* (London: Hollis & Carter, 1953; translated from the French, *La Crise de la Conscience Humaine* Paris: Boivin, 1935). He discusses at length the case of Pierre Bayle whose ten-volume *Dictionnaire historique et critique* was a forerunner of the Encyclopaedia, as mentioned later in this Prologue. See also chap. 9 of Butterfield (1950), 'The transition to the *philosophe* movement in the reign of Louis XIV'.

13. See Voltaire *Philosophical Dictionary* (edited and translated by T. Besterman, Penguin, 1971). (The original *Dictionnaire Philosophique* was first published in 1764.) Besterman, who at one time held the position of research officer of the Society for Psychical Research (SPR) became an authority on Voltaire and the Enlightenment and lost all interest in psychical research. See also Paul Edwards, *Voltaire: Selections* (New York: Macmillan, 1989). A recent biographical study is that by the late A.J. Ayer, *Voltaire* (London: Weidenfeld & Nicolson, 1986).

14. D. Hume, *An Enquiry Concerning Human Understanding*, sect.10 'Of miracles' (1748). Hume, to his credit, did not try to make things easy for himself. He was well aware of the furore that had been produced by recent occurrences at the tomb of the Jansenist priest, François de Paris, in the cemetery of St Médard outside Paris, involving countless alleged miracles and miraculous cures. 'Where' he asks 'shall we find such a number of circumstances, agreeing to the corroboration of one fact? And what have we to oppose to such a cloud of witnesses, but the absolute impossibility or miraculous nature of the events which they relate? And this surely, in the eyes of all reasonable people, will alone be regarded as sufficient refutation.' I discuss Hume's case at length in my book *The Relentless Question* (Jefferson, NC: McFarland, 1989).

15. See John Locke, *An Essay Concerning Human Understanding*, bk.2, chap.8 (first published in 1690).

16. In 1748 J. Lamettrie published his book, *L'Homme Machine*. He was a disciple of the great Dutch pioneer of medicine, H. Boerhave.

17. It was not until the later seventeenth century that the word 'coincidence' first makes its appearance. See Thomas (1971), p.655.

18. Yates (1964) puts it like this: 'The basic difference between the attitude of the magician to the world and the attitude of the scientist to the world is that the former wants to draw the world into himself, whilst the scientist does just the opposite, he externalises and impersonalises the world by a movement of will in an entirely different direction to that described in the Hermetic writings, the whole emphasis of which is precisely on the reflection of the *world in the mens*. Whether as religious experience or as magic, the Hermetic attitude to the world has this internal quality. Hence, may it not be supposed that, when mechanics and mathematics

took over from animism and magic, it was this inter-nalisation, this intimate connection of the *mens* with the world that had to be avoided at all costs? And hence, it may be suggested, through the necessity of this strong reaction, the mistake arose of allowing the problem of mind to fall so far behind the problem of matter in the external world and how it works. Thus, from the point of view of the history of the problem of mind, and why it has become such a problem through the neglect of it at the beginning of the modern period, "Hermes Trismegistus" and his history is important.' (p.455).

At the present time parapsychologists, almost alone among the scientific fraternity, are prepared to face squarely this problem of the role of mind in the universe to which Yates here alludes.

Brian Mackenzie, for his part, has the following to say about the distinction between science and magic: 'In the scientific process, each successive detail is provided for. In the magic process, there are just the wish and the result, and all intermediate steps are omitted. The essential characteristic of magic is that phenomena occur that can be most easily explained in terms of the action by invisible intelligent beings. The essence of science is mechanism. The essence of magic is animism ... ' (unpublished paper).

19. The most powerful organization of its kind, The Committee for the Scientific Investigation of Claims of the Paranormal (CSICOP), has its headquarters in Buffalo, New York State. It was founded in 1976 and has affiliations with other similar sceptical societies in Europe and the United States. It publishes a quarterly magazine, *The Skeptical Inquirer*, and has a publishing house, Prometheus Books. Its foremost spokesman is Paul Kurtz, a philosopher at the University of Buffalo, who is prominent in the American humanist movement and

edits their journal, *Free Inquiry*. He is editor of *A Skeptic's Handbook of Parapsychology* (Buffalo, NY: Prometheus, 1985) and author of *The Transcendental Temptation: A Critique of Religion and the Paranormal* (Buffalo, NY: Prometheus, 1986). Kurtz sees the propensity to 'magical thinking' as the common factor to both religion and parapsychology which, together, make up the 'transcendental temptation'. I would say rather that the common factor lies in their incompatibility with physicalism. Parapsychology, unlike religion, has no doctrine, is not an ideology and issues no imperatives.

Unlike Kurtz, Martin Gardner, another CSICOP stalwart, is a theist but is equally dismissive of parapsychology. See his *Science, Good Bad and Bogus* (Buffalo, NY: Prometheus, 1981). To the general public much the best-known and most active debunker of paranormal claims among the CSICOP coterie is the conjuror, James Randi. See his *Flim-Flam: Psychics, ESP, Unicorns and other Delusions* (Prometheus, 1982). To the parapsychological community, on the other hand, perhaps the most respected and the most knowledgeable of the critics is Ray Hyman, a psychologist at the University of Oregon. See his 'A critical historical overview of parapsychology' in the Kurtz *Handbook* (see above) and his *The Elusive Quarry: A Scientific Appraisal of Psychical Research* (Prometheus, 1989). James Alcock of Glendon College, York University, Toronto, is another influential critic, see his *Parapsychology: Science or Magic? A Psychological Perspective* (Pergamon, 1981).

For a recent overview of CSICOP and what it stands for, see George P. Hansen, 'CSICOP and the skeptics', *J.A.S.P.R.*, 86 (1992) 19–63. Hansen is worried lest, by their indiscriminate opposition to parapsychological claims, they may bring discredit on the very causes they espouse.

20.   Thus it is argued that quantum theory licenses postulating a universal interconnectedness. The authority most often cited in this connection is the physicist David Bohm: see his *Wholeness and the Implicate Order* (London: Routledge, 1982). See also L. LeShan, *The Medium, The Mystic and the Physicist* (New York: Viking, 1974). A case in point is Morris Berman. In his *The Reenchantment of the World* (Ithaca and London: Cornell University Press) he presents an excellent summary of the Scientific Revolution in chaps 3 and 4 under the heading 'The disenchantment of the world'. Then, however, at the start of his 'Prolegomena to any future metaphysics' he writes (p.135): 'we are forced to consider that modern science may not be epistemologically superior to the occult world view, and that a metaphysics of participation may actually be more accurate than the metaphysics of Cartesianism.' He goes on to cite such critics of modern science as Michael Polanyi or Gregory Bateson but, while his message will doubtless find a ready ear among the more fervent environmentalists, his 'reenchantment of the world' fails, I must admit, to impress me. In like vein, David Lorimer writes: 'We may well find that Renaissance Hermeticism and Platonism will underpin the metaphysic of the new science, albeit with the accent on dynamic and evolutionary processes rather than static correspondences' (*Whole in One* London: Arkana, 1990, see p.229).

21.   It is of interest to note that both Goethe and William Blake – two harbingers of the Romantic revolution – took issue with the great Newton.

22.   This aspect is discussed by Isaiah Berlin in his essay 'The counter-enlightenment' in his *Against the Current: Essays in the History of Ideas* (London: Hogarth, 1979).

23.   When George Berkeley, a figure of the Enlightenment, argued that idealism was the logical outcome of a strict empiricism and should be accepted accordingly, he was

regarded as a lover of paradox. Kant, who began the trend in Germany, also reached idealism by seeking to salvage something from Hume's all-embracing scepticism, but the outcome was the creation of a very different type of philosophy, more akin to a religion in its scope and pretensions. Psychical research, on the other hand, was the child of thinkers belonging to the British empirico-sceptical tradition who hoped that, by turning the searchlight of science onto these obscure phenomena, something of value could be rescued from the depradations of materialism.

Select bibliography and references
Butterfield, Herbert (1950) *The Origins of Modern Science*, London: G. Bell.
Debus, Allen G. (1978) *Man and Nature in the Renaissance*, Cambridge University Press (Cambridge History of Science).
Harman, P.M. (1983) *The Scientific Revolution*, London: Methuen (Lancaster Pamphlets).
Hazard, Paul (1953) *The European Mind (1680–1715)*, London: Hollis & Carter (transl. from the French, *La Crise de la Conscience Europeenne*, Paris: Boivin).
Merchant, Carolyn (1978) *The Death of Nature: Women, Ecology and the Scientific Revolution*, London: Wildwood (see especially chap.4 'The world an organism').
Rossi, Paolo (1968) *Francis Bacon: From Magic to Science*, London (transl. from Italian).
Thomas, Keith (1971) *Religion and the Decline of Magic*, London: Weidenfeld & Nicolson.
Vickers, Brian (ed.) (1984) *Occult and Scientific Mentalities in the Renaissance*, Cambridge University Press.
Yates, Frances (1964) *Giordano Bruno and the Hermetic Tradition*, London: Routledge; Chicago: Chicago University Press.
Yates, Frances (1979) *The Occult Philosophy of the Elizabethan*

Age, London: Routledge (see especially chap.15 'Prospero: The Shakespearean magus').

Chapter 1   The mesmeric era

Notes

1. See Ellenberger (1970) chap.2 'The emergence of dynamic psychiatry'.
2. For a description of the encounter between Gassner and Mesmer see Ellenberger (1970) pp. 53–5.
3. For an account of the commissions, see Gauld (1992) chap.1 'The Royal Commissions and the pamphlet war'. Some contemporary documents are included in Shor and Orne's (1965) collection of readings, Part 1: Historical.
4. See Gauld (1992) chap.2 'Puységur'. See also Dingwall (1967) vol.1, pp. 9–14 and Ellenberger (1970) pp. 53–109.
5. See Dingwall (1967) vol. 1 pp. 34–9 and Gauld (1992) chap.3.
6. See Dingwall (1967) vol. 1 pp. 46–58.
7. See Dingwall (1968) vol. 4 pp. 115–21.
8. Dingwall (1968) vol. 4 p. 138 says 'It was known that Esdaile had complete faith in the effluence and pointed to his own work in magnetizing objects as proof of it. For instance he was able to banish pain in subjects who had simply been asked to drink medicated water, which had previously been magnetized by him, without, he stated, any possibility that the patients could have known that any such treatments had been given to their potion.' For Esdaile's own account of his experiences, see J. Esdaile, *Natural and Mesmeric Clairvoyance*, 1852 (reprinted by Arno Press, New York, 1975).
9. Dingwall (1967) vol. 1 p. 115.
10. See Haddock (1851/1975) chaps 5–7.

11. See Dingwall (1967) vol. 1 'The Didier brothers'–Alexis pp. 158–201; Adolphe pp. 201–6. See also Podmore (1902/1963) pp. 154–8 and Gauld (1992) chap. 12 'Topics from *The Zoist*'. The extant contemporary literature on the two brothers is very extensive.

12. See Dingwall (1968) vol. 4 pp. 96–9 and Hands (*The Zoist* 1845, pp. 226–36). Dingwall describes her as 'perhaps one of the most remarkable English travelling clairvoyants of our period and certainly the most remarkable ever reported if we can believe the published reports'.

13. Robert-Houdin is quoted in de Mirville's *Des Esprits et leur Manifestations Fluidiques* (Paris, 1854). Podmore, ever reluctant to acknowledge the paranormal, considers how Robert-Houdin could have been deceived and suggests that Alexis might have been able to read the cards as reflected from the polished table-top although he admits that, with or without bandages, he would have needed 'incredible acuteness of vision'. Podmore himself points out, however, that it is curious that Alexis was in the habit of writing down his guesses (something no conjuror would ever do because it makes it that much harder to explain away mistakes). He suggests that Alexis may have been a natural automatist. See Podmore (1909/1963) pp. 173–5.

14. His report was sent as a letter to Elliotson to use for his journal, *The Zoist*, if he thought fit. It duly appeared in vol.9, Jan. 1852, as 'Recent clairvoyance of Alexis Didier'. Elliotson himself had published his own positive findings with Alexis in vol.6, Jan. 1849 and did so again in vol.10, July 1852. Dingwall discusses it at length in Dingwall (1967) vol.1 pp. 182–5.

15. See Gauld (1992) chap. 12 'Topics from the *Zoist*', p. 239–40.

16. See Dingwall (ed.) (1967) vol.2 'Germany' by L. Moser, pp. 161–74. See also Ellenberger (1970) pp. 79–81,

Podmore (1909/1963) pp.214–17 and Gauld (1992) chap. 8 'Mystical magnetism: Germany'.

17. Ellenberger (1970) p.80.
18. Ellenberger (1970) p.80.
19. Cf. T.X. Barber, *Hypnosis: A Scientific Approach* (Princeton: Van Nostrand, 1969); T.R. Sarbin and W.C. Coe, *Hypnosis: A Social Psychological Analysis of Influence Communication* (New York: Holt, Rinehart & Winston, 1972) or N.P. Spanos and J.F. Chaves, *Hypnosis: The Cognitive-Behavioral Perspective* (Buffalo, NY: Prometheus, 1989).
20. I am not forgetting that numerous mediums have claimed clairvoyant powers and continue to do so but their achievements rarely match the mesmeric somnambules at their best. Even the great Polish clairvoyant Stefan Ossowiecki (see Chapter 4 below) cannot compare in fluency with Alexis in full spate. Ossowiecki sometimes needed a couple of hours of intense concentration in order to ascertain correctly a message in a sealed envelope.
21. See Gauld (1992) chap. 13 'Animal magnetism: Retrospect and reflections'. Gauld also draws attention to the concept of 'therapeutic touch' which has recently gained ground among supporters of alternative medicine.

Select bibliography and references

The two principal references on which I have relied are (*a*) the four-volume work edited by Eric J. Dingwall (1967–8) (see below especially volumes 1 & 2) and (*B*) Alan Gauld's massive recent history of hypnotism (see below). Both sources contain extensive bibliographies of the contemporary literature.

Dingwall, E.J. (ed.) (1967–8) *Abnormal Hypnotic Phenomena: A Survey of Nineteenth Century Cases*, 4 vols, London: J. & A. Churchill. Vol. 1 (1967) *France* by Eric

J. Dingwall; Vol. 2 (1967) *Belgium and the Netherlands* by George Zorab; *Germany* by Liselotte Moser; *Scandinavia* by Erik Bjelfvenstam. Vol. 3 (1968) *Russia and Poland* by Ludmilla Zielinski; *Italy* by Luciano Leppo; *Spain, Portugal and Latin America* by Eric J. Dingwall. Vol.4 (1968) *The United States of America* by Alan Angoff; *Great Britain* by Eric J. Dingwall.

Ellenberger, H.F. (1970) *The Discovery of the Unconscious: The History and Evolution of Dynamic Psychiatry*, London: Allen Lane. See chaps.1–3.

Gauld, Alan (1992) *A History of Hypnotism*. Part I 'The followers of Mesmer', Cambridge University Press.

Gregory, William (1851/1975) *Letters to a Candid Inquirer on Animal Magnetism*, Edinburgh and London, 1851; reprinted by Arno Press, New York, 1975, from the 5th edn of 1909.

Gurney, Edmund and Myers, Frederic W.H. (1885) 'Some higher aspects of Mesmerism', *Proc. S.P.R.*, 401–23.

Haddock, J.W. (1851/1975) *Somnolism and Psycheism: Science of the Soul and the Phenomena of Nervation*, London 1851 (reprinted by Arno Press, New York, 1975).

Inglis, Brian (1977) *Natural and Supernatural: A History of the Paranormal from Earliest Times to 1914*, London: Hodder & Stoughton. See 'Mesmerism' chaps. 15–20.

Podmore, Frank (1902/1963) *Mediums of the 19th Century*, 2 vols, New Hyde Park, NY: University Books. See Vol. 1 Book 1 'The pedigree of spiritualism' chaps. 3–10.

Podmore, Frank (1909/1963) *From Mesmer to Christian Science: A Short History of Mental Healing*, New Hyde Park, NY: University Books. See chaps. 1–11.

Shor, R.E. and Orne, M.T. (eds.) (1965) *The Nature of Hypnosis: Selected Basic Readings*, New York: Holt, Rinehart & Winston. See Part 1 'Historical', containing papers by Bailly, d'Eslon, Mesmer, Deleuze, etc.

Weyant, R.G. (1980) 'Protoscience, pseudoscience, metaphors and animal magnetism', in M.P. Hanen, M.J. Osler

and R.G. Weyant (eds) *Science, Pseudo-Science and Society*, Waterloo, Ontario: Wilfrid Laurier University Press.
The Zoist, 1843–1856, 13 volumes.

Chapter 2   Spiritualism

Notes

1. There is, as can be imagined, an enormous literature covering the topics I touch upon in this chapter. Among recent works that I have found useful and can recommend to the reader are: Oppenheim (1985). This is a truly solid and scholarly treatment of the topic but it is the work of a historian looking at the field from the outside as opposed to a psychical researcher looking at it from the inside. A good example of the latter that has become a modern classic is Gauld (1968). Brandon (1983) is an entertaining though deliberately debunking coverage of this period and should be read in conjunction with Inglis (1977), which presents the positive side. A more specialized treatment of spiritualism from the feminist angle may be found in Owen (1989) and from the class angle in Barrow (1986). Owen writes with a rare sympathy and understanding of the female mediums of that era, mediumship being then one of the few careers open to enterprising women. For a study of the influence of spiritualism on American society see Moore (1977). Among the earlier treatises Podmore (1902/1963, vol. 2) still remains a classic, but Podmore, one must bear in mind, was himself a disillusioned spiritualist.

2. The peculiar ethos of spiritualism is nicely expressed by Alan Gauld (1968, p.76) who writes: 'Spiritualism was comforting cosy, humane. Compared at any rate with the fiercer Christian sects it had a great deal to offer plain men: oratory quite as colourful as any the non-

conformists could provide, but without the disquieting undertones; word, not of a Day of Judgment, but of reunion with those we love; talk not of man's sinfulness, but of the eternity of moral progress which awaits him; above all miracles not distant and dubious, but worked here and now by ordinary people.'

3. Dingwall (1950, p.68) remarks: 'What makes the case of Swedenborg almost unique is the way in which he was able to develop his vast hallucinatory system into one fairly well-coordinated whole.'

4. I owe this information to Brandon (1983, p.19). She, however, takes a thoroughly cynical view of spiritualism in general and of the Fox sisters in particular.

5. In spite of his fame and uniqueness there is still no entirely satisfactory biography of Home. Podmore (1902/1963 chap. 3) tries hard to belittle him; Wyndham's (1937) is an avowedly debunking biography; Burton (1948) is more sympathetic and, more recently, we have Jenkins (1982), which is very readable but is avowedly pro-Home. There is a classic essay by Dingwall (1947, chap. 5) and Inglis (1977) devotes a chapter to Home. In sharp contrast there is Hall (1984) which is, in effect, a series of essays on the more suspicious aspects of Home's career. Although the subtitle of Hall's book is 'the mystery of Britain's most famous spiritualist medium unraveled' we may agree with Dingwall who concludes his review of the book with the remark: 'The chief lesson to be learnt from this book is that the enigma of D.D. Home remains an enigma, and there is no sign of it being resolved' (*The Zetetic Scholar* (1987) pp.154–9). The best biography, in my opinion, is that by George Zorab: *D.D. Home, the Medium: A Biography and a Vindication* but, though written originally in English by the author (and then rewritten in good English by Brian Inglis) it has so far never been published in English but only in Italian and in Dutch

(Zorab 1976 and 1980). Home himself wrote an autobiography *Incidents in My Life* (Home, 1863) and, although one must always treat with reserve anything written by a psychic about him or herself, it consists largely of excerpts from the testimony of others. There is, also, the biography by Home's widow, Mme D. Home (1888/1921).

6. In contrast to Home, Leonora Piper seems a colourless personality who has not inspired biographers. There is a short and reverential biography of her by her daughter, Alta L. Piper, *The Life and Work of Mrs Piper* (London, 1929) and another brief biographical study by M. Sage, *Mrs Piper and the S.P.R.* (London, 1903, transl. from the French). Both books have prefaces by Sir Oliver Lodge. She figures prominently, however, in the works of the psychical researchers who studied her. See, for example, E. Sidgwick, 'Psychology of Mrs Piper's trance', *Proc. S.P.R.*, 28, (1915) 1–657. For a modern assessment of her mediumship, see Gauld (1982) chap. 3 'The mediumship of Mrs Piper'.

7. Given the solidity of Victorian buildings and furnishings it is difficult to imagine how Home could have produced such an effect, and so regularly, without very elaborate concealed machinery. One sitter, on experiencing it for the first time, is said to have exclaimed: 'there is a heart in my chair!'.

8. Home was a particular favourite of the Empress Eugenie and gave many performances in the Tuileries at the court of Napoleon III. He was also *persona grata* with Tsar Alexander II in St Petersburg. The Russian connection was prominent in Home's life. His first wife, Alexandra de Kroll, whom he met in Rome in 1858 and married in St Petersburg in 1860 (where the novelist, Alexandre Dumas, acted as best man) was a well-connected Russian lady. She bore him a son but she died two years later in 1862. He remarried in 1871. His

second wife, Julie de Gloumeline, was a cousin of Alexander Aksakov, an Imperial Councillor who was the foremost Russian authority on spiritualistic phenomena. She was also the sister-in-law of A. von Boutlerow, a Professor of Chemistry at the University of St Petersburg. He carried out some tests on Home which corroborated those of Crookes. Jenkins (1982) has much to say both about Home's French and Russian connections.

9. The nearest thing that I have seen to it are the table-levitations which David Berglas conducted in a television studio! I presume that he makes use of confederates whom he has planted in the studio audience. They could be equipped with metal rods in their sleeves, which could be pushed under the table-top when they place their hands above it, to provide the necessary leverage.

10. In a letter to a Mrs E. Kinney (now in the Yale library) cited by Brandon (1983, p.59). Why Browning, whose celebrated poem, 'Mr Sludge the Medium', mocking Home, was published in 1864, should have conceived such a strong antipathy to him remains something of a mystery which not even Jenkins (1982) can unravel. We know that his wife, Elizabeth, whom Robert idolized, became interested in spiritualism and was an admirer of Home. In deference to her he even withheld publication until after her death in 1861. Yet so strong was Browning's resentment of Home that she dared not mention his name in her husband's presence. But perhaps there was nothing so special in Browning's reaction. Home tended to polarize those who knew him into ardent admirers and fierce detractors! Charles Dickens, like Browning, was among the latter although, unlike Browning, he never so much as attended a seance.

11. There is an excellent recent account of Hare's involvement with psychical research by Rodger I. Anderson (1990).

12. Cited by Fodor (1934/1966) entry: Hare, Robert.
13. Anderson (1990, p.246) gives an example of such a test.
14. See Fodor (1934/1966) entries: Gasparin and Thury.
15. See Crookes (1874, p.3).
16. There is a standard biography of Crookes by his disciple, Fournier d'Albe (1923).
17. See Dunraven (1869/1924) (Adare had by 1924 succeeded to the title of Earl of Dunraven). Adare's two companions were Lord Lindsay (later 26th Earl of Crawford) and Capt. Charles Wynne, his cousin. From the outset, Adare's account provoked heated controversy and it has recently been the target of much sceptical criticism, see Hall (1984) also Brandon (1983). All the same it is not easy to dismiss this trio as just impressionable young officers. Although at that time a guardsman, in 1878 Lord Lindsay became FRS and President of the Royal Astronomical Society. Actually, the fathers of both Adare and Lindsay were more interested in spiritualistic phenomena than were their sons. E.J. Dingwall unearthed an unpublished letter from Lindsay's father, the 25th Earl of Crawford, describing a seance with Home held at a villa in Florence in 1856 with his brother-in-law. It is a remarkable document. We read that, at one point, 'a marble table at the further end of the room – that is a table with a loose marble slab on the top of it – violently rose up to the height of three feet, and redescended in the same manner, and also tilted over – while the slab, and a pencil and paper which lay upon it, remained stationary.' An attempt was made while it was airborne to force it to the ground but this proved very difficult! (*Brit. J. Psych.*, 44 (1953) 61–6)
18. See *Quarterly Journal of Science*, 1 July 1871. The report is reprinted in Crookes (1874).
19. See Karl Pearson, *Francis Galton: Life and Letters* (1914/1930) 4 vols, London, See vol. 2 (1914).

20. See G. Zorab, 'Test sittings with D.D. Home in Amsterdam', *J. Parapsych*, 34 (1970) 47–66.

21. 'Katie' used to sign herself 'Annie Morgan' but there is no evidence that Henry Morgan ever had a daughter!

22. 'Katie', we are informed, was several inches taller than Florence, had different coloured hair (which Crookes insists he had felt down to the roots), immaculate nails (Florence was an inveterate nail-biter) and unpierced ears!

23. Hall (1962/1984).

24. See E.J. Dingwall, *The Critics Dilemma*, Crowhurst, Sussex, 1966 (a privately printed pamphlet) and Brandon (1983) chap. 4.

25. See C.D. Broad, 'Cromwell Varley's electrical tests with Florence Cook', *Proc. of the SPR*, 54 (1964) 158–72.

26. For a rounded view of the case, the Trevor Hall book should be read in conjunction with Medhurst and Goldney (1964) and Medhurst, Goldney and Barrington (1972). The late Zorab attempts a full-scale vindication of Florence Cook's mediumship in a book which has, however, as with his biography of Home, appeared only in Italian and Dutch (see Zorab 1980 and 1988). See also my, 'George Zorab and Katie King' in F. Snel (Ed.) *In honour of G.A.M. Zorab*, NVP, Den Haag, 1986. Crookes' biographer, Fournier d'Albe (1908, p.218) describes the case as 'one of the most remarkable and best authenticated manifestations of supernormal activity on record'. Home, himself, who rarely had a good word to say of any other medium writes (1877, p.350): 'Concerning materialization, I need hardly remind my readers that the carefully conducted experiences of Mr Crookes with Miss Cook were repaid by evidence giving undeniable certainty of the phenomenon.'

27. His cathode-ray tube could also be regarded as a first step in a technology that eventually gave us television. It is worth noting that Thomson, too, was interested in

psychical research and joined the SPR soon after its foundation.

28. See Gauld (1968, pp.108–14).
29. See 'Report of the Committee appointed to investigate phenomena connected with the Theosophical Society', *Proc. the S.P.R.* (1885) part 9, pp.201–400. The report was largely the work of Hodgson. Recently he has come in for strong criticism of his handling of this investigation, see V. Harrison, 'J'accuse: An examination of the Hodgson Report of 1885', *J.S.P.R.*, 53 (1986) pp.286–310 and ensuing controversy in the correspondence columns of subsequent issues. Whether H.P. Blavatsky did or did not possess the paraphysical powers which her followers attributed to her is, however, irrelevant in this context for, unlike Eusapia Palladino, she never collaborated in any systematic research.
30. See Berger (1988) p.24.
31. See Fodor (1934/1966) entry: Pelham.
32. R. Hodgson, 'A further record of observations of certain phenomena of trance', *Proc S.P.R.* (1898) 13 pp.471–2.
33. W. James, 'Report on Mrs Piper's Hodgson-control', *Proc S.P.R.* (1909) 23 or *Proc Amer. S.P.R.* (1909) 3 and reproduced in Murphy and Ballou (1961).
34. In a long letter to Frederic Myers published in the *Proc S.P.R.* (1890) Part 17, and reproduced in Murphy and Ballou (1961).
35. Myers (1903).
36. Curiously, after her death in 1956, extensive communications purporting to come from her were received by the Irish medium, Geraldine Cummins. See Cummins (1965) which has an interesting foreword by C.D. Broad, the eminent Cambridge philosopher and psychical researcher.
37. A useful brief introduction is that of Saltmarsh

(1938/1975). See also the chapter on 'Survival' in Murphy (1961) and Gauld (1982) chap. 6 'Manifestations of purpose'.

38. Cited by Gauld (1982) p.89.
39. For a popular account of this aspect of Brazilian culture see G.L. Playfair, *The Flying Cow*, London: Souvenir (1975), especially part 2 where he discusses that most distinctive product of Brazilian spiritualism (or 'spiritism'): psychic surgery.

Select bibliography and references

Anderson, Rodger I. (1990) 'Robert Hare's contribution to psychical research', *J. Amer. S.P.R.*, 84, 235–62.

Barrow, Logie (1986) *Independent Spirits: Spiritualism and English Plebeians 1850–1910*, London: Routledge.

Berger, Arthur S. (1988) *Lives and Letters in American Parapsychology: A Biographical History 1850–1987*, Jefferson, NC: McFarland.

Brandon, Ruth (1983) *The Spiritualists: The Passion for the Occult in the Nineteenth and Twentieth Centuries*, London: Weidenfeld & Nicolson.

Burton, Jean (1948) *Heyday of a Wizard: Daniel Home the Medium* (with a foreword by Harry Price), London: Harrap.

Crookes, William (1874) *The Phenomena of Spiritualism*, London: Burns.

Cummins, Geraldine (1965) *Swan on a Black Sea*, edited by S. Toksvig with a foreword by C.D. Broad, London: Routledge.

Dingwall, E.J. (1947) *Some Human Oddities*, London : Home & Van Thal.

Dingwall, E.J. (1950) *Very Peculiar People*, London: Rider.

Ducasse, C.J. (1961) *A Critical Examination of the Belief in a Life after Death*, Springfield, IL: C.C. Thomas.

Dunraven, Earl of (1869/1924) 'Experiences in spiritualism with Mr D.D. Home', *Proc S.P.R.*, 35, 1–284 (revised from 1869 edition with introduction by Sir Oliver Lodge).

Fodor, Nandor (1934/1966) *An Encyclopaedia of Psychic Science*, Secaucus: NJ: Citadel.

Fournier d'Albe (1908) *New Light on Immortality*, London: Longmans Green.

Fournier d'Albe (1923) *The Life of Sir William Crookes*, London: T. Fisher Unwin.

Gauld, Alan (1968) *The Founders of Psychical Research*, London: Routledge & Kegan Paul.

Gauld, Alan (1982) *Mediumship and Survival*, London: Heinemann.

Hall, Trevor H. (1962/1984) *The Medium and the Scientist*, Buffalo, NY: Prometheus (new edition of *The Spiritualists*, London, 1962).

Hall, Trevor H. (1984) *The Enigma of Daniel Home*, Buffalo, NY: Prometheus.

Home, D.D. (1863/n.d.) *Incidents in My Life*, Secaucus, NJ: University Books.

Home, D.D. (1877) *Lights and Shadows of Spiritualism*, London.

Home D.D. (Mme.) (1888/1921) *D.D. Home his Life and Mission*, edited with an introduction by Sir Arthur Conan Doyle, London.

Inglis, Brian (1977) *Natural and Supernatural: A History of the Paranormal from Earliest Times to 1914*, London: Hodder & Stoughton. See 'Spiritualism': chaps. 21–5.

Jenkins, Elizabeth (1982) *The Shadow and the Light: A Defence of Daniel Dunglas Home the Medium*, London: Hamish Hamilton.

Medhurst, R.G. and Goldney, K.M. (1964) 'William Crookes and the physical phenomena of mediumship', *Proc S.P.R.*, 54, 25–157.

Medhurst, R.G., Goldney, K.M. and Barrington, M.R. (eds.) (1972) *Crookes and the Spirit World*, London: Souvenir Press.

Moore, R. Laurence (1977) *In Search of White Crows: Spiritualism, Parapsychology and American Culture*, New York: OUP.

Murphy, Gardner (1961) *Challenge of Psychical Research*, New York: Harper.

Murphy, G. and Ballou, R.O. (eds.) (1961) *William James on Psychical Research*, London: Chatto & Windus.

Myers, F.W.H. (1903) *Human Personality and its Survival of Bodily Death*, 2 vols, London: Longmans Green.

Nicol, J. Fraser (1948) 'The Fox sisters and the development of spiritualism', *Journal of the S.P.R.*, 34, 271–87.

Oppenheim, Janet (1985) *The Other World: Spiritualism and Psychical Research in England 1850–1914*, Cambridge, University Press.

Owen, Alex (1989) *The Darkened Room*, London: Virago Press.

Podmore, Frank (1902/1963) *Mediums of the 19th Century*, 2 vols, New York: University Books. See vol. 2.

Saltmarsh. H.F. (1938/1975) *Evidence of Personal Survival from Cross Correspondences*, New York: Arno Press (reprint).

Wyndham, Horace (1937) *Mr Sludge the Medium*, London: Bles.

Zorab, George (1976) *D.D. Home: Il Medium*, Milano: Armenia. (1980) *Home: Het Krachtisgste Medium Aller Tijden*, Den Haag: Leopold.

Zorab, George (1980) *Katie King, Donna o Fantasma?* Milan: Armenia. (1988) *Katie King, Een Geest in Menselijke Gedaante*, Den Haag: Leopold.

Chapter 3 Psychical research: First fruits

Notes

1. Vasiliev (see bibliography to Chapter 6), who set out to vindicate an electromagnetic theory of telepathy such

as had been put forward by F. Cazzamelli in the mid-1920s, ended by showing it to be untenable, much to the dismay of his Soviet sponsors. Even then, however, there were those, especially in the Soviet Union, who clung to it appealing to ELF (extra low frequency) waves as a possible mediator. John Taylor, of King's College, London, adopted it while he was still a believer in the paranormal: see his 'Can electromagnetism account for extra-sensory phenomena?' *Nature*, 275, (1978) 64–7.

2. *Proc. S.P.R.* (1883) 1, p.x–xx 'Objects of the Society'.
3. *Proc. S.P.R.* (1882) 1, p.147.
4. Gurney, Myers and Podmore (1886) vol. 2, chap.13, 'The theory of chance-coincidence', see p.16.
5. Gauld (1968) p.174.
6. *Proc. S.P.R.* (1894) 10, 25–422.
7. D.J. West 'A pilot census of hallucinations', *Proc. S.P.R.* (1990) 57, 163–204.
8. Cf. Gauld (1968) appendix A: 'Early experiments on thought-transference published by the S.P.R'.
9. *Proc. S.P.R.* (1882) 1, p.43.
10. *Proc. S.P.R.* (1882) 1, 38–42.
11. *Proc. S.P.R.* (1882) 1, p.23.
12. *Proc. S.P.R.* (1882) 1, 71–5.
13. Gurney, Myers and Podmore (1886) vol.1 p.30.
14. *Proc. S.P.R.* (1883) 1, p.171.
15. *Proc. S.P.R.* (1888) 5, 270.
16. *Proc. S.P.R.* (1883) 1, 83–97.
17. Blackburn's testimony is quoted at length in C.E.M. Hansel, *ESP: A Scientific Evaluation* (New York: Charles Scribner 1966) p.32.
18. *Proc. S.P.R.* (1883) 1, p.165.
19. See Gauld, Alan, 'Mr Hall and the S.P.R.' *J.S.P.R.* (1965) 43, 53–62 and Nicol, Fraser 'The silences of Mr Trevor Hall' *Internat. J. Parapsych.* (1966) 8, 5–59. For a recent discussion of Gurney's death, see M.H.

Coleman, 'The death of Edmund Gurney', *J.S.P.R.*, 58 (1992) 194–200.
20. *Proc. S.P.R.* (1883) 1, 24–42, see p.24.
21. Gurney, Myers and Podmore (1886) vol.1 52–6.
22. *Proc. S.P.R.* (1883) 1, 33–42.
23. *Proc. S.P.R.* (1883) 1, 39–48.
24. *Proc. S.P.R.* (1885) 2, 424–52, see p.425.
25. *Proc. S.P.R.* (1884) 2, 189–200, see p.192.

Select bibliography and references

Cerullo, John J. (1982) *The Secularization of the Soul*, Philadelphia: Institute for the Study of Human Issues.

Gauld, Alan (1968) *The Founders of Psychical Research*, London: Routledge.

Gurney, E., Myers, F.W.H. and Podmore, F. (1886) *Phantasms of the Living*, 2 vols, London: Trubner.

Hall, Trevor H. (1964) *The Strange Case of Edmund Gurney*, London: Duckworth.

Haynes, Renée (1982) *The Society for Psychical Research 1882–1982*, London: Macdonald.

Turner, Frank M. (1974) *Between Science and Religion*, New Haven: Yale University Press.

Chapter 4   The expansion of psychical research

Notes

1. Berger (1988) chap. 2 'James Harvey Hyslop: A portrait'.
2. Berger (1988) chap. 3 'Walter Franklin Prince: A portrait'.
3. Berger (1988) chap. 4 'Gardner Murphy: A portrait'.
4. Usually referred to in the literature as Baron von Schrenck-Notzing or, more correctly, Freiherr v. S– but hereafter we adopt the abbreviated 'Schrenck'.
5. E.g. Harry Price, *Fifty Years of Psychical Research* (London, 1939).
6. An unflattering portrait of Price is given by Trevor Hall

in his *Search for Harry Price* (London: Duckworth, 1978).

7. Richet won the Nobel Prize for Medicine in 1913 for his contribution to immunology.

8. See Prince (1927/1964) 'Stunts of composition', pp.281–94. For a more recent and popular account of her case, see Litvag (1972).

9. Perhaps the nearest case is that of the Irish medium, the late Geraldine Cummins. She wrote a number of historical novels as an automatist. See Charles Fryer, *Geraldine Cummins: An Appreciation* (Norwich: Pellegrin Trust, 1990).

10. See Tischner (1921/1925).

11. See Inglis (1984) p.152. See also Berger (1988) p.89, who quotes Prince as saying that he had gone to Mexico as a sceptic and come back a 'psychist'! For an appreciation of Pagenstecher, see W.G. Roll 'Pagenstecher's contribution to parapsychology', *J. Amer. S.P.R.*, 61 (1967) 219–240.

12. Eugene Osty, *Une Faculté de Connaissance Supranormale: Pascal Forthuny* (Paris, 1926).

13. See Geley (1927/1975) pp.83–7.

14. See E.J. Dingwall, *J.S.P.R.*, 21 (1924) 259–63 and T. Besterman, *Proc.S.P.R.*, 41 (1933) 345–52. Curiously, when in 1972 I corresponded with these two great authorities, neither was willing to stand by his original endorsement yet neither could offer any coherent reason for changing his mind – a perfect illustration of what Inglis has dubbed 'retrocognitive dissonance'!

15. Carlos Mirabelli flourished in Brazil during the 1920s. If the reports on him could be taken at face value he would undoubtedly rank as the most powerful medium on record, not excluding D.D. Home! However, although these reports were vouched for by a great many persons including medical and professional men, and, although his seances, which included many full-form

materializations of known deceased individuals, are said to have taken place either in daylight or in full electric light, his case was altogether too far out to gain credence outside Brazil. It was dismissed with derision at the SPR although Dingwall declared that he found it impossible to make up his mind about it one way or the other. Some European researchers visited him towards the end of his career, but his phenomena were then in decline and plans to bring him to Europe never came to anything. See Inglis (1984) pp.221–7 and Guy Playfair, *The Flying Cow* (London: Souvenir, 1975), pp.78–110. Recently a photograph has come to light showing Mirabelli in the act of levitating which is definitely faked. See G.L. Playfair, 'Mirabelli and the phantom ladder', *J.S.P.R.*, 58 (1992) pp.201–3. Until further research is forthcoming, the case of Mirabelli is best left in abeyance.

16. The spiritualist view was that light as such was inimical to phantoms and injurious to their mediums. Some modern theorists, however, following K. Batcheldor, argue that strong phenomena demand that element of uncertainty that only darkness can produce.

17. See L.R. Gissurarson and E. Haraldsson, 'The Icelandic medium Indridi Indridason', *Proc. S.P.R.*, 57 (1989) 54–148.

18. *The Reality of Psychic Phenomena* (London: Watkins, 1916); *Experiments in Psychic Science* (London: Watkins, 1919); *Psychic Structures of the Goligher Circle* (London: Watkins, 1921). For a recent appreciation of Crawford see Allan Barham, 'Dr W.J. Crawford, his work and his legacy in psychokinesis', *J.S.P.R.*, 55 (1988) 113–38.

19. See E.E. Fournier d'Albe, *The Goligher Circle* (London, 1922).

20. When I lived in Belfast during the 1950s I tried hard but in vain to meet Kathleen. Her husband, Mr G.

Donaldson (a shopkeeper), told me that for many years after the Goligher circle had dissolved, she and he held private seances in their own home at which Kathleen went on producing ectoplasm (mainly from her vagina). I also met or corresponded with other members of the original Goligher circle.

21. See Geley (1927/1975) pp.198–334.

22. There are many photographs of these in Geley (1927/1975). The original casts are mostly in Paris at the Institut Métapsychique, but a few are in London at the SPR, which also has a set of photographs of those in Paris taken by Mary Rose Barrington. A recent biographical sketch of Kluski, by an author of Polish extraction who is acquainted with the Polish literature, is well worth reading: Zofia Weaver, 'The enigma of Franek Kluski', *J.S.P.R.*, 58 (1992) 289–301. I return to the case of Kluski in my Epilogue (below).

23. See Richet (1923).

24. See A. von Schrenck-Notzing, *Phenomena of Materialization* (London: Kegan Paul, 1920, transl. from the German edition of 1913). The book created a furore when it first appeared in Germany. See also Geley (1927/1975) pp.182–97.

25. Geley was killed in an aircrash in 1923 as he was about to leave Warsaw for Paris. In 1954 Rudolf Lambert, a former associate of Schrenck's, published a report in the *J.S.P.R.*, 37, 380–86, accusing Geley of having suppressed photographs that would have incriminated both Eva and her sponsor, Mme. Bisson. Inglis (1984) 239–42 defends Geley in this connection but the debate continues (see comment by Adrian Parker *J.S.P.R.* (1988) p.91, challenged by Brian Inglis, *J.S.P.R.* (1989) p.301).

26. A. von Schrenck-Notzing, *Phenomena of Materialization* (London: Kegan Paul, 1920), quoted by Douglas (1976) p.198.

27. Harry Price, *Rudi Schneider – A Scientific Examination*

of his Mediumship (London: Methuen, 1930).
28. See *Proc. S.P.R.*, 41 (1933) 255–330.
29. The standard biography of Margery is that by Thomas Tietze (1973). Although he wisely refrains from pronouncing any final verdict on her, the general impression one derives from reading his book is that the mediumship was fraudulent through and through. If so, then her case must surely be unsurpassed in its tortuous perversity, for the Crandons were, after all, a respectable couple.
30. See *J. Amer. S.P.R.*, 19 (1925) p.186 (cited by Douglas (1976) p.224).
31. Inglis (1984) deals with this episode, see pp.166–9. Brandon (1982), a partisan of Houdini, also discusses his attempts to discredit Margery.
32. For the period 1925 to 1927, there is a volume combining reports from the *Proceedings* of the ASPR, vols 20–1, edited by J. Malcolm Bird and profusely illustrated with photographs taken at the seances. The volume was presented to the University of Edinburgh by L.R.G. Crandon himself. One of the foreign visitors during this period was R.J. Tillyard FRS, an entomolgist from New Zealand. Later he published an account of two sittings he had with Margery in *Nature*, 18 Aug. 1928, 243–6. The second of these two sittings was devoted to the production of Walter's thumbprints. The other sitter was a fingerprint expert from the US Navy Yard.
33. Much of this information is to be found in an unpublished book by Mark Richardson, *Truth and the Margery Mediumship*. I am much indebted to his daughter, Mrs Marian Nester, for providing me with typescript extracts from this work. Mrs Nester is a psychical researcher in her own right and a stalwart of the American SPR. Margery was very much part of her youth and her book on the Margery mediumship now awaits publication. She has meanwhile published

one article on the topic in *Fate* magazine, April 1985, 78–88. She, for one, accepted the Walter persona as real: 'Walter spoke by "direct voice", in space; he did not use the medium's vocal cords. He talked throughout every seance, chatting with the sitters, taking a full part in whatever was going on. I can almost hear his voice in my mind's ear, a hoarse masculine whisper with an edge of resonance, perfectly audible to everyone in the seance room. Walter came through as a real person. We never thought of him as "Walter" or as a "purported communicator". He was simply, *our* friend and advisor, an integral functional part of the circle.'

Palladino
34. The literature on Palladino (Paladino) is extensive but much of it is in Italian. The best essay I have read on her is still that by Eric Dingwall who also provides a bibliographical appendix. See 'Eusapia Palladino: Queen of the cabinet' in his *Very Peculiar People* (London: Rider, 1950?). Also to be recommended is 'Eusapia', chap. 10 of Gauld (1968). For a fuller treatment see Hereward Carrington, *Eusapia Palladino and her Phenomena* (London, 1909).
35. See Cesare Lombroso, 'Experiments with Eusapia' in his *After Death – What?* (Wellingborough, Northants.: Aquarian Press, 1988, transl. from the Italian edition of 1908) p.56.
36. One of the Hyères group of islands off the south coast of France near Toulon.
37. See *J.S.P.R.*, **6** (1894) 334–57.
38. For a recent reassessment of the Cambridge sittings see Manfred Cassirer 'The Cambridge sittings with Eusapia Palladino', *J.S.P.R.*, 52 (1983) 52–8, or his more extensive unpublished monograph on this episode in the library of the SPR.

39. E.J. Dingwall *Very Peculiar People* (London: Rider, 1950?) pp. 189–91.

40. An English edition, translated by Carrington who writes an introduction, appeared as *Spiritism and Psychology* (New York: Harper, 1911) see chap. 7 'The case of Eusapia Palladino'.

41. See her review of Morselli's *Psicologia e Spiritismo: Proc. S.P.R.*, **21** (1909) 516–24.

42. Cited by Flournoy, *op. cit.* n.40, pp.109–18.

43. One of the members of the Institut Général Psychologique who undertook the investigation was Yourievitch. Carrington relates the following curious story about him:

    'His father has been dead for some years. At one of Eusapia's seances a solid though unseen body, tangible through the curtain, came to him calling itself father. Now his father had a peculiarly formed finger: it tapered to a point, and the nail was deformed to suit the finger. M Yourievitch asked his "father" in Russian – a language absolutely unknown to Eusapia – whether his father would impress his hand in wet clay that was in the cabinet behind the curtain. Some time elapsed, the medium being held and watched meanwhile. Soon the investigators were told to turn up the light, and when they had done so and examined the clay in the cabinet, they found upon it an impression of a hand, the first finger of which bore identically the same marks of deformity as that of his long-dead father!' ('Eusapia Palladino – the despair of science', *McClures Magazine*, Oct. 1909). Was Carrington making this up (at the risk of being exposed as a liar)? Was Yourievitch having him on? Or did such things truly happen with Eusapia? How are we to decide? [I am grateful to Richard Wiseman (see n.46) for bringing this article to my attention.]

44. A lengthy review of this report appeared in *Proc.*

S.P.R., 23 (1909) 570–89, by P.P. Solovovo, one of the most critical of the SPR personalities. He admits to being pessimistic after reading the report about the prospect of authenticating her phenomena conclusively. Flournoy, on the other hand, accuses Courtier of deliberate obfuscation and prevarication in his efforts to avoid an unequivocal verdict in her favour. The very length of the series shows, however, that the panel were, to say the least, puzzled.

45. Feilding, the Hon. Everard, Baggally, W.W. and Carrington, Hereward, 'Report on a series of sittings with Eusapia Palladino' *Proc. S.P.R.*, 23 (1909) 306–569, see p.357.

46. Feilding, the Hon. Everard, Baggally, W.W. and Carrington, Hereward, *idem* p.462.

47. Gauld (1968) p.243.

48. See *J.S.P.R.*, 14 (1909) 172–6.

49. *idem* 213–38.

50. See his, 'The Feilding Report: A reconsideration', *J.S.P.R.*, 58 (1992) 129–52. His article aroused considerable controversy, see Mary Rose Barrington, 'Palladino and the invisible man that never was', *idem* 324–40; also David Fontana, 'The Feilding Report and the determined critic', *idem* 341–50. Wiseman, in turn, replies to Barrington in *J.S.P.R.*, 59 (1993) 16–34 and to Fontana on pp.35–47. See also A. Matinez-Toboas and M. Francia, 'The Feilding Report: Wiseman's Critique and scientific reporting', *J.S.P.R.* 59, 1993, 120–9 and Wiseman's rejoinder, *idem* 130–140. On a less controversial note see also C.S. Alvarado, 'Gifted subject's contributions to parapsychology: the case of Eusapia Palladino', *J.S.P.R.* (in press).

51. Understandably, the sceptics make the most of her failure in America, see C.E.M. Hansel *ESP: A Scientific Evaluation* (New York: Scribner, 1966) pp.209–16 or,

more recently, Paul Kurtz *The Transcendental Tempta-tion*, (Buffalo, NY: Prometheus, 1986) pp. 344–57. For a sympathetic contemporary account see Hereward Carrington's *The American Seances with Eusapia Pal-ladino* (New York: Garrett, 1954).

52. The offer was published in the *New York Times* on 12 May 1910, see Hereward Carrington, *The American Seances with Eusapia Palladino* (New York: Garrett, 1954) p.248.

53. See E. Feilding and W. Marriott, 'Report on a further series of sittings with Eusapia Palladino at Naples', *Proc. S.P.R.*, 25, 57–69.

54. E.J. Dingwall, *Very Peculiar People* (London: Rider, 1950?) p.214.

Leonard

55. Although she wrote her own autobiography, see G.O. Leonard, *My Life in Two Worlds* (London: Cassell, 1931), most of what we know about her concerns her mediumship and, as with Mrs Piper, most of this liter-ature is to be found in volumes of the *Proceedings* of the SPR, in this case between 1919 and 1934. A book that attempts to cover her case is Susy Smith, *The Medium-ship of Mrs Leonard* (New Hyde Park, NY: University Books, 1964).

56. See W.H. Salter, 'Trance mediumship: An introductory study of Mrs Piper and Mrs Leonard', SPR pamphlet, 1950.

57. See Mrs H. Sidgwick, 'An examination of book tests obtained in sittings with Mrs Leonard', *Proc. S.P.R.*, 31 (1921) 241–400.

58. See Besterman (1968) chap. 13.

59. *idem* chap. 16.

60. See *Proc. S.P.R.* 33 (1923) 606–20.

61. See M. Radclyffe-Hall and Una Lady Troubridge, 'On a series of sittings with Mrs Osborne Leonard', *Proc.*

S.P.R. 31 (1920); see also S. Smith, *The Mediumship of Mrs Leonard* (New Hyde Park, NY: University Books, 1964) chap. 4.

62. A classic discussion of the survival controversy is to be found in Hart (1959) who has much to say about the Leonard evidence. Hart believes that a case can be made for survival, despite the obvious fallibility of mediums, especially if we regard an ostensible communicator as compounded of a dramatic impersonation by the medium interwoven with genuine telepathy from the deceased entity. E.H. Dodds, however, Professor of Greek at Oxford and erstwhile President of the SPR, puts the anti-survivalist case in his oft-cited paper 'Why I do not believe in survival', *Proc. S.P.R.*, 42 (1934) 147–72. Not unreasonably, Dodds asks why the deceased have never been able to give us a convincing account of what existence in that other world is like!

Select bibliography and references

Berger, Arthur S. (1988) *Lives and Letters in American Parapsychology: A Biographical History, 1850–1987*, Jefferson, NC: McFarland.

Berger, Arthur S. and Berger, Joyce (1991) *The Encyclopedia of Parapsychology and Psychical Research*, New York: Paragon House. See esp. Appendix A 'Parapsychology and psychical research around the world'.

Besterman, Theodore (1968) *Collected Papers on the Paranormal*, New York: Garrett.

Brandon, Ruth (1982) *The Spiritualists: The Passion for the Occult in the Nineteenth and Twentieth Centuries*, London: Weidenfeld & Nicolson.

Braude, Stephen E. (1986) *The Limits of Influence: Psychokinesis and the Philosophy of Science*, London: Routledge. See chap.3 'Physical mediumship'.

Carrington, Hereward (1954) *The American Seances with*

Eusapia Palladino, New York: Garrett.

Douglas, Alfred (1976) *Extra-Sensory Powers: A Century of Psychical Research*, London: Gollancz.

Gauld, Alan (1968) *The Founders of Psychical Research*, London: Routledge.

Geley, Gustave (1927/1975) *Clairvoyance and Materialisation: A Record of Experiments*, New York: Arno (reprint of English edition, London: Unwin, 1927 transl. from French edition of 1924).

Gregory, Anita (1985) *The Strange Case of Rudi Schneider*, Metuchen, NJ: Scarecrow.

Hart, Hornell (1959) *The Enigma of Survival: The Case For and Against an After Life*, London: Rider.

Inglis, Brian (1984) *Science and Parascience: A History of the Paranormal, 1914–1939*, London: Hodder & Stoughton.

Litvag, Irving (1972) *Singer in the Shadows: The Strange Story of Patience Worth*, New York: Macmillan.

Prince, Walter Franklin (1927/1964) *The Case of Patience Worth*, New Hyde Park, NY: University Books (originally published by the Boston SPR).

Richet, Charles (1923) *Thirty Years of Psychical Research*, London: Collins (transl. from *Traite de Métapsychique*, Paris: Alcan, 1922).

Tietze, Thomas R. (1973) *Margery*. New York: Harper & Row.

Tischner, Rudolf (1925) *Telepathy and Clairvoyance*, London: Kegan Paul (transl. and revised from *Ueber Hellsehen und Télépathie*, Munich, 1921).

Thomas, Charles Drayton (1922) *Some New Evidence for Human Survival* (London: Collins).

Chapter 5   The Rhine revolution

Notes

1. See Charles Richet 'La suggestion mentale et le calcul des probabilites', *Revue Philosophique*, 43 (1884). See also his *Thirty Years of Psychical Research* (London: Collins, 1923) pp. 96–8. One historian of science, Ian Hacking, regards psychical research as a key area in the development of randomization, as a methodology for the biological and social sciences. See his 'Telepathy: Origins of randomization in experimental science', *Isis*, 79 (1988) 427–51, where he discusses Richet's contributions at some length (I am indebted to Charles Honorton for bringing this article to my attention)

2. The word *parapsychologie* had been introduced in 1889 by the German psychologist, Max Dessoir, and this had caught on in Germany. See M.A. Thalbourne and R.D. Rosenbaum, 'The origin of the word "Parapsychology",' *J. S. P. R.*, 53 (1986) 225–8. See also G.H. Hovelmann, 'Max Dessoir and the origin of the word "parapsychology",' *J. S. P. R.*, 54 (1987) 61–3.

3. Cf. Rhine (1948) p. 114:'But most experienced investigators I believe, have come more and more to accept the view that, while individuals differ greatly in their potentialities, most people – probably all – possess some of the para-psychical abilities in some degree'.

4. For a personal memoir of 'Banks' (as his wife calls him) see L.E. Rhine (1983). The authorized biography is that of Brian (1982). The memorial volume, (Rao, 1982, to which I contribute a chapter on 'J.B. Rhine and the nature of psi') is edited by K. Ramakrishna Rao, director of the successor institute. On Rhine's career, by far the most valuable account is that of two historians of science: Mauskopf and McVaugh (1980), see especially chap.4 'A career in psychical research – J.B. Rhine'.

5. Or so it appeared but Louisa mentions that, in a diary

entry of 28 August 1922, she had noted that, as his life work, botany would never satisfy him (L.E. Rhine, 1983, p.84). One event which influenced the direction he was to take was a lecture he attended during his third year at Chicago given by Sir Arthur Conan Doyle, that indefatigable missionary of spiritualism, who had stopped off at Chicago on a tour of the United States (L.E. Rhine, 1983, p.90). In the light of Rhine's later career it is ironical that the initial impetus should have come from such a source!

6. A useful account of this episode is given in T.R. Tietze's *Margery* (New York: Harper & Row, 1973) see pp.107–14.

7. And yet similar experiments were carried out by F.A. Crew at Edinburgh in 1936 and then by W.E. Agar *et al.* at Melbourne who tested some 50 successive generations of rats over some 20 years (their final report appeared in the *Journal of Experimental Biology* for 1954). In both cases the results *confirm* McDougall's findings. At the same time, as Sheldrake is at pains to point out, *their* rats learned more quickly than those used by McDougall. Moreover the progeny of the *un*-trained parents showed *similar* improvements, thus supporting Sheldrake's own hypothesis of 'morphic resonance' rather than Lamarkism as such; although the Sheldrake effect is no less inexplicable in terms of orthodox biology. See Rupert Sheldrake, *The Presence of the Past* (London: Collins, 1988) p.175.

8. See Warcollier (1938) chap. 4 'Enlargement of our group for long distance work'.

9. I say 'curiously' because Einstein usually distanced himself from the paranormal. In this instance, however, his friendship with Upton Sinclair overcame his reserve. What specially worried Einstein about ESP was its apparent indifference to spatial separation between the parties involved. As he put it, in a letter to the psychia-

trist, Jan Ehrenwald, dated July 1946: 'This is improbable to the highest degree and consequently the result is suspicious'. That there could be phenomena not amenable to a physical explanation was clearly not something that Einstein was willing to contemplate. He was, nevertheless, more impressed with Sinclair's findings, informal as they were, than with Rhine's massive experimental evidence which he thought could be vitiated by 'minute systematic error' (so much for Rhine's pious hope that experimentation is what would impress scientists!). See Martin Gardner, 'Einstein and ESP', *The Zetetic*, 2, 1, (1977) 53–6; also Jan Ehrenwald, 'Einstein skeptical of ESP? Postscript to a correspondence', *J. Parapsych.*, 42 (1978) 137–42.

10. So at least Coover thought but he was not prepared to relinquish the null hypothesis unless the odds against chance were of the order of 50,000 to one! Cyril Burt, who undertook a re-analysis of Coover's data, found that the total number of telepathic trials (where an agent was looking at the card) yielded odds of almost 50,000 to one while in what Coover took to be his control trials, where the agent did *not* see the card face (what would now be regarded as the clairvoyant condition) the odds were still nearly 1,000 to one, a fact that had already been pointed out by the eminent statistician, F.Y. Edgeworth, when he reviewed Coover's book. See Sir Cyril Burt *ESP and Psychology*, edited by Anita Gregory, (London: Weidenfeld and Nicolson, 1975) p.23. Be that as it may, Coover remained sceptical to the end about ESP and about Rhine's experiments which he claimed to have tried to replicate during 1934–6.

11. Zener, however, did not appreciate the compliment so, as early as 1935, Rhine changed the name to 'ESP cards'. Thus did Karl Zener forfeit his one claim to immortality!

12. The drug effect confirmed an earlier finding, that of

Brugmans *et al.* in their celebrated series of experiments at the University of Groningen in 1919 with a Dutch high-scorer, Van Dam, a student. These were perhaps the earliest parapsychological experiments to be carried out under university auspices. Comparison was made between the effects of bromides and the effect of alcohol, the latter (in moderation) *in*creasing the scoring rate, the former *de*creasing it.

13. Pratt's career is described by his friend and collaborator Jurgen Keil in the memorial volume (Pratt, 1987) which he edited. It contains a selection of Pratt's articles.

14. See Ina Jephson, 'Evidence for clairvoyance in card-guessing', *Proc. S.P.R.*, 38 (1929) 223–68. Unfortunately the subsequent series which she did, in collaboration with S.G. Soal and T. Besterman under more tightly controlled conditions, failed to produce positive results, see *Proc. S.P.R.*, 39 (1931) 375–414. Was she, too, a victim of a decline effect?

15. It transpired that Hansel was assuming that the building had the same layout at the time of the Pearce – Pratt series as it had 30 years later when he visited it. Working drawings showed, however, that *no* such window or transome existed in the original layout and Hansel was eventually driven to speculate about Pearce drilling holes in the ceiling above Pratt's room! At all events, the experiment was as water-tight as one could reasonably demand at that period and in his *The Basic Experiments in Parapsychology* (Jefferson NC: McFarland) K.R. Rao, the editor, includes as his first entry the article that J.B. Rhine and J.G. Pratt published in the *Journal of Parapsychology* in 1954: 'A review of the Pearce – Pratt distance series of ESP tests'.

16. Perfect runs, i.e. 25 correct out of 25, were not unknown in the early days. On one celebrated and much discussed occasion Pearce made a perfect run with Rhine as experimenter for a wager (which, in the event, Rhine could

not afford to pay!) see Rhine (1937). But the record for a high-scoring performance goes to Bernard Riess' subject, 'Miss S' at Hunter College. In a long-distance series (about quarter of a mile) from December 1936 to April 1937, she averaged 18.23 hits over 74 runs! She then fell ill and when she recovered she could no longer score above chance. Riess, a psychologist, served at one time as Editor of the *Journal of Parapsychology*.

17. B. F. Skinner, for example, made much of the fact that, in the original printed ESP cards, it was possible to discern the symbol from the back of the card.

18. It was his fellow experimental psychologists, the very people he needed most to impress if parapsychology was ever to gain a foothold in the universities, who put up the stiffest resistance and produced his most implacable critics. See Mauskopf and McVaugh (1980) chap. 9 'Parapsychology and professional psychology, 1934–38'.

19. See Louisa E. Rhine and J. B. Rhine, 'The psychokinetic effect: The first experiment', *J. Parapsych.*, 7, 20–43. See also L.E. Rhine, (1970) chap.2 'The first experiment'.

20. See J.B. Rhine, (1948) foot of p.107.

21. See L. E. Rhine, (1970) chap.3 'The decisive analysis.'

22. See Betty M. Humphrey, *J. Parapsych.* 10 (1946) 78–106 and 181–96.

23. See Gertrude Schmeidler, *J.A.S.P.R.*, 39 (1945) 47–50. See also G.R. Schmeidler and R.A. McConnell, *ESP and Personality Patterns*, (New Haven: Yale University Press, 1958).

24. Louisa Rhine calls it the 'perfect experiment'. It was published in the *Journal of Experimental Psychology*, 50 (1955) 269–75.

25. See Note 23.

26. See L.E. Rhine, (1983) chap.13 'Nonretirement.'

27. It was shortly after his retirement from Duke that I first

encountered Rhine when he invited me to spend the summer of 1965 at the Institute.

28. A useful review of this branch of parapsychology is the chapter by Robert L. Morris in B.B. Wolman (ed.), *Handbook of Parapsychology* (Van Nostrand Reinhold, 1977) 'Parapsychology, biology and and psi'. It was a paper by two French experimenters, see P. Duval, and E. Montredon, 'ESP experiments with mice', *J. Parapsych.*, 32 (1968) 153–66, which first inspired Levy's work. Their experiment dealt with precognition in mice. The mouse could avoid shock by changing its position on the floor of the cage so as to be on the safe (unshocked) side when the current was switched on (which side was safe alternated on a random basis). P. Duval was the pseudonym of Rémy Chauvin, a distinguished authority on animal behaviour at the Sorbonne, Paris. He has been a lifelong champion of parapsychology, but it is a sad reflection on the intolerance of orthodox French science that he felt constrained to publish under a pseudonym! Curiously, the very first investigation that Rhine ever undertook concerned a reputedly telepathic horse: see J.B. Rhine and L.E. Rhine, 'An investigation of a mind-reading horse', *J. Abnorm & Soc. Psych.* 23, (1928/29) 449–66.

29. He told me in a letter that he had been anxious to secure a grant from the National Academy of Science for which he had applied. It did not seem to have occurred to him then that inventing data is the one unforgivable sin in science.

30. See J.B. Rhine, 'A new case of experimenter unreliability', *J. Parapsych.*, 38, (1974) 215–25. See also D. Scott Rogo, 'J.B. Rhine and the Levy scandal', in Kurtz (ed.) (1985).

31. See Carington, W. (1945) pp.27–40.

32. Soal himself spoke of Carington's remarkable pertinacity' in urging him to re-examine his data. In the

light of Soal's subsequent fall from grace, it is worth quoting Carington's own estimation of his fellow investigator (Carington, 1945, p.37): 'Mr Soal is a most remarkable man, for whose work I have the highest possible admiration. Possessed of more than a Jobian patience, and a conscientious thoroughness which I can only describe as almost pathological, he worked in various branches of the subject for many years with nothing but a succession of null results to show for it. So markedly was this the case and so sceptical had Soal become that, when at last in 1939 he announced a highly significant positive result, we all felt, as Professor Broad put it at the time, "Is Soal also among the prophets?".'

33. See S.G. Soal and F. Bateman, *Modern Experiments in Telepathy*, London: Faber, 1954.

34. See C. Scott and P. Haskell, ' "Normal" explanation of the Soal – Goldney experiments in extrasensory perception', *Nature*, 245 (1973) 52–4. They further elaborated their position in the *Proc. S.P.R.*, 56 (1974) 43–72 and in the *J.S.P.R.*, 48 (1975) 220–6.

35. *Proc. S.P.P.*, **56** (1978) 250–77. See also B. Markwick, 'The establishment of data manipulation in the Soal – Shackleton experiments', in Kurtz (1985) chap. 11.

36. See C.T.K. Chari, 'J.B. Rhine and post-mortem survival: A reappraisal and vindication', in K.R. Rao (1982).

37. See Alan Gauld, 'Discarnate survival', in Wolman (1977).

38. See her *Hidden Channels of the Mind* (New York: Sloane, 1961) and her *ESP in Life and Lab: Tracing Hidden Channels* (New York: Macmillan, 1967). See also her presidential address to the SPR, 'The way things look', *Proc. S.P.R.*, 56 (1980) 367–83.

39. In the interests of historical accuracy I feel bound to say that Rhine did not easily brook dissent and many of his erstwhile disciples were alienated by his authoritarian

style. To the outside world, however, myself included, he was the soul of old-world courtesy and charm.

Select bibliography and references

Berger, Arthur S. (1988) *Lives and Letters in American Parapsychology*, Jefferson: McFarland. See chap. 4.

Brian, Denis (1982) *The Enchanted Voyager: The Life of J.B. Rhine* (an authorized biography), Englewood Cliffs, NJ: Prentice-Hall.

Carington, Whately (1945) *Telepathy: An Outline of Facts, Theories and Implications*, London: Methuen. See especially Part 1.

Douglas, Alfred (1976) *Extra-Sensory Powers: A Century of Psychical Research*, London: Gollancz. See Part 3.

Hansel, C.E.M. (1966) *ESP: A Scientific Evaluation*, New York: Scribner. See especially chap. 7 'The Pearce – Pratt experiment'.

Kurtz, Paul (ed.) (1985) *A Skeptic's Handbook of Parapsychology*, Buffalo, NY: Prometheus.

Mauskopf, Seymour H. and McVaugh, Michael R. (1980) *The Elusive Science: Origins of Experimental Psychical Research*, Baltimore and London: Johns Hopkins University Press, (with an afterword by J.B. and L.E. Rhine).

Pratt, J. Gaither (1964) *Parapsychology: An Insider's View of ESP*, New York: Doubleday.

Pratt, Gaither (1987) *Gaither Pratt: A Life for Parapsychology*, selected works compiled and edited by Jurgen Keil who contributes a biography, Jefferson, NC: McFarland.

Rao, K. Ramakrishna (ed.) (1982) *J.B. Rhine: On the Frontiers of Science*, Jefferson: NC: McFarland.

Rao, K. Ramakrishna (1984) *The Basic Experiments in Parapsychology* Jefferson:NC: McFarland.

Rhine, J.B. (1934/1964/1973) *Extra-Sensory Perception*, Boston: Boston SPR, 1934; Bruce Humphries, 1935 and 1964 (paperback revised); Branden Press, 1973 (paperback).

Rhine, J.B. (1937/1938/1950) *New Frontiers of the Mind*, New York: Farrar & Rhinehart; London: Faber, 1938; Harmondsworth: Penguin, 1950.

Rhine, J.B. (1947/1948) *The Reach of the Mind*, New York: Sloane, 1947; London: Faber, 1948.

Rhine, J.B. (1953/1954) *New World of the Mind*. New York: Sloane, 1953; London: Faber, 1954.

Rhine, J.B., Pratt, J.G., Smith, B.M., Stuart, C.E. and Greenwood, J.A. (1940/1966) *Extra-Sensory Perception after Sixty Years*, Boston: Bruce Humphries, 1940 and 1966.

Rhine, J.B. and Pratt, J.G. (1957) *Parapsychology: Frontier Science of the Mind*, Springfield, IL: C.C. Thomas; Oxford: Blackwell.

Rhine, Louisa E. (1970) *Mind over Matter*, New York and London: Macmillan.

Rhine, Louisa E. (1983) *Something Hidden*, Jefferson, NC: McFarland.

Sinclair, Upton (1930/1962) *Mental Radio*, Springfield, IL: C.C. Thomas.

Thouless, Robert H. (1972) *From Anecdote to Experiment in Psychical Research*, London: Routledge.

Warcollier, René (1938) *Experiments in Telepathy*, London: Allen and Unwin. (Edited and abridged by Gardner Murphy from the author's *La Télépathie* (Paris, 1921), comprising his articles in the *Revue Métapsychique*, etc.)

White, Rhea A. and Dale, Laura A. (1973) *Parapsychology: Sources of Information*, Metuchen, NJ: Scarecrow.

Wolman, B.B. (ed.) (1977) *Handbook of Parapsychology*, New York: Van Nostrand Reinhold. See Part 1, chap. 2 'History of experimental studies' by J.B. Rhine.

Chapter 6   Recent developments

Notes

1. Eileen Garrett (née Lyttle) (1893–1970) was herself a prolific writer. Her first book was *My Life in Search for the Meaning of Mediumship* (1938), see also *Many Voices: The Autobiography of a Medium* (London: Allen & Unwin, 1968). As a medium she shot into prominence in 1931 when a 'spirit communicator' intervened in the course of a seance to announce that he was the captain of the ill-fated R101 airship that had recently crashed, and then proceeded to provide copious technical information.

2. In the literature she is referred to simply as 'Fraulein D.' but she eventually became Frau Bender.

3. The Rosenheim case (1967–68) has been described by Bender in his chapter on 'Modern poltergeist research' in Beloff (ed.) (1974).

4. Tenhaeff's posthumous reputation has been badly dented as a result of the work of a Dutch journalist, the late Piet Hein Hoebens, who has shown that Tenhaeff was not above making spurious claims to inflate Croiset's achievements. See especially the bibliography to Hoeben's chapter in Kurtz (1985) 'Reflections on psychic sleuths'.

5. The DMT was invented by a colleague of Johnson's, the Swedish psychologist, Ulf Kragh. It is essentially a projective test, like the TAT (Thematic Apperception Test), incorporating a threatening figure. However, the stimulus is presented tachistoscopically, at increasing time-exposures, to obviate full conscious recognition of the picture. It has been much used by the Swedish Airforce in selecting pilots. For a recent report linking the DMT with ESP see M. Johnson, and E. Haraldsson (1984) *J. Parapsych.*, 48, pp. 185–200.

6. As an executor of the Koestler Estate I was personally

involved in this development. Koestler had specified only that the Chair was to be at a British University but, as Edinburgh showed the most willingness, the executors agreed to bestow on it the Koestler Chair.

7. See, for example, L.R. Gissurarson and R.L. Morris 'Volition and psychokinesis' *J. Parapsych.*, 54 (1990) 331–70.

8. See his *Parapsychology: When the Irrational Rejoins Science*, Jefferson, NC: McFarland, 1985 (transl. from *La Parapsychologie*, Hachette, 1980).

9. See Anita Gregory's introduction to L.L. Vasiliev (1962/1976).

10. Notably the case of 'Leonie' a patient of a Dr J. Gibert of Le Havre. Among those who went to Le Havre to study her was the celebrated French psychiatrist Pierre Janet as well as Frederic Myers from the SPR.

11. A translation was circulated, see V.P. Zinchenko, A.N. Leontiev, B.F. Lomov and A.R. Luria, 'Parapsychology: Fiction or fact?' *Questions of Philosophy*, 9, 1973.

12. See the articles by Thelma Moss and by William Tiller in Mitchell (1974), a compendium published under the name of the astronaut Edgar Mitchell, that reflects the more permissive side of the parapsychology of that period. Mitchell founded his own 'Institute of Noetic Science' in San Francisco.

13. By then, Pratt had broken with Rhine and had teamed up with Ian Stevenson at the University of Virginia. Pratt wrote the definitive monograph on Stepanek, 'A decade of research with a selected ESP subject: An overview and reappraisal of the work with Pavel Stepanek' *Proc. A.S.P.R.* 30 (1973) 1–78. Stepanek even made the *Guinness Book of Records* as the longest lasting 'high-scorer'. However, even his powers deserted him soon after the publication of Pratt's monograph. Then, in 1989, Jan Kappers, an Amsterdam physician with an interest in parapsychology, brought him over to

Amsterdam for testing, but the scoring was at chance level, see J. Kappers *et al.*, 'Resuming work with Pavel Stepanek', *J.S.P.R.*, 56 (1990) 138–47. An attempt to rubbish the work with Stepanek was made by the well-known sceptical writer, Martin Gardner, in his book *How Not to Test a Psychic* (Buffalo, NY: Prometheus, 1989). Pratt was then dead, but Gardner's hypothesis concerning a trick that Stepanek might have perpetrated was effectively answered in some detail by Jurgen Keil who had participated in the test sessions under Pratt at Charlottesville. See J. Keil, 'How a skeptic misrepresents the research with Stepanek', *J. Parapsych.*, 54 (1990) 151–68.

14. For a survey of parapsychological activities and organizations around the world, see Berger and Berger (1991) appendix A.

15. See Leping Zha and Tron McConnell, 'Parapsychology in the People's Republic of China 1979–1989', *J. Amer. S.P.R.*, 85 (1991) 119–44.

16. In keeping with this designation the usual practice was to let the subjects finger the target sheet or put it to their forehead or even screw it up and put it in their ear! From the security point of view this was much to be regretted.

17. See Ullman *et al.* (1973/1989). A good summary of the work is given by R. Van de Castle who took part in it himself, see his chapter on 'Sleep and dreams' in Wolman (1977), especially the section on 'The Maimonides research program', pp.485–90.

18. See Montague Ullman 'The world of psychic phenomena as I came to know it' in Pilkington (1987).

19. Karlis Osis, who later became Research Director for the American SPR, and Douglas Dean who was also soon to become well known in parapsychological circles and has since taken a special interest in psychic healing. Lawrence LeShan, writer and researcher, was also at this period studying Eileen Garrett.

20. See Irvin Child, 'Psychology and anomalous observations: The question of ESP in dreams', *American Psychologist*, 40 (1985) 1219–30. On Child's analysis p < 7.42 × 10^{-8} (i.e. odds of nearly 100 million to one). In this article, Child, a social psychologist at Yale University, takes his fellow psychologists to task for ignoring, or worse still distorting and misrepresenting, the Maimonides findings.

21. See C. Honorton, 'Psi and internal attention states' in Wolman (1977). His article discusses the experimental evidence using each of these three approaches plus that based on the ganzfeld approach described in our next paragraph. For a more recent survey of the field see Rex G. Stanford, 'Ganzfeld and hypnotic induction procedures in ESP research: Towards understanding their success', in Krippner (ed.) (1987). On hypnosis and ESP see E.I. Schechter, 'Hypnotic induction versus control conditions', *J. Amer. S.P.R.*, 78 (1984) 1–27.

22. See A. Mavromatis, *Hypnagogia* (London: Routledge, 1987). The author there discusses some traditional links between psi and the hypnogogic state, see chap.6.

23. Tragically, Honorton died suddenly of a heart attack, on 4 November 1992, at the early age of 46, while working temporarily at the University of Edinburgh. See the obituary by Robert Morris in *J.S.P.R.*, 59 (1993) 62–4.

24. See the ganzfeld debate in *J. Parapsych.*, 49 (1985) with Ray Hyman, 'The ganzfeld psi experiment: A critical appraisal', pp.3–50 and Charles Honorton, 'Meta-analysis of psi ganzfeld research', pp.51–92. The debate was resumed the following year with a joint communiqué from both Hyman and Honorton, 'The psi ganzfeld controversy' plus miscellaneous contributions from: Robert Rosenthal, Irvin Child, James Alcock, Christopher Scott, Gerd Hövelmann, James McClenon, John Palmer and Rex Stanford. See *J. Parapsych.*, 50 (1986) 311–402.

24a. In his 1985 meta-analysis of the ganzfeld research (see above), Honorton lists some 42 studies, conducted between 1974 and 1981, known to Honorton and meeting his criteria of acceptable ganzfeld studies. Then, in 1990, after a further 11 automated studies at his laboratory were completed, including those using 'dynamic targets' (i.e. video-film), Honorton and his co-workers published another article in the *J. Parapsych.*: 'Psi communication in the ganzfeld', 54 (1990) 99–139. In the 10th edition of the well-known introductory psychology textbook *Introduction to Psychology* by R.L. Atkinson *et al.* (New York: Harcourt Brace Jovanovich, 1990) there is a section devoted to parapsychology featuring mainly the ganzfeld work (see chap. 6).

24b. The outstanding exponent of the ganzfeld approach in Britain was Carl Sargent, a post-doctoral Fellow of the Department of Psychology at Cambridge University, see C.L. Sargent, 'Exploring psi in the ganzfeld', *Parapsychology Monographs 17*, Parapsych. Foundation, New York, 1980. Since then, however, a number of unfortunate events have conspired to cast a shadow on the highly successful results obtained by Sargent and his co-workers at Cambridge. After an invited visit to his laboratory in 1979, Susan Blackmore circulated a report in which she mentions certain irregularities in the procedure and suggested a possible way in which cheating *might* have occurred. Then, following another unpublished critical report by Adrian Parker and Nils Wiklund in 1982, the Council of the Parapsychological Association set up a committee in 1984, headed by Martin Johnson, which reprimanded Sargent for failing to respond to their request for information within a reasonable time, with the result that Sargent's membership of the PA was allowed to lapse. By then, however, Sargent had left Cambridge and had abandoned parapsychology and abruptly withdrawn from the parapsychological community – thereby damaging his reputation far more than any critic could have done. See Susan Blackmore, 'A report on a visit to Carl Sargent's laboratory', *J.S.P.R.*, 54 (1987) 186–98; Trevor Harley and Gerald Matthews, 'Cheating, psi and the appliance of science: A reply to Blackmore', *J.S.P.R.*, 54 (1987) 199–207; Carl Sargent, 'Sceptical fairytales from Bristol', *J.S.P.R.*, 54 (1987) 208–18; and Adrian Parker and Nils Wiklund, 'The ganzfeld experiments: Towards an assessment', *J.S.P.R.*, 54 (1987) 261–5.

25. See Targ and Puthoff (1977) chap. 2.
26. Targ and Puthoff (1977) chap. 3.
27. Targ and Puthoff (1977) chap. 4.
28. Marks and Kammann (1980) chaps 2 and 3. See also their letter to *Nature*, **274** (1978) 680–1: 'Information transmission in remote viewing experiments'.
29. See his letter to *Nature* under the same heading: *Nature* 284, p.191.
29a. As an appendix to Targ and Harary (1984), there is a bibliography compiled by George Hansen, Marilyn Schlitz and Charles Tart of remote-viewing experiments published between 1973 and 1982. They also examined unpublished studies and conclude that: 'the success of remote viewing is not due to reporting bias in which vast numbers of unsuccessful experiments go unreported'. A useful assessment of the status of this technique is to be found in Edge, Morris, Rush, Palmer (1986) pp.176–9.
30. See J.P. Bisaha and B.J. Dunne, 'Multiple subject and long distance precognitive remote viewing of geographical locations' in Tart, Puthoff and Targ (eds) (1979). Since 1979 Dunne has been a researcher on the staff of the Princeton Engineering Anomalies Research (PEAR) founded by Robert Jahn (see below). Although his laboratory is best known for its PK studies, it has

also conducted extensive research on remote-viewing ESP.

31. See M. Schlitz and E. Gruber, 'Transcontinental remote viewing', *J. Parapsych.*, 44 (1980) 305–17 and their 'Transcontinental remote viewing: A rejudging', *J. Parapsych.*, 45 (1981) 233–7. Both articles are reproduced in Rao (ed.) (1984).

32. An excellent introduction to the Schmidt experiments can be found in Braude (1979) pp.74–94. The volume also contains a useful set of references to Schmidt's own publications.

33. Schmidt's theoretical position can be found in his seminal article, 'Toward a mathematical theory of psi', *J. Amer. S.P.R.*, 70 (1975) 301–19. We shall revert to the 'Observational Theory' later in this chapter.

34. For a single trial in the Jahn set-up, the REG could be set to produce a number of binary outcomes, i.e. bits of information, varying from 20 to 200 bits per trial.

35. The identity of the 'operators' in these experiments is never disclosed as a matter of policy but it is widely suspected that Operator 10 must be a member of the research team if only because of his/her large share of the output. Could it be Brenda Dunne, herself, whose psi abilities were already well known?

36. Anomalies such as this have given an impetus to an alternative interpretation of micro-PK as 'Intuitive Data Sorting' (IDS). This presupposes that the subject has a precognitive knowledge of the fluctuations in the random series and so can enter the series at a favourable point. See 'Precognition by any other name … ' Broughton (1991) 137–9.

37. At the annual convention of the Parapsychological Association in 1985, Dean Radin and colleagues reported the results of a meta-analysis which they had carried out on *all* the published results in the literature of PK experiments using binary REGs. They write: 'In

our literature review, we found 332 studies published over the years 1969–1984, in 56 parapsychological references contributed by 28 principal investigators. Seventy-one of these experiments were reportedly significant at p < .05, two-tailed, resulting in an overall binomial probability of 5.4×10^{-43}. Taken as *prima facie* evidence, this result constitutes strong evidence for a psi effect' (D.I. Radin, E.C. May and Martha J. Thomson, *Research in Parapsychology 1985*, (1986) 14–17 (abstract)).

As with all such meta-analyses the question arises as to whether the sample is biased due to the fact that non-significant findings are less likely to be published than significant findings. However, applying the formula for what is known as the 'file-drawer' problem, it is possible to estimate how many such non-significant findings there would have to be to reduce the overall significance of the published results to the chance level. It transpires that, in this instance, some 7,778 such non-significant unreported studies would have had to be done (i.e. 18 times as many as the significant studies forming the present sample) in order to negate this overall significance, a quite unrealistic assumption. The technique of meta-analysis has now been applied to most of the major phenomena of experimental parapsychology such as we have discussed in this chapter, and the outcome has been similar. Furthermore, comparisons can be made with such meta-analyses between the more rigorous and the less rigorous experiments and this can dispose of the insinuations, dear to critics, that only sloppy experimentation in parapsychology yields significant results.

38.   Reich, the most eccentric and unorthodox of all Freud's disciples, fell foul of the US Food and Drug Administration and died in prison. He had had the temerity to claim that his orgone accumulators could cure cancer.

He is still revered by many as an outstanding psychotherapist irrespective of his latter-day quest for a universal therapeutic energy.

39. Estabany, who had served in the Hungarian cavalry, used to cure sick horses by dint of stroking them!

40. See B. Grad, R.J. Cadoret and G.I. Paul, 'The influence of an unorthodox method of wound healing in mice', *Internat. J. Parapsych.*, 3 (1961) 5–24.

41. See B. Grad, 'A telekinetic effect on plant growth', *Internat. J. Parapsych.*, 5 (1963) 117–33 and 6 (1964) 473–98.

42. See D. Dean, 'Infrared measurements of healer-treated water', *Research in Parapsychology 1982*, pp.100–2 (abstract). But the matter is still controversial, see P. Fenwick and R. Hopkins, 'An examination of the effect of healing on water', *J.S.P.R.*, 53 (1986) 387–90; D. Dean, *J.S.P.R.*, 53 (1986) 456–7 and Fenwick and Hopkins, *J.S.P.R.*, 54 (1987) 145.

43. Much work along these lines was done by Enrico Novillo Pauli, a Jesuit priest from Argentina, see his 'PK on living targets as related to sex, distance and time', *Research in Parapsychology 1972* (1973) 68–70 (abstract). See also chap. 5 of his book *Los Phenomenos Parasicologicos*, (Buenos Aires: Kapelusz, 1975).

44. See J. Barry, 'General and comparative study of PK effect on a fungus culture', *J. Parapsych.*, 32 (1968) 237–43. Barry worked as a general practitioner in Bordeaux, France.

45. See G.K. and A.M. Watkins, 'Possible PK influence on the resuscitation of anesthetized mice', *J. Parapsych.*, 35 (1971) 257–72; R.A. Wells and J. Klein, 'A replication of a psychic healing paradigm', *J. Parapsych.*, 36 (1972) 144–9; G.K. and A.M. Watkins and R.A. Wells, 'Further studies on the resuscitation of anesthetized mice', *Research in Parapsychology 1972*, (1973) 132–4 (abstract).

46. Two recent publications that support Grad's findings with plants are A. Saklani, 'Preliminary tests for psi ability in shamans of Garhwal Himalaya', *J.S.P.R.*, 55 (1988) 60–70 and A.M. Scofield and R.D. Hodges, 'Demonstrations of a healing effect in the laboratory using a simple plant model', *J.S.P.R.*, 57 (1991) 321–43. Scofield and Hodges, of the Department of Biochemistry, Wye College, University of London, used as their subject Geoff Boltwood, a well-known British healer.

47. See Sister Justa Smith, 'Paranormal effects on enzyme activity', *Human Dimensions*, 2 (1972) 15–19.

48. In his autobiographical sketch in Pilkington (1987) Grad repudiates the idea that there was anything essentially paranormal about the phenomena with which he was concerned, confident that they would eventually be incorporated into conventional science. It becomes clear that Grad belongs to a tradition which stretches unbroken from Mesmer to Reich that seeks to demonstrate energies as yet unrecognized by physics. Braud, on the other hand, belongs squarely with the mainstream of parapsychology which makes no such assumptions concerning the mechanism of PK. Latterly, to avoid any misleading assumptions, Braud has adopted Honorton's suggestion and now refers to Bio-PK as 'direct mental influence' i.e. whether by ESP or PK.

49. See W. Braud and M. Schlitz, 'Psychokinetic influence on electrodermal activity', *J. Parapsych.*, 47 (1983) 95–119.

50. The philosopher Frank Dilley, for example, has argued that telepathy, understood as mind-to-mind communication, is an unnecessary concept: all we need to postulate is (*a*) clairvoyance and (*b*) PK. See his 'Telepathy and mind–brain dualism', *J.S.P.R.*, 56 (1990) 129–37 and his previous article, 'Making clairvoyance coherent', *J.S.P.R.*, 55 (1989) 241–50.

51. Most of the literature on these two women is, naturally, in Russian so I shall mention only accessible English language sources. On Kuleshova, see S. Ostrander and L. Schroeder, *Psi: Psychic Discoveries Behind the Iron Curtain* (New York: Prentice Hall, 1970) chap. 14 'Eyeless sight'; also H. Gris and W. Dick, *The New Soviet Psychic Discoveries* (London: Souvenir 1978), chap. 21 'Dermo-optical perception'. Both books are the work of journalists, not parapsychologists. Unfortunately the latter have had very little to say about Rosa. There is, however, an account by A.S. Novomeisky in English in his article, 'The nature of the dermo-optic sense', *Internat. J. Parapsych.*, 7 (1965) 341–67. The accessible literature on Kulagina, on the other hand, is much more extensive. See J.G. Pratt, 'Soviet research in parapsychology' in Wolman (1977) pp.891–6: 'Investigations of Nina Kulagina'; H.J. Keil, B. Herbert, M. Ullman and J.G. Pratt, 'Directly observable voluntary PK effects: A survey and tentative interpretation of available findings from Nina Kulagina and other known related cases of recent date', *Proc. S.P.R.*, 56 (1976) 197–235; M. Cassirer, 'Experiments with Nina Kulagina', *J.S.P.R.*, 47 (1974) 315–18; H. Gris and W. Dick, *The New Soviet Psychic Discoveries*, chap. 3 'Two telekinetic women'; S. Ostrander and L. Schroeder, *Psi: Psychic Discoveries Behind the Iron Curtain*, chap. 6; articles by the late Benson Herbert on the Kulagina films appear in issues of the now defunct *Journal of Paraphysics*, 1969–1972, which he edited.

52. See Jules Romains, *Eye-less Sight: A Study of Extraretinal Vision and the Paroptic Sense* (New York: Putnam (transl.C.K. Ogden)).

53. In their influential article (see Note 11 above) Luria *et al.* write: 'In Lower Tagil and in other cities in the Urals there have, for some years, been investigations into "cutaneous vision" (the so called Rosa Kuleshova

effect) which often and wrongly is put into the sphere of parapsychological manifestations but in fact has nothing in common with the latter. The upshot of many checks of analogous cases observed abroad, and not long ago in Moscow, give grounds for believing that such a phenomenon, i.e. cutaneous vision, does in fact exist and demands careful study. It is true that up to now one cannot come to any definite conclusions about its mechanism.'

It is of interest to note that Luria's co-author, the psychologist A.N. Leontiev, taught a number of subjects to identify the colour of light when it was shone onto their skin. During Luria's visit to Edinburgh during the 1970s, he told me personally that he was satisfied that Rosa, whom he had himself tested, was indeed genuine.

54. Thelma Moss of UCLA had a blind subject, 'Mary' whom she taught to discriminate colours by touch, see chap. 20 of Mitchell (1974) p.475 (she reported her findings at the annual convention of the Parapsychological Association when it met in Edinburgh in 1972). Carroll Nash (of St Joseph's University, Philadelphia) got some significant results in his experiments, see his 'Cutaneous perception of colour with a head box', *J. Amer. S.P.R.*, 65 (1971) 83–7. However, the most assiduous researcher in this area has been Yvonne Duplessis of the Institut Métapsychique in Paris, who is President of Paris Centre Information Couleur, Commision Sensibilité Dermo-Optique.

55. *Life* magazine, however, sent a team to examine her under Gregory Razran, a New York Professor of Psychology and an authority on Soviet psychology, who wrote an enthusiastic report. See S. Ostrander and L. Schroeder, *Psi: Psychic Discoveries Behind the Iron Curtain* (New York: Prentice Hall, 1970) p.189 and A. Rosenfeld 'Seeing colours with fingers', *Life*, 12 June 1964.

56. See J.G. Pratt, *ESP Research Today* (Metuchen, NJ: Scarecrow, 1973), see chap. 3 'ESP research in Russia'.

57. See H. Gris and W. Dick, *The New Soviet Psychic Discoveries* (London: Souvenir, 1978) pp.40–1.

58. Namely Felicia Parise in the United States, see C. Honorton, 'Apparent PK on static objects by a gifted subject', *Research in Parapsychology 1973*, 128–31 (abstract), also G.K. and A.M. Watkins *ibid.*, 132–4, and Suzanne Padfield in Britain, see B. Herbert, 'The "Padfield effect" '. *J. Paraphysics*, 8 (1974) 137–50.

59. The main source of information on Serios is his chief investigator, Jule Eisenbud. See Eisenbud (1967/1989); and 'Paranormal photography' in Wolman (1977) or chap. 13 of Mitchell (1974).

60. T. Fukurai, *Clairvoyance and Thoughtography* (London: Rider, 1931). The book had originally appeared in Japanese in 1913. Unhappily, his principal subject, Chizuko Mifune, worried by public criticism, had committed suicide by taking poison in January 1911.

61. In his *Paranormal Foreknowledge* (New York: Human Sciences. 1982) Eisenbud discusses cases of spontaneous precognition culled from his therapeutic practice. See also his *Psychology and the Unconscious* (Berkeley, CA: North Atlantic, 1983), a collection of his essays dating from 1953 to 1983.

62. Twenty-nine of these witnesses from the Denver area, all of whom testified to their inability to explain the photographs, are listed on p.71 of Eisenbud (1967/1989).

63. See J.G. Pratt, *ESP Research Today* (Metuchen, NJ: Scarecrow, 1973) chap.6 'Psychic photography'. See also Ian Stevenson and J.G. Pratt, 'Exploratory investigations of the psychic photography of Ted Serios', *J. Amer. S.P.R.*, 62 (1968) 103–29 and their, 'Further investigations of … ' etc., *J. Amer. S.P.R.*, 63 (1969) 352–64. Although these authors are quite properly

cautious about committing themselves in print to the paranormality of the Serios effect, I happen to know from personal communication that they never wavered in their conviction that the phenomenon was indeed paranormal.

64. 'He had gradually become more or less habituated to the thing, he explained, so that now he felt very uncomfortable working without it, although he would do so, he hastened to assure me, if I desired this. I suggested he work in the most comfortable way' (Eisenbud, 1989, p.12). Never, in the history of parapsychology, has an experimenter had to pay more dearly for indulging a subject!

65. Eisenbud (1989) p.78.

66. See David B. Eisendrath, jr., and Charles Reynolds, 'An amazing weekend with the amazing Ted Serios', *Popular Photography*, Oct. 1967, pp.82–158. I am there quoted derisively for saying: ' ... likely to prove the most remarkable paranormal phenomenon of our time' (quoted from the publisher's blurb). Ted was still riding high when Eisenbud's book first appeared and there was, as yet, no reason to think that his powers would prove so ephemeral.

67. David B. Eisendrath, jr., and Charles Reynolds, 'An amazing weekend with the amazing Ted Serios', *Popular Photography*, Oct. 1967, bottom of p.139. For an account of the incident see also J.G. Pratt, *ESP Research Today* (Metuchen, NJ: Scarecrow, 1973) p.115.

68. Eisenbud challenged Randi to come to Denver and make good his claim by undergoing the same treatment as Serios but, as Randi not unreasonably retorted, how could anyone prove that the treatment *was* identical? Only a contest between him and Serios could vindicate the former but, alas, Serios was no longer in the running.

69. For a mention of some of these, more especially of the

Veilleux family of Waterville, Maine, see J. Eisenbud, 'Paranormal photography' in Wolman (1977) pp.427–8.

70. A satisfactory book on the Geller episode has yet to be written. Geller himself has published two books giving his own account of events, see *Uri Geller: My Story* (New York: Praeger, 1975) and, with Guy Playfair who writes the introductory and final sections, *The Geller Effect* (London: J. Cape, 1986). It goes without saying, however, that no psychic should be taken at his or her own valuation. One book that deals exclusively with the phenomena is Charles Panati (ed.), *The Geller Papers* (Boston: Houghton Mifflin, 1976).

On the opposite side there is a vigorous anti-Geller literature, notably Marks and Kammann (1980) see chaps 6–10; James Randi, *The Truth about Uri Geller* (Buffalo, NY: Prometheus, 1982 (revised version of *The Magic of Uri Geller*, 1975) and Martin Gardner, *Science, Good, Bad and Bogus* (Buffalo, NY: Prometheus, 1981) *passim.* The trouble with these critics, however, is that, while they often raise pertinent objections, they write with so much spleen and disdain and with such an air of superiority that one inevitably suspects that something more is at issue for them than just getting at the truth.

71. I recently had occasion to make this point to Guy Playfair (co-author of *The Geller Effect*, see above). He replied that, if it were definite that Geller possessed paranormal powers, his value as a target for terrorist assassination would be greatly enhanced. It was a typical Geller response: hard to disprove but harder still to believe!

72. See A. Puharich, *Uri* (London: W.H. Allen, 1974). Geller, it would seem, did not share his mentor's extraterrestrial enthusiasms and, as Geller became better known, their partnership broke up with some mutual

rancour. Puharich has been quoted as describing Geller as an 'unabashed egomaniac'!

73.   See Mitchell (1974), appendix: 'Experiments with Uri Geller'. These describe some of the preliminary tests by Targ and Puthoff at SRI (see below). This work was funded by The Institute for Noetic Sciences which Mitchell founded following his moon landing. Mitchell first met Geller at Puharich's home in Ossining, New York State.

74.   See *Nature*, 252 (1974). The editors write: 'Perhaps the most important issue raised by the circumstances surrounding the publication of this paper is whether science has yet developed the competence to confront claims of the paranormal' (p.560). For the paper in question, 'Information transmission under conditions of sensory shielding', see 602–7.

75.   See J. Hanlon, 'Uri Geller and Science', *New Scientist*, 64 (1974) 170–85.

76.   See James Randi, *The Truth About Uri Geller* (Buffalo, NY: Prometheus, 1982) chap. 4. In response, Targ and Puthoff circulated a memo listing some 24 misstatements of fact concerning their investigation.

77.   Hans Bender circulated questionnaires to viewers in West Germany and Switzerland who had phoned in, some of whom were then interviewed. Some 402 of them described cases of watches and clocks starting unexpectedly and some 151 of them cases of twisted or bent cutlery including some 36 instances of fractured cutlery. See Berger and Berger (1991) p.155.

78.   See 'A brief report on a visit by Uri Geller to King's College, London, June 20 1974' in Charles Panati (ed.), *The Geller Papers*, (Boston: Houghton Mifflin, 1976) p.214.

79.   Taylor published two articles in *Nature* explaining why the electromagnetism (EM) could *not* account for the alleged ESP and PK phenomena, See E. Balanovski and

J.G. Taylor, 'Can electromagnetism account for extra-sensory phenomena?' *Nature*, 275 (1978) 64–7 and J.G. Taylor and E. Balanovski, 'Is there any scientific explanation of the paranormal?' *Nature*, 279 (1979) 631–3. Having answered both questions in the negative, the authors conclude their second paper by saying: 'the existence of any of the psychic phenomena we have considered is very doubtful'. Taylor's first book, *Superminds* (London: Macmillan, 1975) went into paperback and attained a wide circulation. Following his retraction he published his *Science and the Supernatural* (New York: Dutton, 1980).

80. John Hasted, *The Metal-Benders* (London: Routledge, 1981).

81. At Edinburgh University in the mid-1970s, we too were in pursuit of various mini-gellers who were then around. An amusing account of our efforts to pin down one such is given in Broughton (1991) p.163. Much publicity was given to the use of hidden cameras by H. Collins and B. Pamplin at the University of Bath which showed that most of these children took to cheating when they thought they were not being observed, see, 'Paranormal metal bending at Bath', chap. 6 of H.M. Collins and T.J. Pinch, *Frames of Meaning: The Social Construction of Extraordinary Science* (London: Routledge, 1982). In this book the authors, two sociologists of science, use the geller-effect as a case study of how science tries to cope with the unorthodox while deliberately refraining from committing themselves as to the validity of the phenomenon. As they put it: 'The authors do not know whether paranormal metal bending is "real" or not – nor, as sociologists, do they care. It would make not one jot of difference to the analysis' (see p.184). Only a sociologist, one feels, could be so nonchalant!

82. See John Hasted, *The Metal-Benders* (London: Routledge, 1981) p.39.

83. See Julian Isaacs, 'A mass screening technique for locating PKMB agents', *Psychoenergetics*, 4 (1981), 125–58. Isaacs went on to complete a thesis on PKMB at Aston University, Birmingham, for which I served as external examiner. He was awarded a PhD.

84. F. Bersani and A. Martelli, 'Observations on selected Italian mini-Gellers', *J. Psychophysical Systems*, 5 (1983) 99–128.

85. Girard demonstrated his metal-bending for me when I was in Paris in the summer of 1976 but the conditions were very lax. Brian Millar, then a postdoctoral Fellow working with me in Edinburgh, devised a test object for Girard in which a pair of thin metal strips were enclosed inside a glass bulb. Girard claims that he succeeded in bending the target strips but that someone else later broke the glass bulb! At all events, our test was sadly aborted.

86. See James Randi, *Flim-Flam: Psychics, ESP, Unicorns and other Delusions* (Buffalo, NY: Prometheus, 1982) pp.284–92.

87. See Hans Bender and Rolf Vandrey, 'Psychokinetische Experimente mit dem Berner Graphiker Silvio', *Zeitschrift fur Parapsychologie*, 18 (1976) 217–41 (English summary). The authors conclude that their observations 'made in the presence of magicians' plus the findings of other investigators 'give clear evidence of genuine psychokinetic effects'.

88. This phase of Geller's career is described by him in his *The Geller Effect* (London: J. Cape, 1986) chap. 9 'Big business'. Geller has been quoted as saying: 'People always ask me "If you're so psychic, why aren't you a millionaire?" ' Whether, now that he purports to be wealthy, his credibility is any greater, is another question!

89. The term 'theta psi' was introduced by William Roll for psi effects attributed to discarnate agencies (see

Thalbourne, 1982), theta being the first letter of the Greek word thanatos meaning death.

90. The phenomenon was first noted by a medium, A. von Szalay of Los Angeles, who then brought it to the attention of Raymond Bayless, an investigator with whom he carried out a series of experiments, see *J. Amer. S.P.R.*, 53 (1959) pp.35–9. Three months later, Friedrich Jurgenson, a writer and film director in Sweden, independently reported on the phenomenon. In 1965 he was visited by a German writer and philosopher, Konstantin Raudive. His book *Breakthrough* (New York: Taplinger, 1971) was avidly seized upon by enthusiasts, and thereafter the Electronic Voice Phenomenon (EVP) became something of a craze among amateur investigators. For a critical assessment by an English researcher who visited Raudive see D.J. Ellis, *The Mediumship of the Tape Recorder* (Pulborough, Sussex: Ellis, 1978). For an allied phenomenon see D. Scott Rogo and Raymond Bayless, *Phone-calls from the Dead* (Englewood Cliffs, NJ: Prentice Hall, 1979). Whatever the source of the sounds in EVP, there remains a strong suspicion that their interpretation as speech-sounds is subjective.

91. It was Russell Noyes, a medical professor at the University of Iowa, who coined the expression 'near death experience' about which he published a series of papers in the medical journals from 1971 onwards. But from the parapsychological standpoint, the seminal texts for the NDE are the following: Raymond A. Moody, *Life After Life* (New York: Bantam, 1976) and *Reflections on Life After Life* (Bantam, 1978); Kenneth Ring, *Life at Death* (New York: Coward, McCann and Geoghegan, 1980) and his *Heading towards Omega) New York: Wm. Morrow, 1984); Michael B. Sabom, (Recollections of Death* (London: Corgi, 1982). More recent general accounts of the phenomenon are:

D. Scott Rogo, *The Return from Silence: A Study of Near-Death Experiences* (Wellingborough, Northants: Aquarian, 1989); Margot Grey, *Return from Death* (London: Arkana, RKP, 1985). Raymond Moody, *The Light Beyond* with Paul Perry, introduction by Colin Wilson (New York: Bantam, 1988). Also relevant chapters of recommended textbooks, see Bibliography.

92.   Susan Blackmore offers a naturalistic interpretation of the OBE in her *Beyond the Body* (London: Heinemann, 1982). See also H.J. Irwin, *Flight of Mind: A Psychological Study of Out-of-Body Experience* (Metuchen, NJ: Scarecrow, 1985) or G.O. Gabbard and S.W. Twemlow, *With the Eyes of the Mind* (New York: Praeger, 1984). More recently, Blackmore has tackled the NDE from a naturalistic standpoint in her *Dying to Live: Science and the Near Death Experience* (London: Grafton, 1993).

93.   An early account of this phenomenon is given in W.F. Barrett, *Death-Bed Visions* (London: Methuen, 1926). Among recent studies see Karlis Osis *Deathbed Observations by Physicians and Nurses* (New York: Parapsychological Foundation, 1961) and Karlis Osis and Erlendur Haraldsson, *At the Hour of Death* (New York: Avon, 1977).

94.   See G. Gallup and W. Proctor, *Adventures in Immortality* (New York: McGraw-Hill, 1982).

95.   Two recent studies that attempt to deal with the NDE from a transcendental or quasi-religious angle are Michael Grosso, *The Final Choice: Playing the Survival Game* (New Hampshire: Stillpoint, 1985) and David Lorimer, *Whole in One: The NDE and the Ethics of Interconnectedness* (London: Arkana, RKP, 1990). The experience, however, is not always a blissful one. Noyes reckons that, in about 12 per cent of cases, the effect is negative and the point is emphasized by the cardiologist M. Rawlings in his *Beyond Death's Door* (New York: Nelson, 1978).

96. See J.E. Owens, E.W. Cook and I. Stevenson, 'Features of "near-death-experiences" in relation to whether or not patients were near death'*The Lancet*, 336 (1990) 1175–7. See also I. Stevenson, E.W. Cook and N. McClean-Rice, 'Are persons reporting "near-death experiences" really near death?'*Omega*, **20** (1989/90) 45–54, where the authors conclude that: 'The experiences currently described as "near-death experiences" can occur to persons who, although they may be ill, are not at all near death so far as their medical records show ... we might describe then as having "fear-death experiences" ... .'

97. See R. Noyes and R. Kletti, 'Depersonalization in the face of life-threatening danger', *Psychiatry*, 39 (1976) 19–27 and their 'Panoramic memory: A response to the threat of death', *Omega*, 8 (1977) 181–94. For a more recent discussion from a naturalistic standpoint see G. Roberts and J. Owen, 'The near-death experience', *Brit. J. Psych.*, 153 (1988) 607–17 and S. Blackmore, *Dying to Live: Science and the Near Death Experience* (London: Grafton, 1993).

98. See S.J. Blackmore and T.S. Troscianko, 'The physiology of the tunnel', *Journal of Near-Death Studies*, 8 (1989) 15–28. The tunnel does not, however, appear in all cases. Ian Stevenson informs me that it did not figure in any of the cases in India which he or Pasricha investigated. If so, this would suggest a cultural rather than physiological explanation.

99. In France Col. Albert de Rochas, who became Director of the Ecole Polytechnique of Paris, was a keen psychical researcher and hypnotist. In 1911 he published his book, *Les Vies Successives* which deals with just such past lives as recounted under hypnosis. Reincarnation was a feature of the spiritualist teachings of Allan Kardec (the pen name of Hippolyte Rivail, 1804–1869, a French teacher and writer on education). His version of spiritualism, sometimes referred to as Kardecismo,

later became the dominant one in Brazil.

100. Morey Bernstein, *The Search for Bridey Murphy* (New York: Doubleday and London: Hutchinson, 1956). A useful evaluation of the case is given by the philosopher, C.J. Ducasse, in his article, 'How the case of *The Search for Bridey Murphy* stands today', *J. Amer. S.P.R.*, **54** (1960) 3–22. It is reproduced as chap. 25 of his book *A Critical Examination of the Belief in a Life after Death* (Springfield, IL: C.C. Thomas, 1961). More recently it has again been discussed by the late D. Scott Rogo in chap. 5 'Hypnosis, regression and reincarnation' of his *The Search for Yesterday* (Englewood Cliffs, NJ: Prentice Hall, 1985).

101. The suggestion that her aunt, Marie Burns, might have been a source overlooks the fact that, though of Scots-Irish descent, Mrs Burns was in fact born in New York and only came to live with Virginia's foster-parents in Chicago shortly before Virginia herself left at the age of 18. Even more farcical, among all these innuendoes, was the suggestion that the name 'Bridey Murphy' stemmed from a Mrs Bridie Murphy Corkell who lived across the road in Chicago when Virginia was a child. In fact Virginia never spoke with Mrs Corkell, never knew that she was called Bridie or that her maiden name was Murphy (if, indeed, it was). What *did* transpire, however, was that this Mrs Corkell happened to be the mother of the editor of the Sunday edition of the *Chicago American*!

102. Wm J. Barker's findings were reproduced as an additional chapter to the paperback edition of *The Search for Bridey Murphy* (New York: Pocket Books, 1965) as well as in the *Lancer*, New York edition of 1965, where he responds to her debunkers.

103. In the first of Stevenson's xenoglossy cases, the hypnotist was a physician in Philadelphia and the subject was his wife. The language of the regressed personality, who called himself Jensen, was Swedish of a somewhat

archaic kind. The subject who was from a Russo-Jewish background had never been to Sweden and knew no Swedish. Swedish speakers were enlisted to assist the communication but, for whatever reason, Jensen's speech was very sparse and stilted so it was difficult to draw any conclusions as to the identity of this individual who appeared to belong to a period not later than the seventeenth century. See Ian Stevenson, 'Xenoglossy', *Proc. Amer. S.P.R.*, 31, Feb. (1974) or in the University of Virginia Press edition (1974). In his second case, the so-called 'Gretchen' case, the husband (a Methodist minister) was again the hypnotist and his wife the subject. The regressed personality who called herself Gretchen said she was from Eberswalde in Germany where she lived with her father. She was much more communicative than 'Jensen' but her German was by no means flawless. His third case, the so-called 'Sharada' case, which takes us to India, did not involve hypnosis but was more in the nature of a possession where the secondary personality 'Sharada', who spoke Bengali, would occasionally take over from the subject, Uttara, who could speak only Marathi or English. Both these latter cases are discussed at length in Ian Stevenson's *Unlearned Language: New Studies in Xenoglossy* (University of Virginia Press, 1974).

104. See Jeffrey Iverson, *More Lives Than One? The Evidence of the Remarkable Bloxham Tapes* (London: Souvenir, 1976, with a foreword by Magnus Magnusson).

105. See Melvin Harris, *Investigating the Unexplained* (Buffalo, NY: Prometheus, 1986). But the most comprehensive critique of all the hypnotically elicited reincarnation cases, including the Bridey Murphy case, the Jane Evans cases, and two of the three Stevenson xenoglossy cases is to be found in Ian Wilson (1981).

106. Linda Tarazi, 'An unusual case of hypnotic regression

302 Parapsychology: A Concise History

with some unexplained contents', *J. Amer. S.P.R.*, 84
(1990) 309–44.

107. See chap. 9 'Past life therapy' in Rogo (1975).

108. This is one area of parapsychology where the bibliography tends to be very much a one-author affair.
Indeed, the only book on the topic one can recommend
for the general reader is Stevenson (1987). For the
scholar there are his volumes of detailed case reports
which the University of Virginia Press have issued over
the years, commencing with *Twenty Cases Suggestive of
Reincarnation* 1974 (2nd edn revised and enlarged). This
was followed by four volumes under the general heading of *Cases of the Reincarnation Type: Vol. 1 Ten Cases
in India*, 1975; *Vol. 2 Ten Cases in Sri Lanka*, 1977; *Vol.
3 Twelve Cases in Lebanon and Turkey*, 1980; *Vol. 4
Twelve Cases in Thailand and Burma*, 1983. Stevenson
has, however, acquired disciples who now function independently. See, for example, Satwant Pasricha,
*Claims of Reincarnation: An Empirical Study of Cases
in India* (New Delhi: Harman, 1990).

109. See *J. Amer. S.P.R.*, 54 (1960) 51–71 and 95–117. It was
issued as a pamphlet in 1964.

110. See *Proc. Amer. S.P.R.*, 26 (1966). In 1974 it was published by the University of Virginia Press in a revised
and enlarged version (see above).

111. See Stevenson (1987) p.102.

112. Stevenson (1987) p.104. According to Stevenson: 'The
median interval for 616 cases from ten different cultures
was fifteen months' (p.117).

113. In the abstract to his article, 'The explanatory value of
the idea of reincarnation', *Journal of Nervous & Mental
Diseases* 164, 305–26, Stevenson writes: 'The idea of
reincarnation may contribute to an improved understanding of such diverse matters as: phobias and philias
of childhood; skills not learned in early life; abnormal-
ities of child–parent relationships; vendettas and

bellicose nationalism; childhood sexuality and gender identity confusion; birthmarks, congenital deformities, and internal diseases; differences between members of monozygotic twin pairs; and abnormal appetites during pregnancy.'

114. As of this writing, an illustrated multi-volume work on the birthmark and birth-defect evidence, which Stevenson regards as crowning his efforts in this field, is awaiting publication. It should be interesting to follow its impact on opinion. Stevenson sees a connection between such birthmark cases and cases of 'maternal impressions' where a mother's experiences during pregnancy are thought to show up in the offspring, see I. Stevenson, 'A new look at maternal impressions: etc', *Journal of Scientific Exploration*, **6** (1992) 353–74.

115. See Stevenson (1987) chap. 8 'Variations in the cases of different cultures'.

116. The critics have duly responded to the Stevensonian challenge. See Ian Wilson (1981) chap. 3; W.G. Roll, 'The changing perspective of life after death', sect. 4 'Reincarnation', in S. Krippner (ed.), *Advances in Parapsychological Research 3* (1982); C.T.K. Chari, 'Review of *Cases of the Reincarnation Type. vol. 4 Twelve cases in Thailand and Burma* by Ian Stevenson', *J.S.P.R.*, 53 (1986) 325–9; Paul Edwards, 'The case against reincarnation, part 4', *Free Inquiry*, Summer 1987, 46–53; and Ian Wilson, 'Review of *Children who Remember Past Lives* by Ian Stevenson', *J.S.P.R.*, **55** (1988) 227–34. Some of these critics, i.e. Roll and Chari, are themselves parapsychologists; Wilson is a freelance writer, while Edwards is a philosopher who finds the dualistic implications of the reincarnation hypothesis an insuperable obstacle. Stevenson has attempted to meet some of these criticisms, mostly in the parapsychological journals, but complains that if he were to respond in

full to every critic his own research would quickly come to a standstill!

117. See, for example, Geoffrey Madell, *The Identity of the Self* (Edinburgh: University Press, 1981). Madell arrives at the conclusion that such an identity is unanalysable: 'What is it for a particular ego to be mine?' he asks and replies: 'my claim has been all along that there can be nothing which unites a series of experiences such that they are all the experiences of the one person, *except their being unanalysably, mine (yours, his)*' (p.135) [my emphasis].

118. The late Scott Rogo (1985) discusses these alternative formulations in his final chapter (11) 'Reconceptualizing reincarnation' but such discussions tend to become somewhat strained.

119. The expression 'anomalistic psychology' has been proposed in this connection, see L. Zusne and W.H. Jones, *Anomalistic Psychology*, (Hillsdale, NJ: Erlbaum, 1982). For an overt defence of this approach see S.J. Blackmore, 'Do we need a new psychical research?' *J.S.P.R.*, 55 (1988) 49–59.

120. See J.H. Rush, 'Physical and quasi physical theories of psi' in H.L. Edge *et al.* (1986) or, on a more technical level, D.M. Stokes, 'Theoretical parapsychology' in S. Krippner (ed.) (1987).

121. We have already discussed John Taylor's espousal of the electromagnetic theory and his repudiation of the paranormal once he had abandoned the theory (see note 79 above). Other recent proponents include the Russian physicist I.M. Kogan, who published in a Russian telecommunication journal, and the Canadian Michael Persinger, see his 'ELF field mediation in spontaneous psi events' in Tart, Puthoff and Targ (1979). These latter-day defenders of the EM theory follow Kogan in invoking ELF (extra low frequency waves). For a discussion of the difficulties that confront ELF theories no

less than conventional electromagnetic theories see D.M. Stokes 'Theoretical parapsychology' in S. Krippner (ed.) (1987) pp.114–15). The most recent attempt to defend EM theory comes from Robert O. Becker: see his 'Electromagnetism and psi phenomena', *J. Amer. S.P.R.*, 86 (1992) 1–17.

An associated development is Michael Persinger's Geomagnetism theory according to which spontaneous psi events are more likely to occur when the Earth's geomagnetism level is low. See H.P. Wilkinson and Alan Gauld, 'Geomagnetism and anomalous experiences 1868–1980', *Proc S.P.R.*, 57 (1993) part 217.

122. See Ninian Marshall, 'ESP and memory: A physical theory', *Brit. J. Phil. Sc.*, 10 (1960) 265–86. Marshall's proposal was more or less stillborn but the idea of resonance receives some empirical confirmation in the work of Rupert Sheldrake. See his *A New Science of Life: The Hypothesis of Formative Causation* (London: Blond & Briggs, 1981) and his *The Presence of the Past* (London: Collins, 1988). However, the Sheldrake effect as such refers to the finding that learning is facilitated if others, even though elsewhere in space or time, had previously learnt the task in question. It has no direct bearing on the phenomenon of ESP.

123. See A. Koestler, 'The perversity of physics' in his *The Roots of Coincidence* (London: Hutchinson 1972) p.78.

124. Cf. David Bohm: 'Ultimately the entire universe has to be understood as a single undivided whole, in which analysis into separately and independently existent parts has no fundamental status.' From his widely influential *Wholeness and the Implicate Order* (London: Routledge, 1982), as quoted by S. Roney-Dougal in her *Where Science And Magic Meet* (Longmead, Dorset: Element Books, 1991).

125. For a general exposition of Observational Theory, see J.H. Rush, 'Physical and quasi physical theories of psi'

in H.L. Edge *et al.* (1986) pp. 286–92 or, on a more technical level, see D.M. Stokes 'Theoretical parapsychology' in S. Krippner (ed.) (1987) pp. 139–54.

126. See H. Schmidt, 'PK effect on pre-recorded targets', *J. Amer. S.P.R.*, 70 (1979) 267–92.

127. Braude (1979) p.108. His book contains a detailed critique of Observational Theories, see pp.100–10. See also his 'The observational theories in parapsychology: A critique', *J. Amer. S.P.R.*, 73 (1979) 349–66.

128. An attempt to meet Braude's objections has been made by Brian Millar (a notable proponent of OT, see below) in his 'Cutting the Braudian Loop: In defense of the Observational Theories', *J. Amer. S.P.R.*, 82 (1988) 253–72. See also Braude's rejoinder, 'Death by observation: A reply to Millar', *J. Amer. S.P.R.*, 82 (1988) pp.273–80.

129. See E.H. Walker, 'Foundations of paraphysical and parapsychological phenomena'; H. Schmidt, 'A logically consistent model of a world with psi interaction', in L. Oteri (ed.), *Quantum Physics and Parapsychology*, (New York: Parapsychology Foundation, 1975). Walker had already propounded his theory in Mitchell (1974), see chap. 23 'Consciousness and quantum theory'. Schmidt expounds his theory in 'Towards a mathematical theory of psi', *J. Amer. S.P.R.*, 69 (1975) 267–91. Schmidt is less concerned with interpretation and more with the formalism of his theory. Walker, on the other hand, seeks to anchor his theory to a given interpretation of quantum theory.

130. B. Millar, 'The observational theories: a primer', *European Journal of Parapsychology*, 2 (1978) 304–32.

131. J.M. Houtkooper obtained his PhD from the University of Utrecht with his thesis, *Observational Theory: A Research Programme for Paranormal Phenomena* (Lisse: Swets & Zeitlinger, (1983) [In the Netherlands, doctoral theses are routinely published]. Brian Millar, a Scot, after leaving the University of Edinburgh where

he obtained his PhD in organic chemistry, moved to to Utrecht where for a time he worked at the university and where he eventually became domiciled. Another Dutch enthusiast for OT was a physicist, Dick Bierman, of the University of Amsterdam.

132. Robert Jahn and Brenda Dunne, for example, in their *Margins of Reality: The Role of Consciousness in the Physical World* (New York: Harcourt Brace Jovanovich, 1987) reject any 'direct application of quantum theory to psychic processes' but see it rather as 'a comprehensive metaphor for all forms of consciousness interaction' (see p.201).

133. See vol.8 of the English edition of the *Complete Works of C.G. Jung* (London: Routledge & Kegan Paul). It was published in book form in 1952, along with an essay by the eminent physicist Wolfgang Pauli on 'The influence of archetypal ideas on the scientific theories of Kepler'. The book appeared in English in 1955 under the title *The Interpretation of Nature and the Psyche* (London: Routledge).

134. Jung tried to tie in his theory of synchronicity with his theory of dreams as exhibiting archetypal ideas. The *locus classicus* is his account of a patient of his who was recounting her dream about a golden scarab when just such a beetle began knocking at the window pane from outside (see *The Interpretation of Nature and the Psyche*, London: Routledge, 1955, pp.30–1).

135. Kammerer's 'seriality' never became as widely known as Jung's 'synchronicity'. However, Koestler introduced Kammerer to a wide public with his book *The Case of the Midwife Toad* (London: Hutchinson, 1971). Kammerer was no less unorthodox in seeking to demonstrate the inheritance of acquired characteristics (he committed suicide in 1926 after accusations, that may well have been unfounded, that he had tampered with a specimen).

136. Koestler himself played no small role in propagating the concept, see his 'Seriality and synchronicity' in *The Roots of Coincidence* (London: Hutchinson, 1972, chap. 3) and his section in A. Hardie, R. Harvie and A. Koestler, *The Challenge of Chance* (London: Hutchinson, 1973). He even persuaded the *Sunday Times*, in 1974, to offer a prize of £100 for the best entry dealing with a coincidence. There were some 2,000 entries from which he duly selected the winner. The late Brian Inglis, his partner in the administration of the Koestler Foundation, shared his fascination with coincidences, see B. Inglis, *Coincidence: A Matter of Chance or Synchronicity?* (London: Hutchinson, 1990).

137. I have elsewhere pointed out the weakness of trying to subsume psi phenomena under the rubric of an acausal synchronicity, see my 'Psi phenomena: Causal versus acausal interpretation', *J.S.P.R.*, 49 (1977) 573–82. See also 'The theory of synchronicity' in Braude (1979) pp.217–41.

138. Although, in my capacity here as historian, I have tried to avoid bias, it would be disingenuous of me to disguise my oft-reiterated conviction that only radical dualism can make sense of both the normal and paranormal functions of mind. See my 'Radical dualism' also my 'Voluntary movement, biofeedback control and PK' in Beloff (1990); my 'Parapsychology and the mind–body problem', *Inquiry*, 30 (1987) 215–25; and my 'Dualism: A parapsychological perspective' in J.R. Smythies and J. Beloff (eds), *The Case for Dualism* (Charlottesville: University of Virginia Press, 1989).

139. Most of these doctrines are discussed in Ned Block (ed.), *Readings in Philosophy of Psychology*, 2 vols (London: Methuen, 1980). It is significant that radical dualism (i.e. dualist interactionism) is nowhere represented nor is there any allusion to psi phenomena. In his introduction to vol.1, Ned Block says, *en passant*, 'func-

tionalism (the view that mental states are functional states, states defined by their causal role) is currently the dominant view of the nature of mind.' This is understandable since such a view of the mental puts minds on a par with computers, a view developed at length by Daniel Dennett, here and elsewhere. See also Block's introduction to vol.1, part 3: 'What is functionalism?'

140. The one outstanding defence of radical dualism in recent times is the book which emerged from a collaboration between the philosopher, Karl Popper, and the brain physiologist, John Eccles (*they* use the expression 'dualist interactionism': 'radical dualism' is my own preferred usage). Neither author invokes paranormal phenomena. See K.R. Popper and J.C. Eccles, *The Self and its Brain: An Argument for Interactionism* (London: Springer, 1977). Other arguments for dualism by assorted philosophers, psychologists, etc., may be found in J.R. Smythies and J. Beloff (eds), *The Case for Dualism* (see Note 138).

141. R.H. Thouless and B.P. Wiesner, 'The psi processes in normal and "paranormal" psychology', *Proc. S.P.R.*, 48 (1947) 177–96. This is sometimes alluded to as Thouless' 'Shin' theory of mind as he proposes a neutral expression (the Hebrew letter shin) to denote whatever it is that is causally efficacious in mind–matter interactions rather than making do with a traditional term such as 'psyche'. As the authors there remind us: 'It should be apparent that there is nothing novel in the suggestion that there is some entity which controls the organism in volition and which is informed by the organism in perceptual processes. This was universally believed until comparatively recent times when the idea of a soul or self was discarded by the physiologists and experimental psychologists, and all mental processes, including those of volition and cognition, came to be regarded as merely aspects of the material processes of the organism.'

142. See C. Backster, 'Evidence of a primary perception in plant life', *Internat. J. Parapsych*, 10 (1968) 329–48. A positive assessment of these claims is given by Marcel Vogel (a research chemist) in chap. 12 of Mitchell (1974): 'Man–plant communication'. The claims, however, did not survive such negative assessments as those of J. Kmetz, 'A study of primary perception in plant and animal life', *J. Amer. S.P.R.*, 71 (1977) 157–70 or of Horowitz, Lewis and Gasteiger, 'Plant primary perception', *Science*, 189 (1975) 478–80. Had Backster been vindicated this would no doubt have resuscitated the vitalist controversy but it would have been at variance with radical dualism.

Select bibliography and references
General works, textbooks and compendia
In addition to the comprehensive handbook Wolman (1977), three recent textbooks covering this period can be recommended: Edge *et al.* (1986); Irwin (1989), and Broughton (1991).

Alcock, James E. (1981) *Parapsychology: Science or Magic?*, Oxford and New York: Pergamon.
Berger, A.S. and Berger J. (1991) *The Encyclopedia of Parapsychology and Psychical Research*, New York: Paragon.
Broughton, Richard S. (1991) *Parapsychology: The Controversial Science*, New York: Ballantine.
Edge, H.L., Morris, R.L., Rush, J.H., Palmer, J. (1986) *Foundations of Parapsychology*, London and Boston: Routledge.
Inglis, Brian (1985) *The Paranormal: An Encyclopedia of Psychic Phenomena*, London: Grafton/Paladin.
Irwin, H.J. (1989) *An Introduction to Parapsychology*, Jefferson, NC: McFarland.
Kurtz, Paul (ed.) (1985) *A Skeptic's Handbook of Parapsychology*, Buffalo, NY: Prometheus.

Marks, D. and Kammann, R. (1980) *The Psychology of the Psychic*, Buffalo, NY: Prometheus.

Mitchell, Edgar D. (1974) *Psychic Exploration: A Challenge for Science*, edited by John White, New York: Putnam.

Nash, C.B. (1986) *Parapsychology: The Science of Psiology*, Springfield: IL. C.C. Thomas.

Rao, K. Ramakrishna (ed.) (1984) *The Basic Experiments in Parapsychology*, Jefferson, NC : McFarland.

Thalbourne, Michael (1982) *A Glossary of Terms used in Parapsychology*, London: Heinemann.

White, Rhea A. (1990) *Parapsychology: New Sources of Information*, Metuchen, NJ: Scarecrow.

Part 1 Experimental parapsychology

Beloff, J. (ed.) (1974) *New Directions in Parapsychology*, with a postscript by Arthur Koestler, London: Elek Science. (Metuchen, NJ: Scarecrow, 1975.)

Braude, S.E. (1979) *ESP and Psychokinesis: A Philosophical Examination*, Philadelphia: Temple University Press.

Eisenbud, Jule (1967/1989) *The World of Ted Serios: Thoughtographic Studies of an Extraordinary Mind*, New York: Wm. Morrow. 2nd edn, 1989: Jefferson NC: McFarland.

Gauld, Alan and Cornell, A.D. (1979) *Poltergeists*. London: Routledge & Kegan Paul.

Jahn, Robert G. and Dunne, Brenda J. (1987) *Margins of Reality: The Role of Consciousness in the Physical World*, New York: Harcourt Brace Jovanovich.

Krippner, S. (ed.) (1987) *Advances in Parapsychological Research*, vol.5, Jefferson, NC: McFarland.

Pilkington, R. (ed.) (1987) *Men and Women of Parapsychology: Personal Reflections*, Jefferson, NC: McFarland.

Targ. R. and Harary, K. (1984) *The Mind Race: Understanding and Using Psychic Abilities*, New York: Villard.

Targ, R. and Puthoff, H. (1977) *Mind-Reach*, New York: Delacorte.

Tart, C.T., Puthoff, H.E. and Targ, R .(eds.) (1979) *Mind at*

Large: Institute of Electrical and Electronic Engineers Symposia on the Nature of Extrasensory Perception, New York: Praeger.

Ullman, M., Krippner, S. and Vaughan, A. (1973/1989) *Dream Telepathy: Studies in Nocturnal ESP*, Jefferson, NC: McFarland (1st edn 1973, New York: Macmillan).

Vasiliev, L.L. (1962/1976) *Experiments in Distant Influence: Discoveries by Russia's Foremost Parapsychologist*, edited with an introduction by Anita Gregory, London: Wildwood House. The book was originally published in Russian by the Leningrad State University. An English translation, authorised and revised by the author was privately printed by Anita Gregory and her husband, Clive Gregory, in 1963 under the title *Experiments in Mental Suggestion*.

Wolman, B.B. (1977) *Handbook of Parapsychology*, New York: Van Nostrand Reinhold.

Part 2 Modern survival research

Almeder, Robert (1992) *Death and Personal Survival: The Evidence for Life after Death*, Boston: Rowman & Littlefield.

Edwards, Paul (ed.) (1992) *Immortality*, New York: Macmillan.

Rogo, D. Scott (1985) *The Search for Yesterday: A Critical Examination of the Evidence for Reincarnation*, Englewood Cliffs, NJ: Prentice Hall.

Stevenson, Ian (1987) *Children who Remember Previous Lives: A Question of Reincarnation*, Charlottesville: University of Virginia Press.

Wilson, Ian (1981) *Mind out of Time? Reincarnation Claims Investigated*, London: Gollancz.

Part 3 Philosophical perspectives

Beloff, John (1989) *The Relentless Question: Reflections on the Paranormal*, Jefferson, NC: McFarland [collected essays].

Ludwig, Jan (1978) *Philosophy and Parapsychology*, Buffalo, NY: Prometheus.

Zollschan, G.K., Schumaker, J.F. and Walsh, G.F. (eds) (1989) *Exploring the Paranormal: Perspectives on Beliefs and Experience*, Lindfield, NSW, Australia: Unity Press. (Dorset: Prism Press; Garden City Park, NY: Avery.)

Epilogue

Notes
1. It has been reprinted in G. Murphy and R. O. Ballou (eds), *William James on Psychical Research* (London: Chatto & Windus, 1961). See chap. 7 'The last report'.
2. A. Lyons and M. Truzzi, *The Blue Sense: Psychic Detectives and Crime*, New York: Mysterious, 1991.
3. Pawlowski, F.W. (1925) 'The Mediumship of Franek Kluski of Warsaw', *J. Amer. S. P. R.*, 19, 482–504.
4. R.A. Ranieri, *Materializacões Luminosas*, (S. Paulo: FEESP, 1989) which describes the work of the materializing medium, 'Peixotinho', who flourished after the Second World War. The book contains photographs of the casts of materialized hands similar to those we associate with Kluski. Some of these exhibits have been preserved in an archive in Rio de Janeiro dedicated to this medium. See J. Beloff and G.L. Playfair 'Peixotinko: A latter-day Brazilian Kluski?' *J.S.P.R.* 59 (1993) (In press).
5. Some of his sparse publications include K.J. Batcheldor, 'Report on a case of table levitation', *J.S.P.R.*, 43 (1966) 339–56; 'PK in sitter groups', *Psychoenergetic Systems*, 3 (1979) 77–93; 'Contributions to the theory of PK induction from sitter-group work', *J. Amer. S.P.R.*, 78 (1984) 105–22. See also, J. Isaacs, 'The Batcheldor approach: some strengths and weaknesses', *J. Amer. S.P.R.*, 78 (1984) 123–32.
6. See Iris Owen and M.H. Sparrow, *Conjuring up Philip: An Adventure in Psychokinesis*, New York: Harper & Row, 1976.

Subject index

Names index